Writing the Virus

new work from StatORec

Outpost19 | San Francisco
outpost19.com

Scrima, Andrea and Winner, David Dario
Writing the Virus: New Work from StatORec magazine/
Andrea Scrima, David Dario Winner

ISBN 978-1-944853-77-8 (pbk)
ISBN 978-1-944853-78-5 (ebk)

Library of Congress Control Number: 2020946215

Cover image: Mui Poopoksakul
Cover design: Andrea Scrima

OUTPOST19

ORIGINAL PROVOCATIVE READING
SAN FRANCISCO | @OUTPOST19

Praise for *Writing the Virus*

"We live in the era of the pandemic, more than one million still die each year of TB, 700,000 from HIV and AIDS, nearly half a million of malaria. And since January: COVID-19. As I read *Writing the Virus*, the death toll from this new disease surpassed one million. The scale of this loss is unimaginable. We need to feel it one person at a time, which is precisely what *Writing the Virus* does with its moving diaries and essays, with its psalms of grief. This is a hard issue to read, but it preserves the truth of a bitter, bitter time, maybe it will even help us mourn. A task many of the world's most powerful governments have proven unwilling and even eager not to do."

—John Freeman
author of *How to Read a Novelist* and *The Park;*
editor of the *Freeman's* anthologies

"If a literary remedy could soothe the nested anxieties of our current moment, *Writing the Virus* would be the antidote we've been seeking. This bold new anthology from the editors of StatORec draws on 30 essays, stories, excerpts, and poems published on the magazine's website as the pandemic unfolded. The authors, including Edie Meidav, Uche Nduka, and Liesl Schillinger, share trenchant investigations and paeans to love and survival while the irregular rhythms of locked-down days undulate beneath the surface. This impressive anthology lets readers view the virus, racial violence, and volatile political climate as a triad within a continuum. A testament to the vital role of writers—as witnesses, chroniclers, translators, synthesizers, resistors—during uncertain times, *Writing the Virus* will energize, enrage, and give you reasons to be hopeful."

—Margot Douaihy
editor, *Northern New England Review*

"Covid-19 is the new normal, an unprecedented cultural shift that pressurizes our communities and estrangements, requiring us to reinvent the discourse we use to describe the 'everyday.' This anthology provides us with vital and thoughtful dispatches from inside the virus's transformative, insidious tedium. Vulnerable, bold, tentative, utopic, *Writing the Virus* gave me un-Zoomy succor from some of the best essayists writing today."

—Carmen Giménez Smith
author of *Be Recorder* and *Cruel Futures*

Writing
the
Virus

contents

TO COVID, WITH LOVE

INVISIBLE DANGER

THE FALLOUT

INTRODUCTION
Andrea Scrima

The 31 authors of StatORec's Corona Issue, published in our online magazine from mid-April to September 2020, explore the experience of lockdown, quarantine, social distancing, and the politicization of the virus from a wide variety of perspectives. As an online literary journal with staff based in Berlin and Brooklyn, our purview is circumscribed by our experiences in the United States and in Germany even as we look beyond to the global perspective. As of today, August 29, 2020, we've been living with SARS-CoV-2, the novel Coronavirus, for eight months. Countries that quickly adopted strict, coordinated measures to contain the outbreak saw far fewer infections and deaths than countries whose leaders pursued political strategies of misinformation and denial. And yet here in Germany, whose population has undeniably benefited from good governance, today is also the day that a second "anti-Corona" rally is taking place in the country's capital.

Covid affects people in vastly different ways; it affects nations in vastly different ways. The pandemic seems to have brought every country's worst nightmare back to life. In the United States, the racially motivated violence we've witnessed recently on the part of the police and of white supremacists feels like a resurgence of our original sin, of whatever allowed us to found a nation based on slave labor, while Germany, known for its rational leadership and admired as a shining example of a fully functioning democracy, is currently seeing a reemergence of the dark fanaticism of its fascist past. A volatile mix of the radical right and esoteric-minded, of Coronavirus deniers, conspiracy theorists, Reichsbürger, neo-Nazis, and anti-vaxxers are calling on protestors to "storm Berlin"—spurred on by a group that goes by the name "Querdenker 711" (Lateral Thinkers 711) and calls for the immediate overthrow of the German government and imprisonment of Angela Merkel; the far-right political party Alternative for Germany (AfD), which is exploiting the opportunity to maneuver the movement to its own ends; and other right-wing influencers who see the public health measures as an attack on their personal freedom. Earlier this week, the city's interior minister banned the demonstration, citing grievous infractions of public safety regulations during the first anti-Corona protest on August 1, which deliberately defied mask-wearing and social distancing requirements, conflating them with a nefarious plan on the part of the state to strip its citizens of their basic rights. But at 3 a.m. this morning, the administrative appeals court of Berlin-Brandenburg lifted the ban, and while many have expressed dismay at the prospect of another super-spreader event in the capital, the takeaway is that banning the protest and citizens' right to freedom of assembly will only serve to fuel the movement's supporters. And so, the anti-Corona rally, which is expected to attract more than 20,000 demonstrators from all over the country, will go ahead as planned. With one difference: this time around, calls for violence have been spreading through social media, with far-right supporters advising people to come armed and ready to fight.

Are American Coronavirus deniers comparable to their German counterparts? In Europe, as in the United States and elsewhere, denying the existence of a global pandemic and defying basic measures to contain it can seem like a kamikaze mission, a form of collective insanity. Do they really believe that Bill Gates is conniving with other Illuminati to install a pharma-dictated technocracy to exert mind-control through a legally mandated vaccine? Surely there's another explanation, another set of doubts and grievances fueling the movement. Germany has seen a resurgence of the highly charged phrase "Lügenpresse"—

the "lying press," an older, German version of "fake news" that originated during WWI to counter enemy propaganda and that infamously resurfaced during the Nazi era and again later, as a reactionary anti-immigrant movement rose up in Germany in 2014. We live in volatile times on both sides of the Atlantic; large parts of the population are becoming more polarized than ever before. And yet a dangerous divide has opened up between the measures mandated to contain contagion—the closure of schools, universities, daycare centers, and almost everything else that enables us to live the lives we've known until now—and the ruination of livelihoods and abrupt rise in bankruptcies, foreclosures, homelessness, mental illness, and domestic abuse. Some of the restrictions can seem unfair, while the official reasoning offered to justify them comes across as inconsistent at best. In Germany, theaters and cinemas are allowed to open at reduced capacity and under strict distancing measures, while airlines, evidently the more powerful lobby, continue to pack passengers into every available seat. The restrictions seem at least partly based on economic dictates—culture is clearly less important than the aviation industry or the automobile industry. So are we being lied to?

In the first days of lockdown, a solemn mood prevailed as we watched health workers battle an invisible enemy under inconceivable conditions. Overwhelmed by the sick and dying and forced to adopt triage measures otherwise implemented during wartime to distribute a limited number of ventilators to a far greater number of patients in dire need of them, we wept with doctors and nurses online, their faces bruised by countless hours of wearing PPE, as they described the unbearable reality they were facing. As a new sense of solidarity took hold, we adhered to lockdown and quarantine, we scrubbed our hands and applauded essential workers every evening from our windows and balconies. And as anxiety gave way to an appreciation for the respite the virus was offering some of us, a temporary pause in the ever-accelerating speed of modern life, a new feeling emerged: that the virus's appearance, in spite of all its perils and in spite of all the sacrifices required of us, harbored unprecedented potential. Some said that nature was telling us to slow down; that nature was giving humanity a chance to wake up and finally comprehend the urgent need for change. As the first lockdowns were eased, we watched citizens of countries with large tourism industries retake their streets, and in spite of the economic blow dealt to so many, the images of children playing in piazzas normally packed with foreign crowds seemed, at least to those of us enjoying the comparable luxury of home office, to carry a promise of some kind: a return to a more sane and humane way of living. This state of grace was short-lived, of course; the loss of livelihoods and the collapse of entire economic sectors would soon accelerate a backlash during the course of which a degree of risk and potential contagion would become normalized. Human lives are not, as we're frequently told, merely lost to a dangerous virus, but to broken economies and financial ruin.

But it's hard to ignore the feeling of a lost chance. After years of watching the world's governments fail to work together to bring about the necessary transition from carbon fuel to green energy alternatives; after scientific studies repeatedly revealed that reducing carbon emissions at such a late stage would at best alleviate only a small part of the inevitable devastating effects of global warming, but that this was far preferable to doing nothing and unleashing the worst-case scenario on the world's most vulnerable communities; after watching politicians offer lip service at climate conferences as the status quo remained largely unchanged—suddenly, everything seemed possible after all: industrialized countries were, indeed, rich enough to subsidize entire sections of the population as the skies turned a blue we hadn't seen since the eruption of Eyjafjallajökull, which ten years ago had also brought international air travel to a standstill.

It turns out that we can, in fact, reduce emissions; we can, in fact, slow down production. Why was the virus able to achieve this, while the prospect of an uninhabitable planet was not?

The majority of the texts in StatORec's Corona Issue were written exclusively for the magazine. We reached out to authors we knew and admired, and in some cases asked them to write on specific themes. A sense of urgency prevailed throughout, a knowledge that we were chronicling something, responding to something we'd never experienced before—something that was changing us and the social fabric all around us in ways that we would need time to fully understand. Each of these works responds to the present tense, each shares a sense of vibrating immediacy. For this anthology, we've organized the 31 stories, essays, poems, novel excerpts, and flash fiction into six categories: "Chronicling the Pandemic," composed of essays that track events over a particular period of time and range from the virus's first appearance in early 2020 to the weeks and months of uncertainty that followed; "The Anxiety of Distance," which brings together pieces that capture the strange psychological space of isolation and social distancing; "Writing Against the Virus," a group of works in which the very meaning and purpose of writing comes under scrutiny in the context of a larger crisis; "To Covid, with Love," comprised of essays and an excerpt from a novel-in-progress in which the overriding response to the global pandemic is a renewed focus on personal relationships, caretaking, and love; "Invisible Danger," in which a sense of fear and even paranoia over an essentially unknowable enemy prevails; and "The Fallout," a collection of essays and poems that explicitly address the socio-political implications and after-effects of the pandemic. While each of these works could easily inhabit several categories, we've looked to their underlying mood, an atmosphere that lingers beyond the ideas, facts, and events they describe. The sections themselves—which track the progression from epidemiological threat to the political crisis the virus soon became—sketch out the evolution of Corona's rapidly changing meaning over the past half year. It's our belief that these pieces of writing, composed in unusual times and under considerable pressure, will endure as documents of a particular period of history, testimonies to states of mind we will quite possibly have forgotten as we turn our attention to the new challenges facing us.

As far as Berlin and its anti-Corona movement goes: an estimated 50,000 people took part in the demonstration, more than twice the original estimate; the police barely managed to prevent a horde of neo-Nazis and other right-wing extremists from (literally) storming the Reichstag; and Germany has escaped—for now—a Corona-induced uprising. But at this point in time, while the danger of civil unrest in the upcoming US presidential election season and its aftermath remains a troubling prospect, the effect American instability will inevitably exert on the rest of the world will carry repercussions currently difficult to predict.

Andrea Scrima
Editor in Chief, StatORec
Berlin, September 1, 2020

CHRONICLING THE PANDEMIC

CORONA REPORT
Andrea Scrima

The invisible enemy hit Italy just as I was preparing to leave Florence; containment measures had begun a week prior to my departure. At first the "red zones" of Codogno and other municipalities in Lodi were subject to quarantine, then the whole of Lombardy together with provinces in Emilia-Romagna, Veneto, Piedmont, and Marche. And then, on March 9, the entire country was placed under lockdown. I thought of my room in the Oltrarno, empty; I tried to imagine Piazza Santo Spirito empty, the library at the Piazza Torquato Tasso, filled with students studying for their final exams only the week before, closed, the enormous Palazzo Pitti closed, tried to imagine the Porta Romana crossing empty, the little café on the corner empty, the Via dei Serragli empty. The prospect of restricting the movement of sixteen million people, and then 60 million, seemed surreal—how had reality transformed into science fiction so quickly?—until the understanding sank in that all of Europe would quite likely soon be under quarantine.

The weeks I'd spent there, before the threat of the pandemic's destructive power became manifested in exponential infection curves and a health system hopelessly overwhelmed, seemed as though they belonged to a distant past; the number of dead in Italy had been rising daily ever since. We read reports of wartime triage regulations, of doctors and nurses on the brink of mental and emotional collapse; reports of hundreds of coffins stacked up at the gates of cemeteries and convoys of army vehicles carting them away. Families were losing their loved ones without a chance to say goodbye; funerals were strictly prohibited. In Germany, we were still allowed to go outside if we kept at a distance to one another, but everyone knew that further restrictions were imminent. One evening, at a prearranged time, we stood at our windows and balconies and applauded the empty streets, a gesture meant to express gratitude to the medical profession, but as we began banging pots and cheering and the din reached a feverish pitch, it seemed as though we were engaged in an atavistic ritual, trying to make enough noise to shoo the invisible hobgoblin away.

Although hospitals were still waiting for the deluge to arrive, newspapers already reported shortages of protective gear, masks, disinfectant, ventilators, and staff. Following a two-week period of self-imposed isolation during which I read far too many articles on pandemics, the R0 contagion factor, and virus mutation, I left the apartment to go to the grocery store, and as my hand gripped the bannister and I made my way cautiously down the four flights of stairs (absurdly, I'd tripped in the apartment during my quarantine and sprained my ankle), I realized that I was potentially coming into contact with the pathogen, left behind by the hand of someone entering or leaving the building: no one knew for sure how long the virus could survive on a given surface. The front section of our building counts ten apartments and at least thirty people going up and down the stairs each day, not including postal deliveries. Outside, the hand that touched the bannister was the hand I used to zip up my jacket against the cold; this same hand took the items from the store shelf and placed them in the basket, fished the ATM card out of my wallet and paid and stowed the groceries in my backpack. Leaving the store, I squirted some homemade hand sanitizer onto my hands and rubbed them together, but if I'd picked up the virus, it was on my jacket now, or on the items I'd purchased, or on the handle of the basket I'd returned to the stack at the store's entrance, waiting for the next customer.

We weren't used to the idea of living in times of disaster; we'd been protected for so long that, although comparatively brief in historical terms, the period of post-war peace and prosperity we'd come of age in seemed normal. Other people, people outside the still-stable countries we lived in, had been going through hell for so long that we'd gotten used to the idea that—even if we were living from paycheck to paycheck, even if we were working class—we were somehow, magically, exempt from the world's worst calamities. We watched them on television or on laptops, catching up on the news as we ate our lunch at our desks and closing browser windows when we were finished. Famine, disease, war, plague: these happened to underdeveloped nations or to dictatorships, and not to us.

As the pandemic spread throughout Europe and the rest of the world, those of us who could worked at home and read the news avidly. We stocked up on rice, beans, lentils, and oil, but then, wholly unaccustomed to disaster, for the first time we wondered how we'd cook meals if there were suddenly no water to be had, or no gas for the stove. Should we have been taking our cues from the survivalist movement? Stockpiling canned goods, fuel, water—flashlights and batteries, shortwave radio? Should we have been digging out bunkers? We were only just getting used to the idea of doing without cinema, museums, theater performances, readings, and already we were facing the prospect of mass death and worldwide economic collapse.

Newspaper articles instructed us on how we should be reaching out to the vulnerable, people with anxiety disorder, people who were alone and at risk, as though we weren't already checking in with friends regularly. We settled in for the long haul, began disinfecting the food packages we brought into the apartment, downloaded patterns for homemade facemasks, and wondered if the sectors of the economy that had sustained our freelance existence would survive the impending recession. Our first impulse, when confronted with the online images of refugees trapped in the dangerously overcrowded Moria internment camp on the Greek island of Lesbos, was to turn away: we'd already cried over the thousands of dead in Italy, thousands more in France and Spain, we were waiting in dread for the peak of the curve to arrive, and for the moment, our empathy was limited to wondering anxiously who among us would catch the virus and succumb. Dark thoughts haunted us: it felt like an overdue punishment, as though we, in the rich countries, secretly knew that our wealth and prosperity had been stolen, that we'd been living at the expense of others and had been waiting all along for a calamity to come and take it all away.

Three days before Italy's first recorded death from Covid-19, the UEFA Champions League soccer match between Bergamo and Valencia—which Bergamo's mayor Giorgio Gori would later identify as the decisive "biological bomb"—took place on February 19 at the San Siro stadium in Milan. 44,000 fans crowded together to watch a game that had been heavily promoted as the largest in Atalanta's history, holding up signs that read "Insieme da sempre, insieme per sempre" (always together, together forever) and cheering wildly while thousands more gathered with friends and family to watch the game on TV. Although the first domestic cases had already been confirmed, the Coronavirus was still seen as a Chinese epidemic. Unaware of the danger, a third of Bergamo's population hopped in their cars and chartered buses, clogging the roads and causing three-hour traffic jams on a stretch of highway that normally took forty minutes. When Atalanta won, fans were delirious. Jubilant, they flooded the streets and squares of Milan and crowded into the bars and restaurants of their home towns to celebrate, hugging and singing and drinking well into the night and the next morning and turning virtually all of Lombardy into an epicenter of the pandemic as 2,500 disappointed Spanish fans who'd traveled to Milan for the game flew home, carrying the virus with them. In the press, Atalanta's managing director defended soccer's importance to the country's morale. "Today's results prove us right," he said following Bergamo's 4–1 victory, "and our city deserves it. Our boys will go down in history for society and for all of Italy." By mid-March, when this turned out to be true—albeit not for the reasons the team's manager had envisaged—I realized just how close I'd come to contagion. The day a third of Bergamo's population flocked to the San Siro stadium was the day I left Florence to travel to Greci, the village my grandfather Luigi emigrated from nearly 120 years ago and that he never returned to; that his mother, Maria Luisa, never returned to; that none of his nine Bronx-born children, including my father, had ever seen; none of their children had ever seen. Had I boarded the Frecciargento in Bologna the following morning—the train heading south from Milan—I wouldn't have sat next to Fabio during the four-and-a-half-hour trip, but quite possibly a hungover soccer fan who'd spent the night reveling and was now headed home, snoring in his seat. In which case it's likely that I would have caught the virus and passed it on to Rita and Pino, my hosts, would have passed it on to their son Luigi, who drives the town's ambulance, passed it on to Aldo and the rest of the staff at the Comune, from where it would have spread to Greci's overwhelmingly elderly population. Three weeks later—just as Bergamo counted the highest number of Covid-19 deaths in the country, a third of the Spanish soccer team tested positive for the virus, and the number of dead in Valencia had reached more than three thousand—Bayern München was still planning to play Union Berlin until the Bundesliga, having come under heavy criticism, finally called off the match.

In the case of the Atalanta game, signs of the impending pandemic had appeared well ahead of the event. On the Regionale I took from Florence to catch the Frecciargento in Bologna in the early morning of February 19, Trenitalia broadcast a solemn announcement that it was taking the danger seriously and was implementing all necessary precautions, but when I got up to use the toilet, I was puzzled to find the soap dispenser empty. The first cases had already emerged, but the

Coronavirus was still seen as something essentially Chinese. Italy had already suspended flights to and from China at the end of January, and in Florence, I saw Western tourists trying not to shrink from the remaining groups of Asians crowding the Uffizi and the rest of the city's museums and churches. The prevailing perception was that the virus was something intrinsically alien; people feared that the nearby city of Prato and its huge Chinese immigrant population would become a hotbed of contagion. As it turned out, those first weeks of February were the calm before the storm, a period of incubation. Although the precise starting point of local virus transmission—in other words, Italians infecting Italians—remains unclear, there were ample warning signs that a mass event like the Bergamo vs Valencia match should have been canceled.

While Sinophobia flared up under the threat of the Coronavirus, anti-Chinese sentiment had been brewing for some time. As Chinese immigrant manufacturers successively replaced a once-thriving Italian textile industry, a region that had traditionally voted left now swung sharply right. Successful for generations, family-run artisanal businesses in Tuscany, Umbria, Marche, and Emilia-Romagna went bankrupt as Chinese sweatshops began manufacturing cheap copies of their designs. When Italy's recent trade agreement with China resulted in a total export deficit of twenty billion Euros, populists jumped in to decry the foreign invasion, but then, when the northern countries didn't come quickly enough to Italy's aid, the arrival of the virus brought about a sharp reversal, replacing anger at aggressive Chinese business tactics with a new wave of anti–EU rhetoric.

In mid-March, I was struck by the image of Pope Francis walking through the empty streets of Rome, flanked by security guards. It was a pilgrimage to pray to the Salus Populi Romani situated in the Cappella Paolina in Santa Maria Maggiore, a Marian icon attributed to Saint Luke, brought to Rome by Saint

Helena, and said to have saved the city's people from the Plague during the papacy of Gregory I; Francis then walked to San Marcello on Via del Corso to offer flowers and pray to a wooden crucifixion accredited with having stopped a resurgence of the Plague in the sixteenth century. Two weeks later, in the presence of these two holy artifacts of the Catholic Church, which had been brought to the Vatican for this purpose, Francis gave his Urbi et Orbi blessings in a rainy and deserted St. Peter's Square, reminding "the city and the world" that we hadn't been "shaken awake by wars or injustice," nor had we listened to the "cry of the poor or of our ailing planet." It was two weeks before Easter, and I suddenly recalled that my son and I had been in Rome at this very time the year before, when the Notre Dame Cathedral caught fire and the images of its flaming roof and the smoke darkening the Parisian sky and the startling footage of its spire collapsing branded themselves in our minds like a terrible omen.

QUARANTINE DIARY (EXCERPT)

Matthew Vollmer

Trying to read David Markson's *Reader's Block* during a plumber's visit. Yesterday, E, my son, clogged up the toilet in his bathroom. Upon further interrogation, he admitted that he'd flushed something called a "Magic Eraser" down the commode. Spent twenty minutes pumping a plunger, trying to get the turds of a person I helped create to disappear down the tube. No dice. Got pissed. K—my wife—wondered why I couldn't be more forgiving. She said she didn't understand but didn't finish her sentence. I knew what she meant even though she hadn't said it: she was thinking how unfailingly forgiving my own father is and how strange it is that I hadn't inherited this tendency. According to an article in the *Detroit News*, which was accompanied by a photo of a scantily clad lady wearing a facemask, strip clubs want a cut of the Coronavirus aid. Due to global lockdown, for the first time in three decades, residents in the northern state of Punjab, India can see the Himalayas, which had been obscured by pollution. Tornados and thunderstorms ravaged the southeast last night; this morning is fleecy clouds, blue sky, and intermittent sunshine. On my walk over the nearby golf course hill and over part of a crushed chain-link fence and into the next neighborhood, I spotted my friend Ed retrieving his mail. I yelled his name. We chatted, from a distance. Had he heard that scientists had found six different kinds of Coronavirus in bats? He had. Simple solution, I said. Stop eating bats. At least it hadn't come from pangolins, Ed said. He was tired, he said, of the Chinese eating all manner of creatures so that they could get erections. A retired professor of Virginia Tech's Industrial Design program, Ed, a vegetarian, has been to China many times. "They tried to feed me seahorse soup once," he said. "One guy said it'll make you. . ." and then gestured with his hands in the air as if to make the sign of a giant cock. "I told him I didn't need that," Ed said. "I've been married for forty years!" Another man named Chuck—an unemployed guy who used to volunteer, if my memory serves me correctly, to help homeless men in Atlanta, or maybe he worked with Habitat for Humanity building houses—approached with his two golden retrievers. He asked where I was headed. I told him: the woods next to the quarry. He said he'd just spotted some red flowers, what was their name? He couldn't remember. Name started with a C. "Up in the upper peninsula of Michigan, where we used to live," Chuck said, "you know when they got the news about being six feet apart from one another, they said, why so close?" The three of us shared a laugh. An old man wearing headphones approached us. Behind him, a small SUV was honking its horn. Inside, a woman from the Foreign Language department and her husband, a tall, lanky literary theorist with long, puffy gray hair who commuted to his job at Duke University. They were both gesticulating wildly and indignantly as they passed. The old man just smiled and kept walking. "Columbine," Chuck said, before he left. "That's the flower."

•

"This is a time of collective intensity," Luisa said. Luisa is a shamanic psychotherapist with whom I have worked previously, and I was watching her speak on a YouTube channel about how to widen one's metaphorical riverbed. "Intensity is life-force energy," she said, "and I want to share with you how to keep the power of that energy moving and flowing so it doesn't get stuck. When our energy is flowing, we are more able to grow and evolve through our experience. Intensity is another word for power, another way of describing life-force energy. When things get intense, what happens is very similar to when snow melts in

9

the mountains. . . If there is a very rapid snowmelt, then that melted snow moves with much greater intensity. As humans we are reflections of the natural world. We function as the natural world; we are part of nature. When we are in the midst of great change, we too are experiencing rapid ice melt. The heat is on and the temperature is high and what had been held back is now moving through us with a greater velocity. I want you to feel and imagine there is something coming through the crown of your head. If it gets jammed up, this is when we experience emotions that are stuck, that don't serve us or keep us in alignment with the present moment. As if the riverbed were blocked with old trees and plants or just trash. We're going to work together to clear the riverbed, widen that area so that flow of life-giving water can move through us and create the conditions for us to feel present. When I'm able to be present and breathe, that makes it possible to grow, to transform, to learn, and evolve. And when that happens as a collective experience, there's even more power in that." I listened to Luisa say, "I now align myself with the flow of source." I repeated it. Tried to feel better. Wondered if I did. Hoped I would.

•

"As a Buddhist," the Dalai Lama recently wrote in an official statement, "I believe in the principle of impermanence. Eventually, this virus will pass, as I have seen wars and other terrible threats pass in my lifetime, and we will have the opportunity to rebuild our global community as we have done many times before. I sincerely hope that everyone can stay safe and stay calm. At this time of uncertainty, it is important that we do not lose hope and confidence in the constructive efforts so many are making."

•

Food technologist Eugene Gagliardi, who developed "popcorn chicken," may have foreseen the popularity of his thinly-sliced, frozen steak product "Steak-umm," but could he have ever imagined, at the time of these significant inventions, the *Internet?* Or that the person running the "Steak-umm" Twitter account would represent the voice of reason during an era of conspiracy-ridden paranoia? Would Gagliardi endorse the social media master who, when responding to the questions "Why do people believe in conspiracies? Why do they follow cult personalities or seek contrarian opinions?" had answered, "Because they're vulnerable. They feel bullied or left behind or isolated or exploited or abused or inadequate and they're looking for answers, community, security, and identity" and "When you hold a fringe belief or become part of a tightly-knit outcast group, you feel like you have some secret, valuable information that the world needs. You feel important for knowing it. And anyone on the outside becomes a vague, intangible enemy, often referred to as 'they,'" and "It can be difficult to know what to believe in a time when institutional trust is diminished and the gatekeepers of information have been dismantled, but it's more crucial now than ever before to follow a range of credentialed sources for both breaking news and data collection"? I like to think he would.

•

My doctor, who a friend refers to as "Prescription Pad Chad," called today to discuss treatment of a kidney stone. Two days before, I'd woken up to a familiar pain in my lower back. Wondered if I should go to the emergency room. Nurse at clinic said I could provide urine specimen and then have a phone consult. Peed into a plastic tub that once held Talenti ice cream, twisted lid on, placed in lunch-sized paper bag, and delivered it to clinic's curbside. Two days later, Doc calls. Told him pain had been mild so far but was scared it could get worse. I'd been in emergency rooms before where a dose of morphine hadn't touched the pain. Doc said he'd go ahead and prescribe me some medications just in case, told me—as he had before, and as he had to a great many people, I supposed—that he'd had patients tell him that the pain of passing a stone had surpassed that of giving birth. "It's like getting a grain of sand in your eyeball," he said. "Little things," he added, "can cause great pain." Later, I watched a TikTok where an Asian woman was rolling around the floor of her house while a computerized female voice narrated her predicament: "help I've put hand sanitizer on and forgot I had a hangnail and oh how it burns please help God." I filled up a gallon milk jug with water and chugged. Lacking a strainer, I studied, like some kind of warped fortune teller, my toilet bowl for the tiny particulate that would indicate passage of a stone. But I never found anything. And though the pain seems to have receded, I know it can return anytime.

●

A former student texted me from Scotland. "I've been thinking," he said, "about writing a story about a man shitting on himself on purpose." I wondered what purpose that might serve. "It's just so ingrained in us that shitting yourself is the ultimate faux pas," he continued, "that there must be a sense of liberation in it." I suggested that shitting oneself might represent the ultimate act of defiance, and he said that it would be a kind of Diogenes-like act, and that Diogenes, were he alive today, would probably shit himself in "city center." I didn't know who Diogenes was. My former student explained that he was the best philosopher, and that his favorite quote from the man had been "in a rich man's house, the only place to spit is his face." I texted back that I loved him already and my friend said, "Yeah, he lived in a barrel and used to eat garbage." I typed "Diogenes" into Google, and learned, via Wikipedia, that he had become "notorious for his philosophical stunts, such as carrying a lamp during the day, claiming to be looking for an honest man." Although no known writing of his exists, Diogenes is said to have eaten in the marketplace, urinated on some people who insulted him, defecated in the theatre and masturbated in public. On the indecency of his masturbating in public he would say, "If only it were as easy to banish hunger by rubbing my belly." I agreed that this man seemed like one I should follow.

•

Laura Spinney, in her book, *Pale Rider: The Spanish Flu of 1918 and How It Changed the World*, tells us that some have suggested that The Norwegian artist Edvard Munch's famous painting, The Scream, "sprang from his flu-darkened thoughts. 'One evening I was walking along a path, the city was on one side and the fjord below,' he wrote later. 'I felt tired and ill. I stopped and looked out over the fjord—the sun was setting, and the clouds turning blood red. I sensed a scream passing through nature; it seemed to me that I heard the scream.' By the time Munch wrote those words, the pandemic was over, and so was the millennia-long struggle between man and flu." Or so Spinney thought; 102 years later, here we go again.

•

Because disinfectant is so effective at killing the Coronavirus, the President of the United States of America suggested that "something like it" might be injected into the human body. In response, Twitter users suggested that, according to that logic, perhaps people eat Tide pods; a Facebook user created a fake product called "Clorox Chewables." What to believe? Now that we had "deepfakes," people could choose to believe even live footage of political speeches are doctored. CNN reported that a giant asteroid was headed to earth, and that it looks like it's wearing a face mask—but how am I to be sure? On Reddit,

13

I watched a video: "Girl Goes Viral as She Is Attacked while Trying to Eat a Live Octopus." My nephew Will, who hadn't sent me a text since July of 2019, asked me to look at the YouTube page of the so-called "Ice Age Farmer," who claimed that humans were on the brink of a global food shortage in part due to a Grand Solar Minimum. But when I Googled "Ice Age Farmer" and the only hits were from the Ice Age Farmer's site, I refused to watch any videos, and told my nephew that I was starting to worry about his sources. On the occasion of John Muir's 182nd birthday, *Adventure Journal* posted quotes from the explorer, including "I never saw a discontented tree" and "Few places in this world are more dangerous than home. Fear not, therefore, to try the mountain passes. They will kill care, save you from deadly apathy, set you free, and call forth every faculty into vigorous, enthusiastic action" and "The world is big and I want to have a good look at it before it gets dark."

●

After the sun went down, walked for an hour through fog while talking to my friend Nancy, an ultrasound technician who lives in Montana with her husband and three kids, whom she homeschooled. Nancy thought I should take the Enneagram personality test. So I did. According to my answers, I got "The Enthusiast." My wife, who thought the test was stupid, took it anyway and got "The Challenger." E was "The Helper." "I guess I'm the asshole in the family," K said. Cooked bacon on grill outside in a chilly wind. K opened window to say, "Cooking bacon on a *Monday* morning?" I told her that that was just what a Challenger would say. Ate bacon and eggs and a mandarin orange while re-watching episode four of *The Last Dance*. Checked email. Received PDF of my application for loan forgiveness, though the person from HR who'd created it included the note that said "To Whom It May Concern please sign this and return to me as a PDF." Suited up in winter biking gear and rode to English Department. Fixed PDF. Uploaded it. Visited Patty, a receptionist who had come into the office to work. Told her about the personality tests. Learned that a restaurant in Eggleston, nearly half an hour's drive away, was delivering food to Blacksburg. Had Patty heard about The Bad Apple, the new restaurant in nearby Pembroke? She looked it up on her computer. The dining room was inside a refurbished barn. Stained-glass windows blazed with light. Together, we browsed the menu. "Artisanal cocktails" seemed like something from the past. I showed her a picture I'd taken a few days earlier during a night walk, of a floodlit dogwood, Venus shining brightly in the sky above. I can't stop playing *Days Gone*, even though I'm getting sick of it. Of searching for gas cans to refill my motorcycle's quickly depleted tank, busting opening the hoods of abandoned cars to search for scrap to repair my machete, gathering rags and empty bottles and fuel to craft Molotov cocktails, slashing the throats of endless zombies, staving off attacks by wolves and cougars and infected grizzlies, crafting bandages to heal my wounds during firefights with roving marauders. Of hearing my avatar talk about how he, like me, keeps "losing track of time." Took a break to baste wings—a free ad-on with my subscription to Butcher Box—with Sweet Baby Ray's Buffalo Sauce. Lacking newspaper, I ripped up a Kroger paper bag and stuffed it into the bottom of my Rapidfire Charcoal Chimney Starter, poured briquettes inside, and lit it. Sipped whiskey while watching neighbor girls chatting: one stood on the lawn, the other sat on her front stoop. Remembered the girls I'd seen on a recent bike ride: each standing in their driveways, one across from the other, taking turns flying their paper planes, and when one of the girls had to retrieve her plane from a nearby yard, the other girl yelled her name, and said, "You're getting too close to your neighbor!" A reporter on NPR referred to the virus as "the plague" but talked about it in terms of a forest fire: yes, the devastation was real, but hopefully might pave the way for restoration. According to

AP Science Writer Seth Borenstein, "People were also noticing animals in places and at times they don't usually. Coyotes had meandered along downtown Chicago's Michigan Avenue and near San Francisco's Golden Gate Bridge. A puma roamed the streets of Santiago de Chile. Goats took over a town in Wales. In India, already daring wildlife has become bolder with hungry monkeys entering homes and opening refrigerators to look for food." For most of the day, like most days during the pandemic, my wife and son wore Air Pods in their ears. Which meant that they had been so lost in their own little worlds that when I'd ask them questions, they couldn't hear me, and so they replied, nine times out of ten, by asking me to repeat what I'd already said.

•

A Florida lawyer dressed up like the Grim Reaper to scare beachgoers. Biologists invented a new method of fighting viruses, using llama blood and molecular super glue. According to an article on Patheos, the earth needed a Sabbath. "This might be the first time since the beginning of the Industrial Age that Earth is finally getting a break from the relentless activity and growth of human industrial production," Leah D. Schade writes. "I've noted with bitter irony," she added, "that the virus is using the same tactics against the human body that humans have used against Earth's body. The virus attacks the lungs, multiplying and destroying the 'respiratory tree' down to the tiniest alveoli that enable the exchange of oxygen into our bloodstream. Similarly, humans have pushed into forests and natural areas, destroying the very trees that create the oxygen we breathe." Dr. Schade is the Assistant Professor of Preaching and Worship at Lexington Theological Seminary in Kentucky. She is also a professional harpist with a CD whose title resonates with post-pandemic irony: *Shall We Gather*. There are photos of Dr. Schade online in "Biblical drag"—a costume that resembles the kind of thing someone in the movie *Midsommar* might wear. I wanted to write

16

to her but couldn't find her email, so instead I followed her on Twitter. She didn't follow back. On the same day that I learned that the Pentagon revealed information about UFOs to the public, my friend Evan and his son Jackson watched a line of lights stream across the sky; it turned out to be Space X's Starlink satellites, whose visibility Elon Musk hopes to diminish. My friend Beejay wrote to me to say that her bad lungs had forced her to move from Cairo to Australia, leaving her husband, a diplomat, behind; now she resides in a shed in the back of her parents' house and lives, in her words, out of a suitcase. My students were already writing about the pandemic—some simply mentioned it casually, like "I'm writing this during the pandemic"—and for others it was all they could focus on: the ridiculous amount of money that Jeff Bezos makes per hour, while workers are being fired in droves because farmers have nobody to sell their crops to. The bulldozed fields of lettuce. Our friend Gena and her daughter Nyala stopped by last night before dinner to talk to us. They remained seated in their car. We stood in the yard. After they left, K returned to TikTok. My son disappeared into his room and shut the door. I returned to my office, fired up the PS4, and resumed the slaughtering of zombies.

•

Last night K asked me what it was gonna be like after the pandemic was over. I didn't repeat the sentence by Alan Watts that I'd been thinking of so often: "We are the witnesses through which the universe becomes conscious of its glory, of its magnificence." Instead, I told her that if worse came to worst we could retreat to my dad's house and start a commune. And if things got really bad, we could just fix ourselves vodka cyanide cocktails. I was thinking about the Heaven's Gate cult. Twenty-three years ago this March, thirty-nine members of the Heaven's Gate cult, all of whom were dressed in black pants and black Nikes with white swooshes, chased a concoction of phenobarbital and applesauce

17

with vodka, placed plastic bags around their heads, and died. The night before, they'd all gone out to eat at a Marie Callendar's restaurant, to enjoy their last supper on Earth. According to the *L.A. Times*, one of the waiters there said that they all ordered the same thing, and that everything was set up before they arrived. "They all had iced teas to drink," the waiter said. "Dinner salads beforehand with tomato vinegar dressing. Turkey pot pie for the entree. Cheesecake with blueberries on top for dessert. They seemed very nice, very friendly, very polite. No one seemed depressed at all, or anything like that." And perhaps they weren't. Just as I can understand the allure of absolute and total rebellion—hookers and blow, etc.— so too can I imagine the sweet relief of acquiescing one's will, of handing it over to somebody else, of agreeing to a system of beliefs in which the kind of thoughts one can think are limited. What to wear? Already decided. What to order? Taken care of. A life in which you were so sure of what you believed that you laid yourself down on a bed and died. Whether the members of Heaven's Gate were able, as they surely believed, to fly out of their human containers into a spaceship that was following the Hale-Bopp comet, no one can say. But Nike discontinued the shoes that they wore, pairs of which can still be found on the Internet. If you are willing to pay upwards of six thousand dollars, you too can own a pair of these shoes. "I didn't know Marie Callendar's was a restaurant," my wife said when I relayed this story. She'd only seen the boxed meals in the frozen foods section of grocery stores. Had she heard about "skin hunger"? She had not. An article in *Wired* magazine described how a woman—a 31-year-old director—had been breaking the rules of lockdown to walk to the end of the garden to meet her best friend. "There," the article said, "with the furtiveness of a street drug deal, Lucy hugs her tightly. Alice struggles to let her go. 'You just get that rush of feeling better,' Alice says. 'Like it's all okay.'" And I had to suppose—because I hug K every morning when she kindly brings me coffee in bed—that for at least a minute it felt like it might be.

CORONA DIARY
Joan Juliet Buck

THURSDAY APRIL 2

Woke earlier than I'd wanted, boiled up a compress for the eyes, carried it back to bed. And because my eyes were closed, I meditated. The other day, when I was having the horrors, I got tough love from Anjelica, who said "Don't you have a mantra? Just do it. Don't be sentimental." I can dole out that same cold shower when someone close calls me and I hear more self-pity than distress. I have a radar for self-pity, I know it well, and I know how fast it sinks you. So does Anjelica. I'm too scared of horses to have had much practice getting back in the saddle after I've been thrown, but that's what she does.

I retreat. Retreat. Implies defeat, but you tell me, what constitutes winning right now? If I were still in the hulking fortress on 42nd Street, just north of Hudson Yards where I have not set foot—the cover of *New York Magazine* was enough for me—I would crave air and light, because my view was smothered by a luxury condo built in the manner of a multi-story parking garage. Living in the country is my retreat. Not retirement—"a writer never retires," a sentence that would be more convincing if I had more of an output. A writer never retires. This so-called writer could spend all day looking for food back when shopping was interesting and not alarming, this writer could write practically nothing for a year because her childhood love returned to her and that was more interesting than any words I set down in an effort to reach my agent's expectations of what might earn us both some money in the marketing of this entity that I'd become after the publication of the memoir that, due to some sloppy PR prose, recreated me as fashion icon when that was never the story and never the point and certainly not the point of the book. I felt such a fake trying to write what might be considered enticing, saleable, that I stopped almost at once. There was no need to add to the mess of shit out there. I wanted to live, and love, instead. I'll stop that, we're getting a little near self-pity. You can smell the Poor Little Me creeping in. And that's not the way it is. David Hockney made public his bright, simple iPad paintings of flowers and buds around his house in Normandy yesterday, saying "they can't cancel the spring." Now that the desk faces trees and bushes instead of a blank wall (Oh the self-punishing urge to conflate writing and prison), I can hope that the bush right in front of me is actually a lilac, because I don't know. Dead leaves still cling to the undergrowth, and mauve flowers, too short to pick, with a strange name I never remember.

The meditation gave me the day. I was ready to hand it over to the headlines, then the TV news, then the governor's speech. But now I feel that actually it's mine.

Did the dishes that were piled in the sink. Dr. Stevens told me when I was 23 that I had horror vacui—fear of emptiness. The boyfriends were accumulating at a rate he found unseemly enough to quote Aristotle—"Nature abhors a vacuum"—with an apologetic laugh there in his office behind Harrods, the first Jungian I went to.

THURSDAY APRIL 9

Storm, then sunshine.

Slept well, and late. Much needed.

Bought vegetables today, ginger, and some bacon: $22.

Because I don't need more than that. Right now.

I feel smug about the little systems I've instituted in the kitchen.

Meanwhile, people are going hungry. In the USA. Millions of people. A mile-long queue of cars outside a food bank in Los

Angeles. People wearing trash bags against the rain standing on line for free food.

The money I would have scattered all over the food stores will go where it's needed. Directly to a local food bank.

That will be tomorrow's task.

Today, I made an experimental face mask out of a Number 4 coffee filter, some paper adhesive, and a small silk scarf, tied above the knot on the back of my nylon head-wrap.

I was so proud of myself that I documented the mask on Instagram.

It produces the same delightful effect as the paper bags I used to breathe into when I was hyperventilating with anxiety.

I wore the calming mask to deposit some miniature but useful residual checks, predominantly in the two figures. This meant going to the bank's drive-by, locating which of two metal posts the voice was coming from, then rolling the checks into a clear Plexiglas tube that whooshed up a Plexiglas pipe towards the bank. The beautiful Plexiglas tube failed three times to reach the right hole to penetrate the bank, and came whooshing back to me with a thump.

An apologetic teller had to meet me outside; doubly masked and caped in my love's raincoat, I slipped her the checks in a blue latex hand. Her face was bare. She didn't smirk at the amounts. She apologized: this was a brand-new tube, not yet broken in. A customer had run over the previous tube and smashed it.

Back home, I washed the silk scarf at the same time as I washed my hands, with the same soap, hung it to dry from the shelf over the sink, held it in place with two French glasses.

The landlord went into the basement; he tells me he fixed the lights over the washer and dryer. When I saw him at his truck, he wasn't wearing a mask. I'll wait a few days before I go down to the basement. His grandson cleaned up the flowerbeds, and will grapple with the butterfly bush that now bars all north-south access.

I started writing again this afternoon.

FRIDAY APRIL 10

Today erased itself as it went.

Becalmed, ignorant, retracted, not thinking.

Time shrank at each headline until it was too small to be felt or measured. The number of jobless Americans. Millions. Mass grave on Hart Island. Mass graves in other places. Mass. Graves. The word Trillion. The sound of systems breaking. Trillions. Cogs, wheels, deals, agreements, consortiums, expectations. Trillions. Ptoing! Crash! Boing boing boing, boing. Fizzle. Splat. Trillions.

We need a map. We need testing. Testing for the active virus, testing blood for antibodies. Testing to know where we've been and where we might be going.

Will I dare to wear a tracker?

SATURDAY APRIL 11

Easter is the return. Before Easter, the light is at its utmost contraction to allow darkness to pervade everything. We may awaken, after all this, to a world transformed by our new understanding.

MONDAY APRIL 13

As he began his briefing this morning, Governor Cuomo asked "What day is it today?. . . It ends in Y."

Here are the questions in my head:

1: Are we learning patience and self-discipline?
or
Are we learning passivity?

If we are learning patience and self-discipline, will we emerge strong, wise, and powerful, like Nelson Mandela after 27 years in prison, Vaclav Havel after four years in prison, Denzel Washington in Spike Lee's Malcolm X after 40 minutes screen time in prison? Or as vengeful as the Count of Monte Cristo after 14 years in the Château d'If. Or as nuts as the tigers in Vegas, Women Behind Bars, and Mrs. Rochester.

If on the other hand we are learning passivity, won't our instincts for combat melt into surrender? All we will know how to do is roll over.

which leads to

THE CONSPIRACY THEORY CONSPIRACIES
This Can't Be Happening, Can It?

2: Some of us need to know the news. Maybe, one day out of two. One day pure, self-contained, bored but not alarmed. Next day, news all day long and late into the night. Even if it's broadcast from living rooms, dens, nooks, corners, hallways, Chris Cuomo's basement, green screens. People who need the news are people who believe that objective reality and science exist.
or
Others say paying attention to the news lowers your vibration and makes you sick.

These are the people who are 33% more likely to believe that the Universe has a Plan.

These others: Some read books, some write books, some don't read, some can't read, some have degrees, some read auras. Some are on a higher plane of abstracted bliss, some are baking like fiends, some are clever with dried beans, some do Zoom yoga every day and some believe that vaccines cause autism. And that the white jet trails in the sky are chemicals released as part of a plot to change the weather so as to lower the price of land so that George Soros can buy it all up. Some of these others believe aliens are watching.

Some of these others believe this is all a hoax.

Some of these others don't vote because they say they don't know what to think.

Some of these others don't believe in science.

So I know I'm not in the Others department. But to what degree do I think that—

— This is the revolt of Gaia?

— The clarity of the air and the waters will teach humanity that we can never go back to fossil fuels?

— This is God's way of trying to flush Trump?

— There is a God?

— There is no God?

— Everything's going to be fine?

— Everything is going to be changed forever?

— The children will never get over this?

— The old people will all die?

— They want all the old people to die?

— There will be food riots?

— There will be starvation?

— This is the beginning of a stealthy but complete takeover of our lives and liberties?

— You know you can't renew your passport or get a new one right now, don't you?

— This country will become a right-wing prison?

— We ain't seen nothing yet?

— The Aliens will come save us?

— The Aliens sent it?

— The Internet was invented to carry us through this, and many more such to come?

— And what's with the Swedes?

SATURDAY APRIL 18

I spent the last few days asking myself how it's possible to have feelings without wallowing in self-pity.

Self-pity is self-destruction. Especially now.

It's easier for me, old, to say that, than it is for someone young whose entire load of hopes have for the moment atomized. If I allow myself to feel how much I miss my love in London, it hurts. Our miracle shimmers some days like a mirage; he doesn't always read what I send him, I still haven't watched the scientist's film he sent me about "Nothing."

It took so long for us to come back together, really for the first time, fifty-four years later. Adolescence to advanced age. The unexpected, insane privilege of that, last year. It's been the new time since he went home at the end of February, this is this year, the impossible unthinkable incoherent present, this is what now is like. We are older, and will be older before this is over.

If I allow my feelings to open up and spread out, I'll be in tears. But this isn't me, or me and him, it's everyone at the same time all over the world. All the structures we relied on are breaking along their fault lines, great chunks of our world calving.

So when I cry in the car or cry at the news, I tell myself I'm just crying, and that's that. I'm not crying about me. Or us.

I entertain myself with complaints about the monotony of my own cuisine. I should write out a hundred times "I will not use more than one mixing bowl at a time. I will not use more than one mixing bowl at a time. I will not use more than one mixing bowl at a time."

Stubborn as a dog, I keep trying new recipes, but no amount of non-wheat flour, eggs from Chris and Monique and Tim's hens, hand-held beater or rapidly rusting whisk can change the taste of the food I make into the taste of food made by someone else. Maybe next time, I'll try leaving out the cumin. And the garlic. The miniature twin sinks stayed full for days. The lassitude that overcame me at the sight of bowls and pans crowding the wooden spoons and the two crappy bamboo ones was familiar but not specific.

Then I recognized it as the protective trance of waiting that descends on you when you hear your flight is delayed seven hours and there's nowhere to go but down on your ass on your coat and your wheelie on the floor, where you sit, too obedient to read, zoned out, eating chocolates and letting the wrappers fall where they may. The hibernating dull dedicated non-time. Zoned out because you trust the airline to call your flight and to board you and take off and fly and get you there. Because you know you're in good hands.

The suspended indifferent trusting time of waiting.

This is not that.

Most nights I have to go to bed after four so that I will not wake at four thinking of lines of cars ten miles long queueing for food banks.

So that I will not wake thinking that America still operates on slave labor. Of the 634 workers at the Smithfield's pork processing plant in Sioux Falls South Dakota who tested positive. I wake wondering how many are badly sick, I remember what the head of the local chapter of the AFL-CIO said on TV— that the workers had heard from home about the dangers of the virus a month ago, that they speak 80 different languages. The plant is Chinese-owned, the workers are from 80 countries. I remember something, look up Smithfield's and find Food Inc., the 2009 documentary about another of their plants that had so many undocumented workers that every few weeks they'd let ICE raid a couple of worker's family homes, just to have some peace. The conditions of the pigs weren't much better, and for a while after I saw that film, back in 2009, I stopped eating big agribusiness pork, choosing only to eat small batch, hand-cured, local, nitrite-free, delicate, rich person's choice pork products, or, in a pinch, D'Artagnan.

These informed choices are not enough. They're bullshit. This is a different world now, and to survive, society will have to change radically.

22 million filing for unemployment, the states of the United States are broke, the Federal Government is working against the states.

Malignancy is abroad, and it's not Covid-19.

Night just dropped like the other shoe.

SUNDAY APRIL 19

Late last night, I watched Helen Whitney's beautiful 1983 documentary "The Monastery." The Trappist monks, so holy in their robes and so candid in their interviews, elevated and soothed me. After dinner I started watching the second Helen Whitney documentary I have—I'm to send them to London, they were meant for him—"Into the Night," subtitled portraits of life and death, from 2017.

A mortician. A cryogenic entrepreneur with 141 "patients" in the Alcor "patients bay," preserved in large tubes he calls vessels. A writer who had to shelve a book about death, an astrophysicist who's a lapsed Platonist, a former Islamic extremist. The first of nine—I'm going back to it now, it's too good to leave for tomorrow. There's a "transhumanist designer" whose face reminds me of someone, though I have zero idea what transhumanist designer means.

She's booked to be frozen.

Helen Whitney, whose work I didn't know before, gets subjects to talk about secrets more complex than, say, sexual orientation.

Faith, uncertainty, doubt.

"In our hearts we have these private conversations," says the writer, "so I feel a bit embarrassed but I also feel a bit shriven." Shriven. Feels as if he'd confessed. Been absolved?

27

I miss visiting the Catholics at mass.

Yes I do have to lighten the fuck up.

God, though, the steak was comforting.

THURSDAY APRIL 23

Watch Andrew Cuomo get tough.

The fridge grows empty now that shopping for food is no longer a daily hobby.

Order a pizza from Gigi. Wait in Oblong bookstore parking lot for it to be put in the trunk. Guy forgets to close trunk. We're all a bit off by now.

Eat most of the pizza from the box I've placed on the papers on the kitchen table, and go to the office to sort books, books, papers, plugs, so many plugs, plastic binders, cables, cables. Old iPhones. More cables.

But someone got at the pile of Paris books that I'd topped with Gertrude Stein (because she belongs in Paris).

Today, Gertrude's ziggurat of books about Paris had melted away, and she was incongruously sitting on top of Orson Welles in the movie pile.

All the Paris books—not that many, but maybe 20?—had gone. As had the Quercy et Lot Michelin guide.

I'm not hallucinating: the landlord showed the office to someone on Wednesday, the day I didn't leave the house, and somehow the prospective tenant or the landlord must have created a disturbance in the field of my library system. I wish they'd also taken some plastic file folders. An old iPhone? The landlord is pissed off that I got sick in early March before I could complete the move, and that I'm only paying him for the period up until the original move-out date. I couldn't move alone or get the movers until now. Where'd the effing Paris books go?

Irritating, but no reason to inject myself with bleach: the Paris books were going into storage, antechamber of oblivion.

SATURDAY APRIL 25

On March first, my love called from London to say "come over now. This could last for six months." We decided it would be mad to go on renting the expensive office where I barely went and never wrote—I can't write too far from a kitchen—and that I should pack it up. Storage units rented, movers booked March second. I started sorting, tossing, giving books and pictures away, with a move-out date set for March 13.

Then I got sick on the 9th, and while I lay in bed sweating at 102.6, the portcullis came down, the moat filled up with enemy effluvia, and the world stopped moving.

I don't know if I had it. I might never know.

London would be, for the immeasurable time being, impossible.

But I had a project.

This entire period I have been consumed with the impending, yet for weeks impossible, move out of the office. I dragged my head, arms, feet, and only returned the modem via UPS a few days ago. But for almost two months every day I've had the move on my mind. The must of the move. The maybe London is beyond the move or maybe he'll come back here where it's country, but speculation and planning both useless in the face of what's going on.

And the thing was, never mind the outcome, I had a project: the move. End of the office. All I need is a table, the rest is all crap from Staples to reproduce the props of a real office. But I had a project. A mission. A thing to worry about. A thing to not do quite yet but it's number one on the agenda but I'd rather take a walk to build my strength back up, I'd rather disparage the forsythia and the unkempt trees than sort out the old pictures notes mementos manuscripts and clips.

All of which had kept me from darting to London when he said "come now."

I had a project, so I'd be OK. As long as I had a project I

couldn't watch Homeland without him, I couldn't read the paper or pick up after myself because I had a project. And when I went back to the office to tackle the project, I'd stand perplexed in front of an open page in a notebook with the New York address of an old associate of my father's, who'd called to give it to me after Dad's death 19 years ago so that I could send him something. Did I ever send whatever it was? Should I throw this out?

I know why I rented an office big enough to run Vogue from. I was hoping someone would give me an assistant so I could decide what to do about Mr. Pick's New York address on the page of a pale blue notebook from Staples.

Moved my last things out of the office today. Correction: Movers moved today. Steve and Larry moved. I was at home sorting keep-donate-give-toss, pawing through ribbons and socks and that effing Tom Sachs T-shirt printed with a gun and "Kill all Artists" that I can neither frame nor wear nor toss. I was handing the Dansk desk over and now had to make the second big room ready for the long French farm table and the other table from the office, both very old, worn, and wonderful.

But first I had to make sure that what I gave away went to the right home. Who needed, liked, wanted, desired, hoped for, would accept, would keep these things?

It came to me that my problem—this particular problem—began when recycling became mandatory, how long ago? Before that, I gave the better rejects to charity shops, and if I wanted to throw something out, I threw it out. I didn't try to divine how to recycle my discards, who might be happy to receive the old shoes or the gloves, before recycling I didn't stand by a bed trying to figure out who would like the yards of silk ribbon I brought back from Paris in 2001. Etc.

To snap out of the need to categorize my overflow and

discern what was really garbage, I poured baking soda all over the big room carpet and then I vacuumed it up on the Turbo setting. The optical illusion of making a difference may not be borne out, but who cares?

The desk went away, the tables came in, the room is quarantined for a few days, and for the first time in. . . eight years—I am all in one place. Unless I count storage.

Zoom cocktail. New faces, old friends. I was still hungry; on the phone, Linda counseled me not to complicate the salmon, just bake it in a 400° oven with salt and pepper.

SNL from home.

Ate like a pig today. Nux Vomica 6 CH, and bed. Night off.

Oh my god I don't have a project any more.

SUNDAY APRIL 26

Watched two episodes of Homeland so that I'll be caught up for the finale next weekend, and he and I can watch it together in real time, if not real space.

If the asteroid doesn't hit us. How timorous I'm becoming. Have to acknowledge that little clutch of fear about a firm rendezvous for one week ahead. Planning anything for the immediate future is oddly more alarming than long discussions about UK versus USA versus EU, if there's any left by the time they let us out.

Homeland is not soothing. I pull at the fuzz of the hide at my left, and wonder if a wire pet brush might fluff it up. While Carrie Mathison is ruining her career, I check out how you comb a sheep hide, compare the special £4.30 brush from the UK with the $14.00 dog or cat brush from Amazon, and make Jeff Bezos a little richer while endangering a whole chain of overworked, underpaid, unprotected people from warehouse packer to forklift operator to delivery driver, so I can fluff up my sheep hides while I watch TV.

MONDAY MAY 11

Woke late. Recorded but have not yet watched governor Cuomo. The thrill of the disaster movie has worn off.

This is what life is, this is what it is going to be.

London call; we are both flattened by the monotony.

When you drop the bravado of This Is the Opportunity to Work on Myself and Grow as a Person to Heal and Create a New World, everything suddenly weighs tons: feet, arms, head, the air, the day, the time.

Even the blue plastic bag that sheathes the NYT for delivery weighed a ton today. It was so heavy that it was sloppy, it was in fact full of water, water that the newspaper had marinated in for so long that it was almost papier mâché.

Another day of WTF.

I briefly wondered who could have wanted to drown my *New York Times*.

Prepared for a long period when no one will be watching. Or present. Or playing. Put away the movie books, brought forward the psych books that I used to hide, placed the box of remotes within easy reach of the loveseat, stashed away the useless and highly contagious board games—monopoly pieces, scrabble tiles, boxes of racing demon playing cards. All that touching, shouting, scrambling, snatching, pushing, spitting, yelling. Bliss. Forget it. Attended Ariadne's webinar about Procrastination so I wouldn't have to work.

Familiar faces in the Zoom rectangles. But I think procrastination is as shameful for each of them as it is for me, so I didn't wave. Must be like AA.

Walked with Joseph. Tried some word games on him. He didn't enjoy playing Essences or Botticelli. "I'd rather gossip," he said. But about what, dear Joseph, what on earth is there to gossip about?

Zoom cocktail. One piece of good news about a friend. Each one there (or here, there, everywhere) as fed up with the dormitory aspect of our—so far—comfortable lives. Gloom if not doom and maybe more doom coming.

France reopened, partially. Provincial hairdressers were overrun, but nothing like the scene French TV news showed, with an editorial smirk—the Colorado eatery jammed with jostling barefaced patrons. They missed showing the one with the guys standing at the Subway in North Carolina carrying automatic weapons and a rocket launcher.

Those French, they just don't get it. Tomorrow, right here, Caligula's horse gets named emperor for life.

THURSDAY MAY 14
Over 36 million people have lost their jobs since March.

WE ARE DREAMING OF THE FUTURE SEASON
Steven Cheslik-DeMeyer

J and K, the owners of the house, come out to greet us when we pull into the driveway. They live next door in another house mostly hidden by trees. J, a big man in jeans and suspenders, keeps at least ten feet from us. K hovers another ten feet or so farther back. With her straight grey bob, she doesn't exactly remind me of my mother but she looks like someone my mother would like. They both look like the kind of people who would give you a hug or at least take your hand in both of theirs to shake it. J warns us that the top rack in the dishwasher is a little stubborn. They tell us to text if we need anything. After we lug our stuff into the house, J comes back with a Tupperware container of homemade granola, "from a *New York Times* recipe," he says.

•

We left the city on an impulse and in a hurry.

At first, in early March, C's company divided his department into two teams that would take turns working from home for a week, then a week at the office, but a few days later they just sent everybody home indefinitely. *I always* work from home, as far as that expression describes what a writer does. After two weeks together all day in our one-bedroom apartment, on Saturday the day before my birthday, C was sitting on the couch with his iPad, and he said, "We don't have to stay here. We can do this anywhere. Why don't we go somewhere?"

"Where?"

"Michigan?"

Michigan seemed far away and we'd have to fly.

"How about Maine?" I said.

34

We talked it through—in New York, we share a building with thousands of other people, many of them over 70, over 80, we share the elevators, the hallways, laundry room, and we share the streets and grocery stores with the whole neighborhood. It's impossible to maintain six feet of space between us and everyone; whereas in Maine we can isolate ourselves for 14 days to make sure we aren't infectious and, after that, even if we venture out for a hike or to the grocery store, we'll see very few people—and we came to the conclusion that regarding both our own chances of contracting the virus and our chance of spreading the virus, in a remote location on the coast of Maine was a better place to be.

Within what seemed like minutes, C got a reply to his inquiry about a house he found on a vacation rental web site. "The property is available, and I'd like to invite you to stay! Please come, relax and enjoy the peace and quiet of rural Maine. K." Though the house would not be ready until Thursday, C booked a rental car to pick up on Monday. The governor was shutting down one industry after another and we were worried that rental car agencies might be next.

On Tuesday an article appeared in the *New York Times*, "The Wealthy Flee Coronavirus. Vacation Towns Respond: Stay Away," followed by what felt like a fusillade but was probably only three or four articles here and there along the same theme. A town on Long Island contemplated closing a bridge to keep outsiders out.

We wouldn't have called what we were doing "fleeing," but in the days following our decision to go to Maine, we'd become part of an unpopular exodus. Our thoughts veered from "maybe we should cancel and stay home" to "we need to get the hell out now." For a while (and still, but now we're used to it) the world seemed to change from hour to hour, over and over some new piece of information would force one to recalibrate every plan, aspiration, opinion, what to do for the rest of the day, everything.

•

I don't think either of us realized how secluded the house would be.

•

We emptied our refrigerator and freezer and cupboards of food, packed it all up in bags and boxes, the frozen stuff in a Styrofoam box that Omaha steaks, a gift from C's brother and sister-in-law, had been delivered in and that we had saved seemingly for this occasion. Having no idea what I would want to read while waiting out a pandemic in a rented cabin on the coast of Maine, I brought Edmund White's biography of Genet, Flannery O'Connor's *Collected Stories*, Proust's *In the Shadow of Young Girls in Flower* (the new translation), *City of Night* by John Rechy, and Philip Roth's *Nemesis,* a late short novel about an outbreak of polio in Newark in the 1940s. I packed empty notebooks, sketch pads, drawing pencils and pastels, my guitar, and a week's worth of clothes (there's a washer and dryer there) and we threw everything into the car. We joked, though it wasn't funny, that we were afraid they might not let us out. Of the city, of the state. But nobody stopped us. Traffic was lighter than you'd expect but there were plenty of cars on the roads. We drove straight through, it took eight hours, and here we are in a charming rough plank cabin surrounded by spruce and birch trees, with a fireplace and a wide porch in back facing a cove on the western side of an island off the coast of Maine. For five weeks which will turn into seven.

What will we come home to?

•

I *do* feel guilty that we are sitting out the pandemic here in this beautiful place, while friends, many of whose incomes disappeared overnight, are stuck in their tiny New York apartments for who knows how long. Because of social media, I don't have to speculate on whether or not they are struggling, while here, at the edge of the world, it hardly matters that it might be the end of the world; in fact it seems like it *is* and it's *okay*.

•

The trees thin out as you get closer to the shore, but there are still lots of them. A massive spruce stands just out the back door, between the house and the water, and everywhere dozens, hundreds of skinny white birches. It was through a screen of these birches that we first saw the water, vertical bands of shimmering cerulean between the trees, when we drove up to the front of the house on Thursday just before sunset and parked on the gravel. But through the sliding glass doors in back that lead out to the deck, the water is (notwithstanding that big spruce) fully visible. Its surface—luminosity, color, shape, reflectivity, transparency, motion—changes from hour to hour, and, in the morning and evening light, from moment to moment. At high tide the water looks like it might spill over the rocks and come right in the house. Low tide reveals several tiny islands of rock just a few feet off the shore.

Ducks float patiently in groups of two or three. One will suddenly upend itself and disappear under the water for 20 or 30 seconds, then resurface with a small fish in its beak. Sometimes a gull or two, twice as big as the ducks, will join the floating group and wait for a duck to surface with a fish, steal it, and fly to one of the little islands to wolf it down. The only time the ducks weren't hunting was during the storm.

•

All day I've been sluggish and on the verge of tears. I woke to email from the Korean producers of my musical with e-tickets

37

attached for a June trip to Seoul. When we knew we would be unable to go in April, we discussed June as an alternative. I guess I just didn't, seeing how the epidemic has evolved, imagine anyone was still planning on a June trip to Seoul. It's true it's safer in Korea now than New York, but Trump is shutting down *all* immigration, so won't the international airports be a mess?

•

It's snowing this morning. About an inch of it has accumulated on the deck and the big spruce and the rocks farther down. I watch the scene revealed incrementally as the sun slowly lights the deck and the cove and across the water to the island opposite.

•

Before we left, before we'd considered the possibility of being met with hostility here in this idyll, I put in a forwarding order with the post office, but a few days after we arrived, we decided to cancel it and lay low. I read that mail delivery is fucked up for everyone in New York right now, so I guess I shouldn't worry about it.

•

I've moved my office to the kitchen table. I was sharing the dining table with C, but he shakes his leg and the whole table vibrates, and he breathes loudly and sighs while he works. Used to our little New York apartment, it didn't occur to me for several days that there were other places I could sit. C is only about fifteen feet away, I can see him, and I have a view of the water here. This place is so heart-wrenchingly beautiful.

•

Yesterday the governor of Maine issued an executive order prohibiting rental accommodations: hotels, B & Bs, vacation houses, all of it. Bookings already made can be honored but no new ones. We paid through May 2, so we're safe for now, except that the order indicates a hostility toward outsiders that feels threatening in contrast to the hospitality of our hosts. On Thursday (four days from now) our 14-day quarantine is over and we'll have to get some groceries. Will they know we're not from here?

•

C and I have been married for eight years but I've never seen him at work before now. He's an attorney and he takes phone calls all day long, stomping back and forth through the house, speaking forcefully in a patois I don't understand but that I am mesmerized by. I've never loved him more than I do in this house.

•

I start habits but don't follow through: daily walks, practicing guitar, working on new songs, writing in my journal, writing *anything*. But I've always done that, stabbed at habits but stopped short of killing them.

•

Our self-isolation period—the Maine governor has recommended that anyone entering Maine from out of state stay inside for 14 days, though that was our plan all along—will be over at six o'clock tonight, and we had planned to go to the grocery store tomorrow, but we ran out of alcohol on the 12th day, so we're going tonight. We pass very few cars on the half hour drive to the supermarket in Bar Harbor. We tie scarves over our faces and take two carts from the young man whose job it is to sanitize each cart as it's returned. We want to lay in enough food for the rest of our stay, three more weeks. We spend over two hours in the store.

We buy lemons and limes, beer, whisky, potato chips (bags and bags of them), tortilla chips, avocados, local Cheddar, butter and milk, half and half for coffee, seven pounds of coffee, sugar, middling olive oil, good olive oil, all the sad herbs they have, parsley and cilantro, dill, and onions, celery, and carrots, mushrooms, asparagus, broccoli, several bunches of scallions, ground beef, ground pork, pork chops for the grill, chicken legs, bacon, eggs, garlic, locally made rye bread, beer, Diet Coke, peanut butter, and small jars of cumin and oregano because I didn't bring any spices from home except a bag of dried New Mexico chilies—I remember thinking when we were packing, "I won't need spices," like I pictured my days spent reading big dense books and eating meals seasoned with just salt and pepper. The only things we can't find are sweet vermouth and flour.

The staff, but very few customers, are wearing face masks. As the cashier behind the Plexiglas rings up our groceries and sends them down the conveyor belt, a woman about my age puts them in bags. Not thinking, I reach out to grab one of the bags and put it in the cart, but mid-reach I realize I've come within inches of her hand. "I'm so sorry, I wasn't thinking." She says "Pfff. I don't care. I have to wear the mask 'cause it's the rule, but I don't care," and she rolls her eyes and smiles at me.

The sky was cloudy on the way to the store, but as we come out with our two carts loaded with plastic bags, it's full-on snowing big wet clumps of snow and we're soaked by the time we load the car and pull out. Several inches of snow have already accumulated on the winding two-lane highway back through the national park to our house. The headlights seem to be aimed straight ahead, illuminating the blizzard flying at the windshield but not the road. Several times the tires lose traction and the car skates until it finds a grip again. Steep ditches but no shoulders run along both sides of the highway. I think about what we're wearing (will we freeze to death?), at least we won't starve, but if we're injured in a crash, where is the closest hospital and will anyone stop to rescue us? Two New Yorkers driving into a ditch in a little snow in April is such a ridiculous problem. Is there even room for our little car accident when the world is on fire?

•

Venus appears every night before sunset, before any stars are visible, in the same part of the sky where the sun will disappear behind the island on the other side of the cove. It is so bright and clear you can see its roundness, like a tiny moon, and it occurs to me—it should have been obvious but it wasn't to me—Venus is not, like a star, shining its own light on us, but a planet illuminated by the sun so we can see it from here.

•

I am primarily a theater artist. Several licensed productions of a musical I wrote, called "Lizzie," were either running or planned as the epidemic started. A large production in Sweden closed early when the government shut down the theaters. Two college productions were canceled, and other small productions were postponed indefinitely. The biggest, in Seoul, is still running. Audience members are required to wear masks and are forbidden from cheering.

•

I have made macaroni and cheese, two quiches, baked pasta, mushroom risotto, casseroles, potato salad, pound cake, chocolate cake, two batches of oatmeal cookies, chicken and dumplings, shrimp and chorizo over polenta. C prepares the coals in the little Weber grill and I grill two pork chops rubbed with garlic and salt. I bake chicken legs like I do at home, 500°

41

for very crispy skin, but the smoke alarms all go off at once, so I finish them on the stove with some mushrooms and deglaze the pan with dry vermouth. I am cooking like there's no bathroom scale and no tomorrow, and I think, "Why is our life at home so pinched? *This* is how I want to live, how I've always wanted to live, like the days are all special, and when this is over there will be cake every day and cheese on everything and we'll wear caftans and drink like fish and smoke like chimneys and we'll be big not small and we won't be afraid to *fucking eat*."

Leaving New York was a rupture we are still in the middle of. Will I want to or need to or be able to pick up work in progress later? It certainly doesn't feel at all like I will be doing the same thing but "remotely," like so many people with other kinds of jobs surely will be, but more like I will be starting over. Like everything is either going to end or start over, or end and start over.

•

J tells us a big storm is coming, bring the deck chairs inside. The eerie grey light, the roiling water, the spray on the rocks, the loud drama of it, it's like a Turner seascape. I make a short video and post it on Instagram. Watching it later, out of context, it looks like what you'd expect the coast of Maine to look like, waves crashing against rocks, spray. It doesn't look like a remarkable storm at all.

•

The day after we got here, J came by with a bird feeder on a pole and pounded it into the ground where we could see it from the kitchen window. He said it would take a few days for the birds to find it. The next day I sat in my kitchen table office and watched a pair of finches and one chickadee fly in and out of it, but they didn't stay long and they didn't return, and this afternoon J moved the feeder to the back of the house.

•

Today Trump tweeted: "In an attempt to create conflict and confusion, some in the false media say that it is the decision of the governors to open the states, not that of the President of the United States and the federal government. Let it be understood that this is incorrect." Let it be understood.

•

Today it has been sleeting or something all day, started in the middle of the night. The view across the water is grey and foggy. Later it changes to snow.

•

I have a sort of burning, though burning is too strong a word for it, sensation in the back of my left nostril or possibly deeper in my sinus. It feels like how it feels when you've been chopping chilies and touch your face without thinking and later it sort of stings a little and it takes a moment to recall why; in fact that's what I thought I must have done except that it's lasted for weeks now. It's very mild, most of the time unnoticeable. It's been there since about a week before we left the city.

•

I sit for hours with my guitar in the loft bedroom looking out at the water. A fragment of melody, an unusual chord progression that I can't name (I'm pushing myself to try odd things, "bad" things, go somewhere other than where my fingers and my voice want to go) and two lines of lyrics that suggest more, suggest a fuller idea, to me. Sometimes that's all I need and everything else builds out naturally from that, hangs on it, and sometimes it's just what it is, a fragment, a few evocative words that lead to nothing.

The endless sky
My love and I

Can a day be too beautiful to write a song about? I take a nap.

●

At the beginning of March, I organized a reading of a new musical I've been writing for the last three years based roughly on my high school diary. The reading was scheduled for April 14th, but within a couple weeks of setting the date, casting, booking the space, I had to cancel it because gatherings of, I think at that point more than three people, were prohibited by the mayor. I told everyone it was postponed but it's not likely we'll do it any time soon. Half the cast were college students uncertain if and when school would start again, or if they'd be in New York for the summer or back next year. The other half were old friends, colleagues of decades I only see when we do such things together. A friend who knows how offered to help me arrange a reading by video conference, which was generous, but I couldn't bear the thought. I want to be in a room with people and my play. That's what theater is.

I'll argue with you until I am blue in the face how essential, how elemental, the arts are, but I still wonder if the cancelation of my reading is a loss notable to anyone but me.

●

When we do such things together.

●

I am sleeping better here than I have in years at home. I'm still waking up intermittently through the night but I must be sleeping soundly in between because I am alert in the daytime and able to read for long stretches without dozing. It's not unusual for me to sleep better when I'm away from home—at hotels, when we visit family, in vacation houses, etc.—but I feel truly relaxed here. I guess there's nothing odd about it, here by the vast ocean and sky and quiet and nothing pressing or unpleasant to do.

•

The recycling bin fills with empty wine bottles, gin bottles, beer cans. C jokes that he's going to drive out and find a dumpster in the middle of the night to dispose of our recyclables so J and K don't know how much we're drinking. Isn't everybody drinking too much?

•

Four deer walk by the kitchen window as I sit at my computer. They stay for a while, three young, one older. It's a wet day. One sits down on a mat of pale green moss on a large flat rock twenty feet from the window surrounded by spruce seedlings. Another eats from the bird feeder. The younger ones look soft as kittens, with large heads and wet curious eyes. One, just feet away from the window, locks eyes with me, neither of us afraid.

•

My friend M sent me a link to a story about a group of armed vigilantes a couple islands over from us who cut down a tree and dragged it across a driveway to prevent the residents of the house, temporary construction workers from New Jersey whom these year-round residents had decided were infected with the virus, from leaving.

•

When we first arrived, I thought I'd write new songs, a whole batch of them, not theater songs, not part of a show but connected to nothing except my heart and an impulse to say something. But I find myself drawn instead to scour my computer for forgotten sound files and images, to organize, catalog, preserve my old work, or at least what I have here: music I made with bands in the eighties, some of my first theater music, a random assortment of demos. Instead of writing, I am cataloging and archiving. For what? For whom? I start up an email correspondence with my old bandmates, one of whom was my boyfriend though most of my twenties, and we listen to the old recordings and reminisce.

•

Well, I had a terrible time trying to sleep last night. I thrashed for a couple hours, my back hurt, I itched all over, finally got up and went to the downstairs bedroom and slept fitfully for a few hours and finally at 5:30 I just got out of bed.

•

I've started taking late morning walks, after my shower, down the rocks behind the house to the shore. At low tide, the rocks are covered with mussels and barnacles. Walking through this landscape, feeling like I'm in the presence of geological time, like I'm in the presence of a god I don't believe in, thinking, as I bring to mind each little component of my former life: will that survive? Will that survive? Will we still do that? Will I need that?

•

We have weekly Zoom calls: Monday and Friday happy hour with C's family, Thursday with mine, a Saturday afternoon call with friends I went to Parsons School of Design with, and a

Sunday call with a group of C's oldest friends. I see and talk to my friends and family more frequently now than I have in decades. We talk mostly about the pandemic and what we're watching on TV. C and I are catching up on Schitt's Creek. These Zoom conversations are so unexpectedly intimate I am almost in tears just to see their faces on my computer screen, hear their voices, their laughter.

•

C found out that an old friend, a classmate from acting school, contracted Covid-19, is in the hospital in New York, and will be put on a ventilator.

•

J has asked us two or three times if we know our plans in May. No one has booked the house after us, and he will hold it for us if we'd like to stay. No one wants us to go back to New York. Worried that we'd be scolded for leaving, we've found just the opposite. Everyone we've told has exhaled deeply and said I'm so glad, that's such a good idea. My friend S who lives in Vermont sends emails trying to persuade us to stop on our way back and stay for a while instead of going home.

•

We receive regular email updates from our coop management and board, including increasingly stern warnings that, because the maintenance staff are sanitizing the common areas in our buildings twice a day, anything left in the hallway will be thrown away. We've likely lost a few packages that were delivered right after we left (a set of cheap whisks from Amazon, a large order of heirloom beans from Rancho Gordo, other things I can't remember), and who knows where our mail will be?

We hiked one of the trails in Acadia National Park yesterday. The park roads and facilities are closed, but many of the trailheads are accessible from the highway. Beautiful day, sunny and 50°. The guidebook described this trail (the Acadia Mountain Trail) as "moderately strenuous." It was a long scramble up a steep pile of rocks and a long scramble down the other side. We passed two or three people and stepped off the trail to let them pass; everyone is friendly and doesn't get too close. We lingered at the top for several minutes, looking out over the trees and water, mountains and the ocean in the distance. I pondered what I would do if C fell on the rocks and broke his leg or sprained his ankle. Or what he would do if I did. I don't think either of us could carry the other down. The hike took two hours and we were exhausted when we got home and very sore this morning.

•

Franklin Graham is setting up a tent hospital in Central Park and requiring volunteers to swear they disapprove of gay people. It's the Chick Fil-A of hospitals; people want the sandwich, but why does it have to come from proselytizing bigots?

•

Last night I cut my thumb. I sharpened my own knives and brought them here from New York because rental kitchens never have good knives, and I've been very careful using them, knowing this is not a good time to be in an emergency room. But I was washing one with a very stiff new sponge and the knife slipped out of my hand and slid quickly across the pad of my thumb. I knew it was a bad cut immediately, so much blood, a long cut and deep, but I don't think dangerously so. I pressed a wad of paper towel on it for at least half an hour before the bleeding slowed, and then C put two Band-Aids on it. The cut, in normal times, would need a few stitches.

·

It was sunny this morning, and the water was still, but clouds have been gathering all day and the wind is picking up, and the forecast says rain. I feel heavy.

·

C is anxious. Since his friend was put on the ventilator, there's been no news from his wife or any of their mutual friends on social media about his condition.

·

I'm watching cookbook author and food blogger David Lebowitz's live "Apero Hour" on Instagram at noon (6 p.m. in Paris, where he lives) almost every day. It's just David in his kitchen making a cocktail and talking about it. Paris is shut down and everyone is sheltering at home. The other day, he was obviously frazzled. He explained that he'd had a "meltdown," argued with his partner Romain who is shut in with him, but then he decided to let it go "because that's what you do when you love someone, you let it go." But he was noticeably shaken, in that way that, after a big fight with your partner, even after you've come together, forgiven each other, and agreed to move on, your body takes longer to recover than your mind. There in his kitchen, with the sounds of a city (even in lockdown, there are city sounds, cars, bits of conversation when people pass by his kitchen window) and his tall white kitchen cabinets behind him, and his earnest, goofy smile, it was such an intimate confession, such a small gesture, a sharing of the burden, and I cried watching him.

•

K brought us chocolate chip cookies. Twice.

•

Every night after dinner, C hauls armloads of firewood in from a small shed outside and builds a fire and we sit in two wicker armchairs with a table with a lamp on it between them, and we drink a bottle of wine and watch TV for a couple hours. Once we stumble onto a religious station, but it's not like the Christian TV I know from Tennessee and Texas, it's Catholic TV with nuns and the Pope, and the visual aesthetic is very 1950s, like Highlights Magazine or like one of those religious tracts or an illustrated children's Bible come to life. C finds it less fascinating than I do.

•

C's friend died. He finds out when his friend's wife posts the news on Facebook. He spent two weeks on a ventilator, recovered enough for it to be removed, but a few days later his condition got worse and he died. He was in his forties.

•

Even though it's cold, late most nights we open the back door and step onto the deck to look at the moon and stars as long as our necks can stand it, until we're shivering and have to come back inside.

•

I don't know what to do because I don't know what will exist in its former form, or, if changed, how? Into what? What will be important? *Doing something*, anything—chronicling my

50

days, writing, practicing guitar, contemplating new songs, even reading— is an act of hope I'm not sure I have. Hope that there will be a familiar venue for my work, that the things I write about will still matter or even mean anything, that there will come a time when I'll be glad that I learned that thing, that I know that story. The future extends as far as what to make for dinner. It's likely we'll still be here in an hour and hungry.

•

It is our eighth wedding anniversary on May 5th. We're in Maine; we should have lobster! On the roads we've passed lots of signs for lobster pounds and fresh seafood, but nothing looks open. J came by for something else, I don't remember what, and C asked him if he knew where we could get two live lobsters. He lingered to chat on the back deck, at a safe distance. We all feel the strangeness of that distance. It's just enough beyond a normal distance that people who have only recently met but like each other would put between them when they're chatting about nothing in particular in such a lovely spot. J tells us there's not a lot of "fin fish"—they're overfished. He tells us about his business, a store that sells outdoor equipment. Everything used to be made locally, but now most of it is imported from China. He used to visit China every year but he thinks his trip last year—to Wuhan—was likely his last. He says he'll put some thought into it and let us know about the lobsters.

•

Trump muses in his daily press conference on the possibility of injecting disinfectants into people to kill the virus. Perversely, the despair, weariness, fear, and spiritual exhaustion we were all experiencing already just from enduring years of this monstrously cruel man looming over every moment of our days tempers the shock of the pandemic.

•

My friend, who lives alone in a small apartment in Brooklyn, watches Governor Cuomo's press briefing every morning and posts a detailed summary with charts and graphs. Number of new cases, number of deaths, hospital capacity, etc. My friend was divorced two years ago. He has a steady girlfriend he hasn't been able to see, or touch, or hold, for weeks. He posts on Facebook a photo of a visit with his 21-year-old son—they wear face masks, meet in a park, and stay six feet away from each other.

•

Sometimes iTunes on shuffle is like a Tarot reading. Just now Bruce Springsteen singing the old Baptist hymn:
  Through all the tumult and the strife
  I hear the music ringing
  It finds an echo in my soul
  How can I keep from singing?

•

C texted J to say that we'd like to stay an additional two weeks, through mid-May. We will have been away from home, or, more specifically, left our apartment untended, for seven weeks. Neither of us could come up with a reason why seven weeks is worse than five.

•

J came by with another container of granola and a box of green recycling bags.

•

Yesterday's hike: the Gulley Trail to the Long Pond Trail. The first two-thirds mostly followed a not completely dry creek bed, thick with exposed tree roots and piles of large rocks, every step landing at a different angle. The last stretch was flat, along the edge of the pond, but by then I had triggered my bad ankle and had to limp most of the way back.

•

Headline this morning says, "Nearly Two-Thirds of Artists in the United States Have Lost Their Livelihoods as a Result of the Coronavirus, a New Survey Says." I swing back and forth between enjoying the disruption, the feeling that everything is askew—the constant striving, or the feeling that I *should* be constantly striving, has eased up; I feel released—and then remembering that the reason I feel like this is that I have no clear hope for the future, not just in the regular "you never know" way, but *at all*.

•

I found two YouTube videos, one demonstrating how to cook lobsters, the other how to eat them. It surprised me that they came in a paper bag, two of them sort of curled up, wet and sluggish. I think I expected a cage. A man delivered them early in the afternoon, so we put them in the refrigerator. I made potato salad. When we opened the fridge later to retrieve them, they were lively and crawling around. The video suggested putting them in the freezer (first it said for 10–20 minutes but later in the instructions said 30–60 minutes, so I settled on half an hour) to "put them to sleep" before boiling them. As C pulled them out of the freezer, one of their arms fell off. Just fell off onto the floor. We took the rubber bands off their claws and dropped them into the pot of boiling salted water and watched. The one on top, the one that had lost a claw, was sort of squirming, and then quite clearly trying to climb out. A stream of white liquid seeped out from under its shell and coagulated, like an egg white, or semen in a hot shower. I pushed it down with a set of long metal tongs. It climbed up again. I held it down. After the recommended cooking time (I think it was nine minutes, but I've forgotten), I pulled them out and plunged them into cold water. They smelled foul, but I reminded myself that lots of foul-smelling things are delicious, like fish sauce. I washed as much of the white stuff away as I could, put the lobsters on plates, C opened a bottle of wine, and we sat down to eat. As the video instructed, we grasped them by the body and tail and twisted to remove the tails. C's looked like the one in the video. Mine, as soon as I twisted, emitted a flood of black viscous matter all over my plate. Nowhere in either video was there black sludge. C laughed. I jumped up from the table. We argued.

•

It snowed thick, wet snow that didn't accumulate on the ground and wind blew hard all evening, but later I opened the back door and the giant spruce in the dark, with every branch articulated by a layer of snow, was alive, undulating, waving slowly, speaking in a language we couldn't hear. What was it trying to tell us? We stood and looked at it for a long time, terrified but giddy.

•

Staring at the computer, reading another prognosticating think piece about *this uncertain time*, another and another and another. I declare a moratorium on reading the literature of prediction. You don't know. Nobody knows. It will get worse. It will get better. You don't know. I will be 60 years old in nine months. This was supposed to be the home stretch.

•

I toggle between, "I'm done. I've done enough. I don't have

another reinvention in me," and "I can work with this. It's a puzzle I can solve." I put it in the general context of disappointment and suddenly I'm sitting in a familiar room. Disappointment is the air artists breathe.

•

An email from the National Alliance for New Musicals this morning: "On behalf of our Festival Selection Committee, I want to thank you for submitting your new musical for consideration for our 32nd Annual Festival of New Musicals. You were a part of a record-breaking year for the Festival, with 343 quality submissions from all around the world. We were in awe of the energy and commitment put into each submission, and it was our privilege to read them. Unfortunately. . ." and so on, you get the gist. Why can't they just start these things with "Sorry, but no." My first thought was, "Okay, thanks and good luck with your old paradigm," which was followed by, "What's to become of us all?" It is no consolation that this is the least disappointing rejection I've ever experienced.

•

Woke to a dream, holding a friend, but it is a homunculus, exposed and raw, sentient but silent, I say over and over, it's okay, it doesn't matter, it doesn't matter, it doesn't matter. A tender ache that seemed to lack location. Is the ache in me? In the homunculus I'm holding? The air all around us? I was so worried. It felt unbearable. I was worried in a way I knew I couldn't sustain, and I was worried knowing that.

•

The water in the cove this morning is bottle green and looks like moving glass in this wind and clear sun. The storm windows rattle in their frames all day.

My brother helped my father get on the Zoom call. We're all surprised to see his face pop up. He has video but no audio. We ask him if he can hear us and he writes "YES" on a piece of paper—in the block letter handwriting he's used since his first job out of the Army as a draftsman for an engineering firm in Waukegan, Illinois—and holds it up. We can't hear you. He listens to us talk for 20 minutes and then his image disappears.

•

I got a request by email today for a "perusal copy" of the Lizzie script from a small theater company in Washington D.C., with the subject line, "We are dreaming of the future season."

•

Lying in bed trying to fall asleep, I'm watching the black silhouette of the spruce trees against grey sky and water, no visible horizon, no perspective, just a field of grey. The water is present, you can hear it crashing ashore, smell it, feel it, but it is not discernible. This landscape is unlike anything I've ever seen, more mysterious than any other landscape. Withholding, unconcerned with your opinion of it. I trust this landscape. It is not a needy landscape.

•

It's almost May. Spring is coming, but so, so slowly and I think that's for the best.

•

J texted yesterday that he was smoking some chickens, and did we want him to throw one in the smoker for us. Yes. We ate it for dinner last night and cold the next day with a yogurt sauce with lemon and herbs. Later I made stock with the bones and cooked black-eyed peas in it. How old are J and K's children? How old are J and K? She seems about my mother's age, the age she was when she died five years ago. The way they are taking care of us makes me think they miss their children. I want to stay here forever.

•

I am flossing my teeth every night. Is that hope?

•

We are leaving in two days. We want to hike up Cadillac Mountain today. Till today we've chosen trails that are accessible from public roads, but we really want to do this one— it's the highest peak and the most popular trail. We read that people usually drive up most of the way and then walk to the top, where there's a paved viewing area, but there's also a hiking trail up. On the map, the trailhead looks to be a short walk from a residential street in Bar Harbor. We leave the car, over my protestations, in the parking lot of a golf club, and walk through the neighborhood that butts up against the park. I'm very anxious—we've kept our noses clean for seven weeks I don't want to have a run-in or get our car towed two days before the end of our stay—but C dismisses my apprehension and I follow him up a street that looks like a driveway to me, where we find what looks like a path into some young woods and set out. We have no idea if we are in the park or someone's back yard, but eventually we can tell with Google Maps that we are near the trail and in a few minutes my nervousness wanes when we start to see the blue-painted trail markers.

The hike up is about two hours, all uphill, all rock, some solid table rock but also a lot of piles of smaller boulders. It's only 50° or so but sunny and the trail is exposed. I take off my long-sleeved shirt and tie it around my head. We encounter no one on the way up, and one man on a bicycle at the top. We wonder, as we stroll around the paved loop at the top, looking out over every island and inlet, the town of Bar Harbor, and the ocean blue and flat in the distance, how many people in the decades since this park was created have been alone at the top of this mountain. We can see *everything* from here.

We decide, instead of taking the same trail down, to walk down the park road and see what other vistas it offers. The silent, empty paved road with its freshly painted yellow line down the middle, switch-backing down the mountain, is unexpectedly poignant, full of menace and sadness. My husband watches *The Walking Dead* and says the setting looks familiar. My ankles, and C's too, start to hurt, the smooth paved road somehow harder on our joints than the steep, uneven rocks and tree roots on the way up. We round a sharp bend and see an older couple, dressed in sportier outdoor wear than ours, coming toward us on the other side of the road. As we pass, they both smile and say hello. C says, "Don't speed!" and we all laugh.

•

Back home in New York, the Blue Angels are flying over our apartment building scaring the crap out of everyone and Jared Kushner has declared the crisis over and the government response a success. Covid-19 deaths in New York City are down to just under 300 per day and are still climbing in rural areas.

•

Email from our coop's management:

> We have had several staff members contract the
> virus, some were quite sick for a number of days. All are

now in recovery or back at work. . .

It now seems clear that both the Governor and Mayor are intent on opening segments of the state and city according to a plan that continues to track new infections and hospitalizations. . . . We will move cautiously, because as everyone knows, there has not been a building within our coop that has not experienced illness and loss. How do we come out of this? We will begin to answer this question in the coming days.

•

C has decided that when we leave here he will drive to North Carolina. His mother has pancreatic cancer. Before the pandemic, he was flying down every other week to see her, but now it's been two months. Since we have been virtually isolated here for several weeks, this may be the safest time for him to visit her. Should I go to North Carolina? I want to see my mother-in-law and I worry about how long it could be before another opportunity comes. But I want to go home.

•

We're leaving tomorrow. I had planned to spend today packing but I realize that we brought so little I don't need much time. All that's left of the food and booze are a few half-full bags of different kinds of rice and lentils and half a dozen cans of beans, tomatoes, a couple boxes of pasta, half a bottle of dry vermouth, bitters. Half the clothes I brought I never wore. *Nemesis* is the only book I read and I didn't touch the art supplies. Notebooks, my guitar. It doesn't amount to much.

•

We waited and waited and just as we're leaving spring is finally apparent here: buds on trees and the scrubby bushes along the path from the house to the rocks down to the water. Walking down, it feels crucial not to damage or disturb a single branch for fear of knocking off the tiny, fragile red buds. Two or three days have been sunny and a glorious 48°, otherwise cold. The only actual leaves so far are on the sticker bushes beside the gravel spot where we park the car.

•

The trip to Korea in June is canceled, of course. They will remount the show next year and invite us to come then.

•

Leaving, driving through town up the peninsula to meet the highway, forsythia is *everywhere*, huge wild bushes of it, all blooming, like forsythia *always* does, every year, to signal spring. Some trees are barely budding; from a distance like clouds or swarms of pale green and pink on their branches. The roads are lined with ancient graveyards, some big, some just a few tombstones half fallen down but cared for, the grass cut around them and fences in good repair.

•

Traffic is not light, but it never stops, driving into the city. We find a parking spot across the street from our building. Street cleaning has been suspended for now, so the car will be fine there until morning when C will leave for North Carolina. As we unload the trunk, the neighborhood erupts with cheering and applause and banging on pots and pans. They do this every night at seven o'clock to acknowledge the nurses and doctors, the transit workers, ambulance drivers, cops. It goes on for several minutes.

•

When I step out of the elevator on our floor, I see a neat pile of packages in front of our apartment door along with two large stacks of mail bundled and held together with rubber bands, waiting for us.

•

My first night alone, after C leaves for North Carolina, I wake from a dream in which I wake and open my eyes to find a young man, a teenager, sitting at my bedside holding a long gun aimed at the middle of my face. The boy is calm and silent. I am perfectly still. It is a moment in perfect balance. And then I wake up.

•

I keep pots of herbs and flowers on the balcony. When we left, the season was just beginning when I'd have put in new plants and the old ones would show new growth. I reconciled myself to the fact that the perennials would all be dead after seven weeks of neglect. But the thyme and chives are full and bushy and green. They look better than they ever did last year, probably because I haven't been snipping them every day and they've had a chance to grow. If I'd had time to plant anything new, it would surely have died, but the thyme and chives are thriving.

IN THE TIME OF "IN THE TIME OF":
AN AUTO-FICTIVE STUDY OF THE SOCIOCULTURAL INFLUENCE OF NOSTALGIA/SENTIMENTALITY AND DESPAIR/DENIAL ON THE DEVELOPMENT AND ACCEPTANCE OF LINGUISTIC AND METALINGUISTIC RESPONSES TO TRAUMA VIS-À-VIS THE COVID-19 PANDEMIC OF 2020

Joseph Salvatore

Abstract. The terms nostalgia / sentimentality / despair / denial and the development and acceptance of linguistic and meta-linguistic responses to trauma in culturally and socioculturally contextualized spaces as modes and manners of managing intangible historical events such as the 2020 Covid-19 pandemic are as specifically connected to one another as the terms nationalism/national identity / privilege / power are connected to totalitarianism / bromides / clichés / propaganda / newspeak / disinformation. The coupling, colliding, combining, and collocating of all these terms as denoting a process of language change can be closely related to the spatiotemporal instance in which and when such intangible historical events are experienced both subjectively and publicly as trauma. Such trauma, this paper will argue, leads to the use of ideological linguistic structures as a way to displace the denial, dissociation, dread, and despair brought upon the traumatized subject, rather than leading to the creation and establishment of new forms of language to identify, express, and confront the psychic devastation, national injury/ need for grief/mourning, and personal-identity deconstruction brought on by said trauma, replacing opportunities for individual or social change or resistance or the creation of alternate social orderings. In this study, I intend to focus on the influence of nostalgia and sentimentality as responses to despair and devastation as it regards the development and expression of linguistic and metalinguistic trauma.

Keywords: nostalgia, sentimentality, despair, denial, linguistic, metalinguistic, trauma, cholera, plague, Covid-19, Coronavirus, collocation, pandemic, grief (unexpressed), loss (un-mourned), cliché, fiction, prayer, Queens, Jackson Heights, Elmhurst, New York City.

Methodology

Autometafictive scholarship of this kind is a genre favored by the emotionally squeamish, the reticent, the shunned, the forsaken, the fearful, liars, lovers, and thieves. Those who prefer—'prefer' is perhaps the wrong word, and so is 'choose'—Those who *must* live in the head, so to speak, do so as a way to avoid engaging with the body. For as the saying goes, the body keeps the score. We know from the work of neurolinguists and the imaging technology they are now able to use in their study of the brain, namely MRI and PET scans, that different parts of the brain light up on imaging screens at different times for different tasks and functions—even if those tasks and functions are related to the same field. Take, for example, language: *vocabulary*, the part of the brain involved with learning words (nouns, verbs, adjectives, adverbs, etc.), is located in one part; while *grammar*, the way those words are used, is located in another; and in yet a third area of the brain (on the other side, actually) resides *syntax*, the way we arrange words into grammatical strings or chunks of units of meaning and melody (phrases, clauses, sentences). Why the different areas for one field? It is because language is so infinitely complicated that the brain sorts these tasks into areas of relative subsets, which utilize similar working pathways. For example, vocabulary, which is located on the opposite side of the brain from syntax, reveals far less illuminated activity in brain scans because they are units functional largely unto themselves, whereas syntax involves so many different tasks and activities (not only vocabulary and grammar) in order to produce language that it is located closer to the regions of the brain that produce music. Yet even with all that information at our disposal, such technology still can't tell us who or what is the source of all those functions. And so that persistent romantic question still nags: Who sends the signal to the brain calling forth to perform a certain 'function' that illuminates those different lights? Who generates the expressive linguistic impulse that the brain labors so complexly to produce? For whom? For what purpose? To put it another way, the brain is a construction site with contractors and subcontractors and laborers breaking up one large job into discrete tasks at different nodes. But who is the architect? Who is the one that turns on those lights, like so many bright stars in the night sky? (Alas, such questions seem hopelessly romantic or sentimental or nostalgic for a sense of a "self" or "essence" or "soul.")

The lights in brain scans may be compared to security lights in darkened properties coming startlingly ablaze at night when someone enters the sensor's zone. The lights tell us a perpetrator is there, but they may not tell us who that startled perpetrator is if that person (or animal) escapes. To extend the metaphor, as we live out our always-complicated days and months and years, we don't have brain scans to indicate what parts of that ultimately unknowable organ are being activated by this or that perpetrator or (to be less punitive) agent. What information about ourselves could be gained by knowing more about the way our brains function? But we don't need those external scans, for we have our own internal system, our bodies. Our bodies, better than any brain scan but far less interpretable, not only know what parts of the brain are being activated; they know *who* is activating them. They know the agent. Intimately. They know us. Our bodies, ourselves. Neither malevolent nor punitive, neither judgmental nor authoritarian, the body—not the brain—nonetheless serves as doctor and lawyer, shaman and exorcist; it is, at once, the

64

light grid and the light source. It is the ledger and the assets, the liabilities and the owner's equity, it is the account of all revenues and expenses. The body keeps the score.

So somewhere in the autometafictive scholar's head is an awareness of this predicament. And while the autometafictive scholar may well be hard at work to address this mind-body problem in, say, weekly sessions and settings, he, she, or they will often try to keep those efforts hidden, even going so far as to employ multiple pronouns as a way to shield the writer himself, herself, or themselves. As with much metafiction, such methodologies and the sources attributed therein are often fictive assemblages of faux texts (e.g., Borges's "Pierre Menard, Author of the Quixote," Nabokov's *Pale Fire*, Maryse Condé's *I, Tituba, Black Witch of Salem*, Carmen Maria Machado's *In the Dream House* and *Her Body and Other Parties*). In the case of autometafictive scholarship, they may be more rightly termed *autopastiches*, assemblages of both faux and real-world documents: quasi-letters, "found" texts, pseudo-interviews, questionable quotes, fraudulent artifacts that threaten the stability of a text like symptoms of an illness threaten the corpus. (N.b. The American term 'autosamplings' does not offer the fuller historical context and significance of the term French scholars prefer, *autopastiche*. This paper will use the latter.) Consider the poet Donald Justice. A note at the end of Justice's 1973 book *Departures* indicates that some of the poems in it came "in part, from chance methods." "Chance methods" are what current autometafictive scholars would consider a form of autopastiche. As one critic described Justice's methodology: (It is) "an ingenious system of quotation and transformation of lines from other poems." Jonathan Lethem calls this technique "the beauty of second use." Bob Dylan calls it "Love and Theft."

Introduction

Before the pandemic, I had begun taking steps to lessen the effects of what had been professionally classified as generalized anxiety disorder. It was suggested by certain people that holistic approaches could yield positive results: meditation, exercise, diet, no screens before bedtime, switching from coffee to tea. I began drinking green tea. At first the transition was difficult, due not only to the change in my energy levels and focus, but also to the horrible headaches I experienced. But soon green tea worked not only as well, but better than coffee. The energy was clearer, the somatic effects of coffee, which I hadn't noticed when I was regularly drinking it, disappeared, and the anxiety backed off to manageable levels. A slight compulsive tendency was lessened as well, with the exception of my green tea. It was pointed out to me that my feelings for green tea were not quite in the same neighborhood, but perhaps in the same borough as *cathexis*. Because I felt like one could cathect things far more unhealthy than green tea, I considered it a form of self-care and, in February, when I found them on sale at my local supermarket, I stocked up, buying 8 boxes of 20 bags, only one of which I allowed myself every morning.

On the morning of March 2, 2020, I drank my green tea, dropped my kids off at school, held office conferences in person with students and advisees, dropped in on a few colleagues in their offices, taught my in-person class (which modifier I never would have added to describe my class), and that evening, I attended, along with another writing colleague, the PEN American Literary Awards Ceremony at a sold-out Town Hall, on West 43rd St., in New York City's Times Square. The event was hosted by Seth Meyers, who joked that it was sold out because writers have such a lonely, isolating job that they would jump at the chance to gather with a large group of people crowded together in one room—even, he added, during a pandemic. I looked at my friend, who was sitting next to me in the front row, our elbows sharing the same armrest, and smiled. After the event, a massive group of attendees repaired to a massive nearby bar and restaurant, where we all crowded toward the bar, waiting a half-hour, four-people deep for service. Drinks finally acquired, we made our way to the long food buffet tables in the warm and stuffy rear of the establishment, where we politely handed each other plates and utensils and talked closely to each other's faces because it was so loud, and sampled each other's food and occasionally sampled this or that interesting cocktail.

On March 15, the mayor held a press conference and announced that he was closing all of the schools for the city's one million students (my children among them) with the hope of reopening them on Monday, April 20. As of that afternoon, five New Yorkers had died from the Coronavirus and 329 had been infected, the mayor said. I told my spouse, a public high school history teacher in NYC, that we and our children (ages three and five) would be able to handle a month of remote learning. That morning I broke my rule and had two bags of green tea.

On March 17, I walked home from my office, during what would normally be rush hour in NYC—Saint Patrick's Day, 6 PM, on Seventh Ave., between 22nd and 23rd, only a few cars cruised along, some pedestrians, and me. From behind me, a gravel-grinding racket filled the air, a sound that otherwise would have been drowned out by the roar of bumper-to-bumper traffic. Along came a lone skateboarder, a thin young man in tight camouflage jeans and a leather jacket and pink bandana, riding past me on the nearly empty street, playing air guitar and gliding serenely over the asphalt, all while the entire globe was being brought to its knees. In 1975, photojournalist Craig Stecyk, writing in *Skateboarder Magazine*, wrote a series of articles chronicling the adventures of the Zephyr Competition Skateboarding Team (a.k.a. the Z-Boys) who, during a two-year period of drought and water conservation in Southern California, rode the empty swimming pools of the wealthy as the region dealt with severe water restrictions. As I watched the skateboarder disappear to the north, I thought of Stecyk's words: "The true skater surveys all that is offered, takes all that is given, goes after the rest and leaves nothing to chance in a society on hold and a planet on self-destruct."

On March 19, my daily tea bag intake had gone up to three and my anxiety levels had returned to the days when I was drinking coffee. And then, while in a closet reaching up to a high shelf for a new box of tea, I knocked over a box of pasta, which fell toward my face, the corner of which struck the center of my left eye. An eye injury is scary anytime. But during a pandemic, it's terrifying. And my doctor said a virtual exam wasn't going to cut it. I had to go into the city and have my eyes dilated so she could check the retina. The retina wasn't torn, thankfully. But I had to limit screen time for the next few days, which made my Zoom training and preparation for the following week's online educational restructuring a challenge.

That following week my slightly compulsive habits returned to escort my anxiety through the darkened parlor of my shadowy un-scanned brain. And so, with my children now at home all day, our babysitter gone until school reopened, I found an activity that was somewhat comforting—calculating the number of green tea bags against the days remaining until the schools reopened. The mayor had said a little over three weeks; that worked out to be 20 days—and here before me was an unopened box of 20 green tea bags. For an obsessive, such coincidences feel like a cool breeze on a fevered brow. I imagined the day when I would tear open that last tea package. Twenty days from now—a whole new month: April, the season of renewal and hope. The schools reopened, my children back to their routines, life as it had been finally restored. And surely there would be some change, perhaps even improvement from what was going on a whole twenty days earlier. A new awareness of where we had gone wrong, perhaps? New safety guidelines, maybe? Good! I hated germs in a way Monk would empathize with. The counting and calculating seemed like an act of faith, a ritual. It brought comfort because it was concrete, factual. To my mind, faith was not so much belief-despite-proof as much as scientific certainty, like of gravity's surety, of the inexorability of things. If I leave a full pint of ice cream out on the counter tonight, I have faith that tomorrow it will have melted. Of that I have no doubt. And prior to Corona, my sense of that kind of faith was as solid as the frozen ice cream had been the night before. Fairly soon, however, upon the arrival of the pandemic, my faith in the inexorable certainty of things began to change, change utterly. It wasn't so much that I thought I would find the ice cream on the counter still frozen the next morning or some other speculative possibility; it was rather that when I went into the kitchen to check the ice cream, it would be gone. Not sucked into some vortex of alternate reality, but plainly stolen, taken from me. Never to return.

Autoethnographical Interlude:
Six Degrees of Education

From Journal, March 23, 2020: Things are challenging here in our one-bedroom home with our 4- and 5-yr-olds, getting them set up with the DOE's technology for their online education while keeping them from jumping off the walls. Doing this while my spouse and I are also doing our own online training and work to move all our teaching completely online, all with only two computers. Doing the math, it's nearly impossible for all of us to be online at all the times we're supposed to be, but we're keeping faith.

From Journal, March 24, 2020: Thank goodness for small miracles—my eye is slowly getting better. I still have weird stray floaters and streaks across my field of vision, but the pain has finally lessened to bearable levels. However, I am personally taken down to near-depression levels at how unable I am to find time to write. Not blocked—worse, far from it! It's Sartrian: Hell is desperately needing to write, but having neither the time nor the place to do it. (I can feel the impulse pushing itself forward even in the writing of this entry.)

From Journal, April 1, 2020: A memory of Father Antonio Checo of St. Marks Church, Jackson Heights, NY, the priest at my kids' school, who just died from Covid-19. I had dropped my kids off for school on a bright, crisp autumn morning, and stood outside the church adjacent to their school building. I stood there alone, holding my son's scooter in one hand, looking into the dark, beautifully lit church. I was thinking of my mother walking me to my own parochial school. Just then Father Checo approached me, asked me if I wanted to go inside and pray. I paused, considering the question. "Or we could just pray here," he said. Together. I told him some of the things I was thinking about, my mother, her faith—quiet, strong, private—my children and my own childhood. He shared his story about his mother and his faith, and then we stood there. Together. Silently. I used to think of that story as a story about my spiritual development, how an unexpected encounter opened up some things inside me. But now it's just another pandemic story.

From Journal, April 5, 2020: I feel like there's so much to consider and reflect upon, and yet I can't open my psyche to it, the demands of the day being so intense. We are four people in a one-bedroom with two screens and need daily to educate others online and to be educated ourselves online. The terrible lack of life quality to online education is a topic for another time, but for now everything depends on not only wrangling a 4- and 5-yr-old in front of a laptop on a dining room table but opening their minds and spirits toward learning. It's a complicated system that requires infinitely more resources than we have as a family.

From Journal, April 21, 2020: Jess is baking and has asked the kids to help her but they keep coming into our bedroom where I'm working and interrupting me, almost a dozen times since I started working on this article. I understand their neediness, but it doesn't make it any easier. I have friends whose children are grown and gone, and friends with kids still under the same roof but old enough to already have their own identities and developmental stages somewhat fairly well laid out; they're operating with their kids in what I'd describe as "maintenance mode." Certainly there are difficult challenges for that mode, but it feels quite different from what's going on with our children at this particular age. Their needs take so much of our focus and energy and time under the best and most normal of circumstances, and this current situation is so far, far beyond normal that I don't even have a word for it. And, of course, add to that the individual needs our kids have and it gets exponentially more stressful. My son just turned four and my daughter is five and a half, which doesn't seem like a big difference, but when we're all on top of each other as we are now, without parks to blow off steam in, it is actually a huge difference and sometimes a negative one. When they're not stuck in front of their DOE screens, my daughter is super verbal and very assertive about her desires; my son has developed some verbal disfluencies and a stutter since the shutdown—and he's more passive and needs a very different environment around him to thrive: quiet, slow, deliberate, attentive. It's the exact opposite of the environment my daughter wants and needs: She likes it when I have NPR on and she likes to read aloud and make up songs and make things and perform little plays, and she wants my son to be a part but then she gets frustrated when he can't keep up or doesn't understand her rules, and then they're at each other's throats. I know all siblings do this, but it's setting his progress back, and it's killing me to witness this. And in fact, since he's lost his preschool schedule, he's gotten worse. Jess and I are obviously anxious about it because we want our daughter to thrive and use her imagination and play creatively as screen-free as possible, and we want our son to thrive in his own way and we need to care for him in a focused way, but right now neither of us can do that. We have to be online so much. I barely know how to discuss this aspect of our experience with my colleagues at university. There's barely been any discussion of it in all the many meetings we've had. And while I'm fully aware that, from other perspectives, we're so lucky to have these jobs and the technology to keep them, it still seems so overwhelming. And now the closure of schools feels so demoralizing. Jess and I take turns taking the kids out early, like 8-ish, which I think helps a lot to offer them a regular daily routine and some activity. We try to find areas of sidewalk that are spacious enough for them to ride their bikes or scoot or kick a ball around (how pathetic that sounds—*sidewalks!*).

From Journal, April 24, 2002: This morning, I took my kids out early, as usual, to get a little air after breakfast, and my 4-yr-old son's bike chain came off while he was biking on the sidewalk. He jerked the handlebars sideways and fell over. And despite wearing his helmet, he managed to hit the base of a streetlight with the front of his face. His nose bled and might be broken, and his gums and teeth were bloody, too. I was alone without Jess and freaked out because of all the recent talk about the new inflammatory health risk to children due to Covid. Elmhurst Hospital is only two blocks away, and yet I just didn't want to bring him there if we didn't absolutely need to. But his mask was soaked red, and he was scared and screaming, and my daughter also started crying. But mercifully, thankfully, I reached his pediatrician's office and they did a virtual doctor's visit to check if his nose is broken and/or if he had a concussion. I had to calm him down enough to do all the things they needed him to do as he stared at my phone. And now we have to watch him for the rest of the day for signs of excessive sleepiness or slurring or lack of balance or vomiting.

From Journal, April 27, 2020: Overheard a man in line outside the supermarket, on his cell phone, in a heated exchange: "Are you fucking shitting me, man—*this is worst-case scenario!* I don't give a shit that he's low-balling us or making a grab. Call him back now and accept his offer. We've got to sell."

From Journal, May 3, 2020: There's nothing open here but a food store and a liquor store. Parks are closed; and schools, of course, are now closed for the rest of the year. I am so brokenhearted about this. I know that Jess and all her colleagues—as well as my kids' teachers—have been working their asses off and doing heroic work. And I'm so grateful for their effort. But truth be told, the kids were thriving in their brick and mortar schools in so many ways—intellectually, artistically, socially, culturally, athletically, emotionally—ways that sitting in front of a computer screen cannot even remotely touch (pun intended).

From Journal, May 9, 2020: Things are grim here. The area of Queens I live in is less than a mile away from Elmhurst Hospital (I can see its roof when I step out of my building), and right now we're the hardest hit, as the *Times* reports. A 90-year-old woman in our building was taken out of here to Elmhurst Hospital by paramedics two weeks ago. Her son told us yesterday that he never saw her again after that, until they called to say that she's now in a refrigerated truck outside the hospital. No visits with her body, no funeral allowed. They'll let him know when the body can be released. He was not only sad when he told us this, but visibly anxious, stuttering, repeating himself, apologizing for having done nothing wrong. He wore a military-grade gas mask and total body coveralls, as he took a few things from her apartment. We stayed at least 15 feet away from him. No pats on the arm, no handshakes, certainly no hugs. My children are now educated about things they might not have needed to learn until later in life; you cannot shield them from anything anymore. They are homeschooled in tragedy. You are always with them, they are always with you. There's nothing open here but a food store and a liquor store. Parks are closed, and schools, of course, are closed and so are their meager school playgrounds that used to be open to neighborhood children. Each day there's a line of pale-blue surgical-masked neighbors waiting six feet apart snaking around to the back of the supermarket. The wait to get in can be an hour sometimes, and then once you're inside, the shelves are empty and people are scrambling to grab the last item of whatever is left. As I left the apartment to go food shopping tonight, my daughter yelled through the closed door, "Daddy, do you have your mask on?"

From Journal, May 12, 2020: Every evening at 7 PM, my family opens our windows and bangs on pots and pans with wooden spoons, hooting and cheering for all the front-line workers who are putting their own and their family's lives at risk every day. We cheer for these heroes along with our neighbors in this Queens neighborhood, only a few blocks from Elmhurst Hospital, where some of our friends and neighbors work every day and where some of them have gone to die (of the latter I'm thinking especially of Father Antonio Checo of St. Marks Church). This is intensely real for us here. It's no media plot, it's no global conspiracy. The refrigerated trucks and mass graves are real and as necessary as the masks we should all be wearing and the distance we should all be keeping. Jess and I teach our two children to respect and be grateful to these front-line heroes, and they are entirely so (their own grandfather was a lieutenant in the fire department and, were he still living, would have been at

74

work through this crisis, too). The kids have drawn those vibrant rainbows that decorate so many windows as a small visual sign to those workers that we appreciate and honor them.

From Journal, June 10, 2020: In the past few months, I've had several friends my age share with me stories about increases in sleep trouble, disordered eating, increased drinking, heightened anxiety, depression. For me, the first thing that changed was my sleep: insomnia, crazy dreams, low startle threshold. The anxiety was so intense in March and April that for a while there, when I finally fell asleep, I felt like I was awake, so alert was I to any trouble with my family throughout the night.

> "One sign that he hadn't been writing enough, Garp knew, was when he had too much imagination left over for other things. For example, the onslaught of dreams: Garp now dreamed only of horrors happening to his children."
> — John Irving, *The World According to Garp*

From Journal, May 19, 2020: My father, Giuseppe Salvatore, would have been 95 years old today. He died just before Sept. 11, 2001. I used to comfort myself by saying that at least he didn't have to witness the events of that dark day. Now I think, thank Christ he and my mom aren't around to endure this thing we call the world in 2020. What kind of world do we live in when you're thankful your loved ones are not alive to see it? And yet, of course, the truth is, every night I say a prayer wishing they were, somehow, still here. I don't know any rational way to reconcile that. Seems the human heart is at even the best of times always a fearful muddle, built to hold two opposing beliefs at once within its aching chambers. Happy Birthday, my dear good father. May we see each other again someday.

Home Schooling

I cross paths with my five-year-old daughter in the hallway outside the bathroom of our one-bedroom apartment.

"Daddy, did you know that the word 'shit' is another word for poop?"

Acting nonplussed I reply, "You're right; that's true. Where did you learn that word?"

"In a book in the laundry room."

Suspicious a book was not the origin of her learning, I say "Hey, great. So can you spell it for me?"

She keeps her eyes on me concentrating. "S-H-I-T."

"Well done!"

She smiles.

"So," I say, "is that a long-vowel-'I' or a short-vowel-'I'?

Her smile weakens slightly as she considers this. "Um, short?"

We high-five each other. She heads back to the living room, I to my bedroom/office-for-the-foreseeable-future. Then I stop and say "Hey, honey. Do you know what 'bad words' are?" She says she does and then we have a brief discussion on the topic of appropriate contexts for their use—basically, we decided together that I'm her only appropriate context. At least for the foreseeable future.

"In the grammar school of my hometown, Appleton, Wisconsin, in the early 1880s this was, we pupils in our stiff shirts were suffered at our small desks to learn to write a grammatically correct English sentence. But rule-bound language and defining words were, for me and my family— and I think for many immigrants—always a straightjacket to wrestle out of, to escape from, to shake off, to make a spectacle of . . . My father changed our family name from Weisz to Weiss; mine from Erik to Ehrich. And I, when my time came, changed my own to Harry 'Handcuff' Houdini.

I realized in that small classroom back in Appleton that language and the rules of grammar were the original pair of ironclad cuffs from which my restless young wrists first sought to slip."

— Erik Weisz (a.k.a. Harry "Handcuff" Houdini)

Pedagogy of the Possessed

Nearly forty years ago, sociolinguist Dell Hymes wrote that "the United States is a country rich in many things, but poor in knowledge of itself with regard to language." Since Hymes wrote those words, the state of the country's language awareness has not only remained impoverished; it has, in its impoverishment, like certain voter blocks, become ignorant of its own ignorance. Embraced it, in fact, celebrated it, produced it, packaged it, sold it, voted for it, elected it, died for it. Yet in this time of such massive historical catastrophes—both national and global, biological and politico-economical—an understanding of linguistic diversity and the need for expanded social and cultural knowledge have become essential for the survival both of our democracy and our planet. Alas, one of the myriad unnamed victims of the Covid-19 pandemic has been the English language. (Here I'm taking a descriptivist position that sees language use as neither correct nor incorrect, but rather effective or ineffective, accepted or stigmatized. This view allows us to understand grammar not as a set of rules to be memorized and produced, but rather as a set of tools, about which we might become more aware and over which we might deliberate with thought and care.) As James Sledd said, "Outside the classroom, there is violence in the street. All over the world, the haves are consciously choosing to ride the haven'ts harder, so that the rich grow richer as the poor sink deeper into poverty. The primal, though perhaps not irremediable, fault is that justice in an unjust society is rendered ever more remote. Meanwhile the masters demand of teachers that they uncomplainingly do what the masters make impossible, but the motives for such teaching must be carefully considered. To teach the standard language as supposedly a means to upward mobility in the mainstream culture is to fight on the wrong side in the class war, to teach students to put their neighbors' noses out of joint by getting and wasting more than their neighbors can get and waste. It is wiser to teach (language), and to teach its nature, as a tool, a weapon which the dominant have too commonly used for purposes of domination but which the dominated can use for purposes of resistance and of access to the best values of multiple cultures and traditions. If they are ready for abstractions like subjects and predicates, they are ready for the abstractions of race and class."

"To recognize that we touch one another in language seems particularly difficult in a society that would have us believe that there is no dignity in the experience of passion, that to feel deeply is to be inferior, for within the dualism of Western metaphysical thought, ideas are always more important than language. To heal the splitting of mind and body, we marginalized and oppressed people in an attempt to recover ourselves and our experiences in language. We seek to make a place for intimacy. Unable to find such a place in standard English, we create the ruptured, broken, unruly speech of the vernacular. When I need to say words that do more than simply mirror or address the dominant reality, I speak black vernacular. There, in that location, we make English do what we want it to do. We take the oppressor's language and turn it against itself. We make our words a counter-hegemonic speech, liberating ourselves in language."

— bell hooks, *Teaching to Transgress: Education as the Practice of Freedom.*

In the Time of "In the Time of"

Many consider Camus's *The Plague* the ur-text of the pandemic, but if the true test of a literary work's contagion is its invasion into a culture's language, then that text would have to be *Love in the Time of Cholera*, by Gabriel García Márquez. The ubiquity of its titular syntactic construction, most markedly since March 2020, reveals both its durability and its flexibility, and its ability to render any event in a patina of nostalgia and sentimentality. Its linguistic spread is, like the virus it seeks to contain, exacting a psychic toll, providing the linguistic affordances of denial and dissociation.

Unlike *The Plague*, García Márquez's 1988 novel is not a story about an epidemic; that's its backdrop. Rather, the book is primarily about romantic love, long unrequited (fifty-one years, nine months, and four days, to be exact) but faithfully awaited by the romantic hero, Florentino Ariza, and finally consummated with the object of his passion, Fermina Daza. Such subject matter permits a certain sentimentality in its handling. Reviewing the book for *The New York Times*, Thomas Pynchon remarks its use: "In the postromantic ebb of the '70s and '80s, with everybody now so wised up and even growing paranoid about love, once the magical buzzword of a generation, it is a daring step for any writer to decide to work in love's vernacular, to take it, with all its folly, imprecision and lapses in taste, at all seriously."

There are, however, more troubling and problematic issues in this novel than "folly" and "lapses in taste"—such as sexual assault and statutory rape—that the book also romanticizes. While waiting over fifty years for Fermina, Florentino has sex with 622 women, including his maid, whom he impregnates and then bribes to name another man as the father of his child, allowing Florentino to avoid responsibility. As well, he has sexual relationship with a 14-year-old of whom the 60-year-old Florentino has been given custody. But all this happens "in the time of cholera," and so both the book and the romantic language in which it is written would have you feel, as Pynchon does, that this material is "daring" when rendered in "love's vernacular." Another aspect of the novel's taking place "in the time of cholera" is that it seems, if not to exonerate, then certainly to lessen the blame on Florentino, for the symptoms of the plague are close to those of love: fever, dizziness, nausea, aches, and anguish, as if the victim is possessed and therefore not fully in their right mind. A doctor in the novel, after examining a young man whose mother complains to him that (her son's) "condition did not resemble the turmoil of love so much as the devastation of cholera," concludes that "*once again*" (my emphasis), "the symptoms of love were the same of those of cholera." Love itself, it seems, might be the more unstable signifier when it occurs "in the time of cholera."

Urban politics in the time of the plague are also fevered and dizzying and painful. García Márquez's training as a journalist helps counter some of the novel's romanticism not only with the realism of sexual misconduct but also of political corruption and racial bias. Cities, characterized by their density, have long been associated with plagues, especially in those areas occupied primarily by the poor and minorities. A doctor in the novel feels "alarmed at the possibility that the plague had entered the old city, for all the cases until that time had occurred in the poor neighborhoods, and almost all of those among the black population."

We see the same thing happening on Manhattan's Upper West Side, where wealthy residents pressured the mayor in early fall 2020 to relocate a population of 300 homeless men who had been housed in The Lucern Hotel during the Corona lockdown. According to the New York Times: "Covid-19 has disproportionately affected Black and Hispanic populations, which also represent most of the estimated 80,000 people who are homeless in New York." Racism and elitism in the time of Covid.

The book's title "Love in the Time of Cholera" is a noun phrase. It lacks a completing verb phrase, which would turn it into an independent clause, a complete sentence, or as composition 101 taught us, a complete thought. It could be the subject of a sentence or the predicate. It could say "We found *love in the time of cholera.*" Or it could say "*Love in the time of cholera* produces symptoms that are difficult to distinguish one from the other." In other words, without a predicate, no comment can be made about the topic. It's all theme and no rheme. Nonetheless, that singular noun phrase is remarkably suggestive of the promise of a majestic story. Let's parse these six words: *Love* is not only the novel's great theme; it is also its central conflict—as well as the reader's. For, as Pynchon puts it, Florentino's at times heinous actions, "we find ourselves, as he earns the suspension of our disbelief, cheering him on, wishing for the success of this stubborn warrior against age and death, and in the name of love." Next: *Cholera*, the word not only names the extremely virulent disease that, according to the World Health Organization, can kill within hours if untreated; the disease is also responsible for seven pandemics throughout history and remains a global threat to public health. In the novel, Cholera also functions symbolically as a reminder of Florentino's long-suffering lovesickness, which creates its own kind of wasting, depleting misery for the sufferer.

Between these two poles, between the highest of human ideals and the lowest of human suffering, is framed the prepositional phrase *in the time of.* The phrase offers the promise of story, a certain romance, conjuring exploits contained within a frame of history, during which much of what happens will be explained by the sheer fact that it happened during that historical frame. *What happens in the time of the plague stays in the time of the plague.*

The title is reinforced by its construction. García Márquez's novel is built for the backward glance of nostalgia and sentimentality. It begins when the characters are very old, and then goes back over fifty years to the time of the cholera epidemic, when passions and fevers were running high. Everything is viewed through that sepia-toned lens. "At nightfall, at the oppressive moment of transition, a storm of carnivorous mosquitoes rose out of the swamps, and a tender breath of human shit, warm and sad, stirred the certainty of death in the depths of one's soul. And so the very life of the colonial city, which the young Juvenal Urbino tended to idealize in his Parisian melancholy, was an illusion of memory." History teaches us that how we remember the past affects the way we view our present.

In the time of—linguists call this kind of formulation a *collocation,* which Steven Pinker defines as a string of words that are remembered as a whole. Pinker goes further and associates collocations with idioms and clichés. The irony is that the brain is designed to love the very thing it is specifically designed to be critical about. That is, the brain loves rhythmic units, putting them into small chunks of meaning. Part of that has to do with the fact that collocations and clichés appear closer to the language modules nearer the music module; there is rhythm to collocations; they're catchy for the reason that music is catchy. We use them as absentmindedly as we might hum a jingle while we're tying our shoes. Let's test the theory: If I say *He was killed in the line of* _____. What word would finish that sentence? How about *The patient told the doctor she was in excruciating* _____. If you guessed *duty* and *pain,* you hit the nail on the _____. Collocations are easy because our brain has chunked them so many times that they have lost their meaning. (In the United States, in 2020, there are two such competing phrases that are on their way to becoming collocations: the first is *Make America Great Again* and the second is *Black Lives Matter.* On their surface, they denote one thing. But what they now connote is something much deeper, ongoing, and evolving.) But try the same test with *in the time of.* The collocated phrase allows for the speaker or writer to fill in the front and the back. Recently, I was invited to attend a webinar on the topic of

Narrative Revival in the Time of Remote Learning. Not bad, I thought. The phrase has certainly knocked the previous reigning champ off its perch: "What we talk about when we talk about Narrative Revival and Remote Learning" doesn't quite have the same ring to it.

The current ubiquity of the phrase *in the time of* is remarkable. A search on the Internet since March 2020 yields a result over 1,180,000,000 (compare that with a search for, say, "if the flood of love," which yields three results). However, if we wanted to dig deeper, we would need a more sophisticated, more powerful tool than Google. We'd need to do corpus linguistic analysis, which is the examination of textual patterns in a selected body of naturally produced texts. Corpus linguistic analysis can uncover unexpected patterns of speech and writing and also confirm or complicate pre-existing intuitions or assumptions, for instance those related to linguistic responses to historical trauma, such as the one we are living through in 2020.

The tool we used for this study is the online Contemporary Corpus of American English (COCA hereafter), which contains over 450 million words. A search of COCA for the "in the time of" collocation reveals that the frequency of *in the time of* has increased incrementally since the release of the novel (24,000 hits in 1988, the year the book was released, with a yearly increase of roughly 3.52 percent, a statistically significant difference ($p > 0.00003$) per year, with a dramatic drop in the years immediately following September 11, 2001. A theory for this might be that the events of 9/11, though globally horrific in the immediate aftermath, were not romanticized in the same way, perhaps because the event itself seemed to be ended with the war in Iraq and the death of Saddam Hussein.) However, since March of 2020, the frequency has increased by 89.25 percent. What could account for that rise? Could that number reveal the intense need we have to narrate the events of the Covid-19 experience as though they already had an ending? The research is inconclusive because the research is still ongoing. The researcher confesses here and now that he is afraid to peer more closely at the data, afraid to do the field research, afraid to admit that what seems more important now is finding some way not to deny the trauma but turn toward it.

Conclusion

In writing this autometafictive faux-paper, I realized the subject matter is much more personal than I had ever understood. Distancing myself though a series of fraudulent artifacts and "found" texts and lifted lines did not shield me. Writing about my terrified children, my overworked and at-risk spouse, a dead priest, literary gatherings, all things I've cherished and have lost has activated some long-held-back grief, restive and uprising, needing to come forth. Much has been said about how the current leader of the U.S. is not acknowledging or admitting the seriousness of this pandemic; that he's not acknowledging the deaths, and by not acknowledging the deaths, he's not acknowledging our nation's need to mourn those deaths. I agree with that theory. But writing this piece has also made me realize that neither as a nation nor as individuals have we been allowed to grieve and mourn the loss of our old lives. Re-reading that PEN Award scene and thinking about my old office at my university and recalling the warmth of other bodies in crowded cafes hit me with the realization that not only is all of that gone, but the memory of that time and place has been forever altered. Like that poor dead priest, like my university workspace and collegial relationships, like Times Square and social gatherings, our lives have a new memory frame: it's all *pre-pandemic* now. As my parents (both born in the 1920s) used to say, "Oh, I knew that family *before the war.*" Or "I used to love going to the movies at lunch break *before the war.*" I understand that need for the collocation now in a way I did not as a young man.

"Grief is a cruel kind of education. You learn how ungentle mourning can be, how full of anger. You learn how glib condolences can feel. You learn how much grief is about language, the failure of language and the grasping for language. . . Grief was the celebration of love, those who could feel real grief were lucky to have loved."
—Chimamanda Ngozi Adichie

Remembering the pre-pandemic world, it's as if we were looking at a star, and didn't see the actual star but rather the shimmer of a thing that is already dead. Not possible any longer. In many ways, it feels like a thing that is not merely forgotten, but something that could never happen again.

THE ANXIETY OF DISTANCE

HALTED TIME
Christian von der Goltz

Behind the news, behind the curves and theories, behind the ongoing argument over who says what, behind all the noise of the internet, a ghostly silence has been spreading into every aspect of daily life. More than all the talk of numbers and statistics, it's this silence that is changing people's behavior. Social distancing isn't the cause of this silence, but it's helped to spread and intensify it. Ubiquitously, wordlessly, it follows us with the beautiful spring weather like a mild breeze. We all know where it comes from: people are dying, we read about it every day, and there will be more. But all we hear and see is the spring in the air: birds are chirping, flowers blossoming, people are strolling in the parks as if the worst were already past. The eerie silence seems to grow with the number of dead. There are so many dead now that new graveyards have to be dug out with bulldozers.

Silence is the soundtrack to the virus's global spread. It's the first force capable of interrupting global capitalism's voracious greed, and remarkably, nearly everyone obeys: politicians, CEOs, religious authorities, even Pope Francis obeys. They do it almost shamefully. It's the first time we've been forced to follow measures that haven't been dictated by financial interests, but by another category altogether: the necessity to protect human existence.

We live from day to day; we feed our imagination and our thirst for explanation with statistics and speculation. When I look back in my journal, I can trace how the exceptional conditions have come over us gradually, week by week, and yet it feels as though they've arrived overnight. Things we thought only a day or two ago now seem naïve. We're confused; nothing is the way it used to be, and it remains to be seen whether anything will ever be the same again. Some politicians have begun using military metaphors: "we are in a war and doomed to win it," said French president Macron. In a way he's right: in wartime, during all the bombing and destruction, the time afterwards seems unimaginable, yet it's this vision that people cling to: afterwards is the utopia. But war, as we know it, comes with atrocities, devastation, filth, ear-splitting noise. Pandemic arrives without a soundtrack or visible effects; apart from internal organs, it doesn't overtly destroy anything—and so we're not wading through blocks and blocks of rubble from demolished buildings, but worrying, in silence and largely alone, over the prospect of ruined livelihoods and dangerously destabilized economies. Hospitals do their part to keep the scourge invisible; apart from the occasional shocking video of a nurse or doctor posted late at night after a grueling shift, we see and hear nothing. We're told to be nice to each other, to take walks, to read books, to eat healthy foods: visions from a better life we've never quite had.

In the midst of all this, there are people who refuse to obey the virus because it challenges their pride or their right to freedom. On the political stage we see the die-hard reality deniers, the Trumps and the Bolsonaros and their supporters, fail on a royal scale—in spite of their tremendous arsenals of worldly power—while their unfathomable ignorance causes thousands of innocent people to die. But the pandemic cares neither about power nor opinions; it's unconcerned with what people claim or think. Perhaps there is a lesson to learn in all this: that within this new silence, and all the suffering it conceals, there was also something missing in the time *before*—during the era of untamed capitalism and greed, the era of ever-expanding growth and progress, the era of glittering events and *the-show-must-go-on*—a state of mind which seemed as outdated as the only word we have for it: humility.

For many, these past two months have been the hardest

two months of their lives: people hopelessly alone, or stuck with bored and screaming kids in cramped apartments, forced to simultaneously home school and home office; people not allowed to visit their elderly parents in nursing homes. Doctors and nurses battling what we're not supposed to see; people in the service industries forced to go to work without being provided with the requisite protection. This contrast between a quiet spring for those not on the front line of the pandemic and the nameless horror taking place behind it feels like we're living in a science-fiction movie.

In the never-ending stream of Corona news, two images have opened my eyes to the full scope of the tragedy: one was an erratic cell phone video clip taken inside a hospital in the Iranian city of Qom. The floor was covered with the bodies of people who had died the night before and were wrapped in black garbage bags ready to be hauled away; all around them, staff were hurrying back and forth in seemingly helpless agitation to make room for the never-ending supply of new corpses. The other image revealed a long convoy of black military trucks waiting in line in the middle of the night with their engines running, loaded with corpses that had been picked up at the hospital in Bergamo, destined now for improvised cemeteries in surrounding towns, since there was no room left for the dead in Bergamo. What hit home was the sobering fact that people are dying in numbers unknown during times of peace. Our societies are taking the greatest care to distract our attention from this most obvious fact of all. We read the numbers and statistics, but numbers remain numbers, and the curves reveal nothing about the tragedies unfolding behind them even as reports emerge to caution the heedless young that it's no longer merely the elderly who are succumbing. This unspoken edict preventing us, who are still healthy, from seeing the ill, the dying, and the dead, is part of a strategy to avoid mass panic, to keep our society functioning.

From the moment I saw these videos, I wished to be told

to stay home in the harshest tone; I wished for the severest form of quarantine. How was it, I kept asking myself, that I was longing to be imprisoned for my own protection? The wish was there the very moment I saw the videos, I didn't have to talk myself into it, it was as though it had been hiding there all along in some remote corner of my subconscious. It was as though I'd been longing for something—and this was the weird thing I hadn't been able to admit to myself, let alone to anybody else—as though I'd been longing for "normality" to finally come to an end. And then, when the German government offered its so-called "creatives" financial assistance to weather months of cancelled freelance work—the envy of many other countries where small businesses promised assistance have been left with empty hands—this sudden freedom, this unreal life felt like a gift from heaven, a once-in-a-lifetime-experience of halted time.

I've been struggling with a book project on my mother's childhood during World War II, which she, as the daughter of a Norwegian politician, spent in house arrest in a tiny German village near Berlin. She herself never told her story to anyone, behavior typical of people who have experienced war, imprisonment, or torture in childhood. In the larger picture, she didn't have it all that bad, but what she did see was apparently enough to keep these memories sealed up inside her. This is a story from another time and place, and yet I see a similar psychological mechanism at work, a maxim, never openly declared, that everybody—from ordinary people to government officials—have to obey: no one shall see the horrors happening all around us. Societies remain peaceful as long as people can be induced to think that everything is fine. This peace helped create the prosperity I and all my contemporaries grew up in. The religion of our society was progress, and it was as beautiful as it was false: something profound and elementary was always missing, but it was as though we weren't allowed to talk about it. That progress, which was supposed to last forever, has now come to a sudden halt, and nobody dares speculate on what will come after. But when I see the first signs of the German economy rebooting, when I see the automobile manufacturers resuming production and masked workers grateful to have their jobs back—when I consider that things are likely to continue as they were before—I realize that some of us will mourn the lost chance this interlude of silence offered us to reevaluate what our societies are based on—and to make changes that have long been urgent, self-evident, and necessary.

THE DAISY ASSASSIN:
INCIDENT FROM A TIME OF PLAGUE
David Dario Winner

1

For years now, I've run up and down stairs in Brooklyn parks. An attempt to stave off a middle-aged paunch has morphed into a serious endorphin addiction.

My favorite steps lie on Lookout Hill right behind a statue of George Washington in the eastern corner of Prospect Park. Sometimes, I climb with my big yellow mutt. Sometimes, I climb alone, not focusing much on passersby except when joggers, families with children, and those damn birdwatchers get in my way.

Then came Covid.

2

My eighty-eight-year-old father, alone in Charlottesville, told me he wasn't so concerned about protecting himself as he'd lived a long life and was content to die. And my uncle in Rome (nearly blind in his mid-sixties) ran out of food in the midst of the Italian catastrophe and was taken in by friends at the eleventh hour.

Back in Brooklyn, I grew concerned about my six feet of separation, just a little less than the space between people if they hewed to the edges of the stairs on Lookout Hill. Bravely I traipsed up and down, risking my ankles if I were to mis-land and my skin if I were to tumble into the thorny vines off to the sides.

3

Foucault famously discussed "an enclosed, segmented space," in the time of plague, "observed at every point, in which the individuals are inserted in a fixed place, in which the slightest movements are supervised, in which all events are recorded."

The stairs did not resemble the space that Foucault describes, a circular medieval prison called a panopticon. And no one other than myself is observing the young white family that blocks my way one morning. Not the little boy, seven maybe, moving dangerously close to me as I boil with self-righteous rage. And imagine their attempts to reason with him in the parlance of educated Brooklyn parents. "Do you really think you should be getting so close to that man, Harrison, can we discuss this?"

4

At that very moment, while I am fighting the good fight in Prospect Park, a friend's body in Sunset Park hurts so much that he can barely move. All essential activities (urinating, defecating, swallowing) seem impossibly painful. And in England, in Leicester, the brother-in-law of a friend gasps for breath. Weeks later, well after his ostensible recovery, he staggers onto my friend's Skype session and staggers away, exhausted by the effort.

5

Another family on the path kindly but firmly direct their kids to stay away. When I run by the handsome blond father, both of us keeping to the edge of the stairs, I praise his and his wife's childrearing as if I were broadcasting from my lookout post in the panopticon, encouragement for correct behavior, punishment for infringement.

6

My college closes, and I start teaching remotely. Shelter in place is mandated. Most stores close but liquor stores remain open, making affluent Park Slope resemble '70s working-class black Washington according to an acquaintance's Facebook post.

7

Largely Hasidic Borough Park is one neighborhood away from me. Many New Yorkers, particularly secular Jews like me, view Hasids as insular, patriarchal, just plain weird. But I once flew from New York to Warsaw on a plane full of Lubavitchers who were visiting the ancient village of their rebbe. Over the Atlantic in the middle of the night, I was awakened by dozens of dancing, chanting, exhilaratingly mystical men.

While the overseers of the panopticon are on a break, hundreds of members of the Hasidic communities of Borough Park and Williamsburg attend a wedding. Infection spreads through the descendants of Holocaust survivors determined to repopulate the Jewish race. More than six feet, I try to give them twelve, those carriers of the plague.

8

Dawn, my wife Angela's cousin, Bob, her husband, and their teenage daughter all have it. They seem okay but share a house with Angela's 97-year-old aunt. They self-quarantine, but they could already have given it to her. Meanwhile, my father goes one last time to Whole Foods. Those over sixty are supposed to stay home, and he's nearly three decades past that. I imagine the market ringing with disapprobation as he clings to his cart like a walker, but he tells me that no one seemed bothered.

9

My leadership position in the Corona panopticon is out of character. I'm not generally so obedient. I bike through red lights and onto sidewalks. My dog can be the only one off the leash in the park. Not a risk taker, just a minor-league law breaker.

But back in the park in the last day of March, I come up

with a list of rules. Winner's Rules of Order govern running up and down Lookout Hill. Perhaps I can create a makeshift signpost that demands that in the name of public safety:

1. All families must congregate in open areas to avoid blocking trails and stairs.

2. All children over the age of three must be informed that they should stay out of people's way. And be given (no, not beatings, I'm a liberal guy) heightened time-outs if they fail to comply, some offshoot of Guantanamo's heightened interrogation.

3. No individual shalt pay so much attention to their phone as to ignore social distance.

4. All couples must. . .

And so forth. Perhaps the park can build me a treehouse, so I can root out disobedience from above. Really, though, the primary rule breaker is myself, or at least I am exploiting a loophole. Dog-walking and exercising shouldn't entail so many hours away from home running up and down stairs.

10

Far from Lookout Hill, authoritarian governments exploit the crisis. Viktor Orbán has seized even more power in Hungary. Jeanine Áñez Chávez has postponed Bolivian elections. A friend I've made in Iran tells me that, "Our government and regime don't give a fuck about the people. We are hostages, not citizens." Stateside, Trump's bizarre populism may be more dangerous than his authoritarianism. Denying, lying, and stalling as Corona spreads.

11

I don't know whether he's still calling it the Chinese virus because I can't stand to listen to him. The wife of a friend, an RN from the Philippines, takes a car service from Queens to Mount Sinai in the Upper East Side, not so much because she fears infection but because Asian people are getting harassed on the train and around the hospital. The parents of a Filipina student of mine have been mistreated in Rome, but I guess I can't blame Trump for that.

12

One night, Angela and I get mad at each other. "But I cook all the meals," I scream, though it isn't true. "But they're terrible," she rejoins, which *is* true though she later takes it back. A text chimes. Dawn's husband, Bob. Dawn's blood oxygen is at 86% and they fear intubation. When Angela's father was dying from COPD and lung cancer and when my mother was rasping for breath in her last days, their levels were nowhere that low. This is terrifying.

Angela's phone dies, and we (still mad at each other but panicked) search madly around for a charger, scaring our poor dog. We find it, power up, and text Bob back, but he does not respond.

My cousin Frank in the West Village also has it. Not nearly so bad as Dawn, but he is in his seventies and smoked much of his life. His job (trumpet player for the Metropolitan Opera, sometimes on stage in ancient Egyptian attire) may have kept his lungs strong.

13

My father and his much younger half-brother in Rome always complain about the media hype of hurricanes, blizzards, and the like. In the early days of the plague, I joke that if they somehow survived WW3, they would pick themselves out of the rubble and declare it a "cable news exaggeration," a favorite phrase of my uncle's. My father and I receive a dictated e-mail from him declaring that it is good that he is "semi-blind," so he can't see that Italy's "great humanitarian effort" is "folly." My father, alone and anxious, has jumped off that bandwagon. It no longer seems exaggerated.

14

The peak is upon us, and I refrain from Lookout Hill.

15

Dawn is better. After several days in the hospital, she is being released. She is exhausted, though, and speaking is difficult. Frank continues to improve but tells me that his recovery has not been "linear."

My uncle cannot return to his own apartment because Corona has been discovered in the condo, and the place has been quarantined. He writes to say that the TB epidemic of 2018 killed more people but that nobody wants to listen.

16

Without my Lookout Hill endorphin fix, I'm getting depressed, irritable. I return to the park, wearing a mask even though it's uncomfortable, swearing to stay not six but nine feet away.

Most risks have immediate consequences. If you get caught in a riptide, you drown. Not that afternoon, not the following month, but right then. But if I catch a dribble of Corona sputum on Lookout Hill, I may wake up one morning two weeks later not with one of the mild sore throats that have been scaring me but a deep exhaustion so I can barely make it to the bathroom to pee. A compression in my chest so I can barely breathe.

17

On the stairs, a man deep in his phone approaches me. He walks right in the middle. Even if I slide by him, hewing to the side, I'll be much closer than six feet. So I jump off the stairs into the underbrush, feeling morally superior. *Look what I've done to avoid infecting you*, I silently address him. I glance down at my feet to see what's below them in case I might trip on vines or stones. There aren't any. Just dozens of beautiful spring daisies.

18

"When you were very little and we lived on Wertland Steet," says my father, more and more upset by the administration's response, "there was a woman who lived across the street, quite mad and a nymphomaniac. She came over in the evenings with absurd stories of people on the street plotting against her. One couldn't call the police. She's Trump!"

19

It is a glorious sunny day in the park, mid-Passover. There are hundreds of people and many Hasids. It is slow-going on the stairs. I have to stop often to keep proper distance. Sometimes, I have to jump off them, steering clear of daisies. Friendly dogs come my way, but I must not pet them. They may carry the virus on their fur, or I could be carrying the virus, bringing it to their owners.

A Hasidic girl (fourteen or fifteen maybe) and a Hasidic boy of about ten are walking below me on the steps. I have paused to allow them to pass, but the boy inexplicably turns around and dashes towards me. When he is only a couple of feet away, I plunge off the stairs, losing my balance and possibly murdering more flowers.

The boy has turned around again and begun to head back to his sister when the words "excuse me," flee my mouth without proper input from my brain. No adult is around. The girl is the closest thing. I can see her hesitate. She hears me but doesn't know what to do about the strange man addressing her.

"Excuse me," I say again, and she stops and looks up at me.

"Can you tell him?" I pontificate, gesturing towards her brother, "can you tell him to stay away from people?"

The expression on her face still haunts me. Confusion, fear. I must have looked so terrifying in my sweaty gym clothes and ridiculous mask.

She may not have seen how close her brother had come to me. She may not have known what this was all about. This could be the anti-Semitism that she's been warned about. Do I want her to wear a gold star? Will I shatter her family's shop windows? Drag her, her brother, and her parents to someplace resembling the camps from which her great-great grandparents had escaped.

20

Trump urges people to liberate themselves from quarantine in Michigan, Texas and Virginia.

As the two people who look in on my father in Charlottesville may be Trump supporters, I beg him to keep clear.

There is silence on the phone.

"Well," he says, "I'll do my best."

There is nothing more I can do. I can bark down at the disobedient from my treehouse. I can terrify teenage Hasidic girls, but Virginia is hundreds of miles away, far from my panopticon.

21

The next time I find my way to Lookout Hill, I regard Washington's ominous words emblazoned upon his statue. "Good God! What brave fellows I must this day lose!"

Of course, I don't know the future of myself and the other not-so-brave fellows (and females) on the stairs.

But the community college classes I've been teaching remotely for weeks have taken a dark turn. My students live two rivers away from me in impoverished, ungentrified neighborhoods in Jersey City. My middle-aged white mug appears on their computer screens like some Big Brother figure as I feel obligated to show myself, but very few choose to reveal their faces or their living spaces. Fewer and fewer of them log on, only about twenty still participating out of sixty-odd students in three classes.

Awkwardly, I've asked my classes how everyone was doing and have received bracing if non-committal responses: *okay*, *fine*, *okay*. Then I get an e-mail from Gregory, living with his mom and stepdad. He's too upset to deal with the stupid assignment I've concocted about Corona because his cousin and his aunt have died, and his mother has tested positive. Tears well up in Gregory's eyes the next time we encounter each other on Zoom.

Two students have it in an evening class. One participates from home. The other sleeps through most of the days. A student from Turkey and another from Morocco report to the class about the shitshows in their countries.

The following day, April 23, I learn that sweet Adriel, who came from Ecuador as a toddler, is doing poorly. His father, who is younger than I am, has just died from it. Angela and I speculate about what we don't know. Adriel's father may not have had the luxury of working from home. For him and so many other immigrants from the Global South, the problem may not be being over-zealously monitored in a panopticon but being sent out to work in the dangerous world outside.

THE DOUBLE FEATURE
William Cody Maher

To go out with me for fresh air or for some sun and to listen to
the birds. . . to go out with me is to watch behind my back to be
anticipating what is ahead to look for kids suddenly lurching out
of the bushes out of my mind. . . to be out with me is not to be
out with me and I don't know how I can change that unless all
the stop lights remain green and no one waits at the stop lights
and no one stands before us or alongside of us or behind us or
anywhere near us and it is not two meters says the expert it is
four meters when the jogger or the bicyclist is exhaling depending
on the wind factor the velocity. . . so how can we go out together
with the masks that are of little value but of some value to
someone but not for us here in Schloss Park. . . no longer the
park that I knew or Tarkovsky knew. . . who hated Berlin to
death he hated it and the only place he loved was Schloss Park
where the herons stand and the turtles sun themselves and the
Japanese tourists who are no longer in Berlin who are back in
Japan and the handful of people I would see in the park during
the week are not mouthfuls of people hundreds of mouthfuls
of people that remain silent in my eyes because they cannot
speak and should not speak so it has become a silent world a
world that is kept silent through the use of masks or no masks
and the sense of neighbors when they are potential carriers and
no longer identified in any other context despite all efforts to the
contrary or why when K who is a hairdresser abruptly approached
my wife and I unconscious of my or her reaction or he negligent
of the meaning of his drawing within the three-meter radius or
was it two meters and the sirens go off and the pulse rate
quickens and the baby fortunately I noticed the baby who was in

its cradle directly in front of me and it was munching on a postcard and it had become very cute though initially it had no features that you could attribute to cuteness so noticing the baby I turned my attention to it as K then retreated into his hair salon and his young wife continued talking with us and so I felt I had overcome the initial fear but that was some time after we had returned from the park where the crowds of joggers and bicyclists and the groups of kids grouping or groping together and that awareness of these groups nearby and then the shock of the ball suddenly in our midst can you imagine a ball kicked in our midst and the little boy running to it and my abrupt standing and kicking the ball well I could have missed the ball and kicked the kid and the young father fortunately not seeing the frightened face of the old man who kicked the ball and the stadium of fear in my head with everyone rising to exclaim that it is a crime and not allowed to kick the ball anywhere near a moving or still target which any old person is and that the police where are the police I thought and told my wife who has had enough of the police and my hands up in the air at the infractions of the rules but what were the rules were the rules four meters today and six meters tomorrow or no meters in the nightmare when dreaming a life of normal perceptions or meters apart the lovers holding hands with no meters between them where is the measuring stick to take my tantrum I mean take my temperature my stick where is my stick to walk the straight and narrow sidewalk. . . where is the logic and the madness of language not even that can straighten this out if it were simply the madness of consciousness that would have the ability to reflect and to upstage the madness of reality there would be the beginning of hope but no. . . no madness can outdistance the social distancing not respected by the joggers whose breath is eternity if they be the ones or the bicyclists if they be the ones and the police must enforce and practice social distancing and have no idea where to draw the line and now the mind is left on its own and has decided it has no place to jog and no escape and now after everything has been considered and that day has passed. . . that day in the park where I was unable to find any peace and afterwards perhaps just for a moment only the baby who was playing with the postcard in her mouth from some distant location from some sweet dream of eternal innocence and my hands with the white gloves still with the key in the door head half turned and then seeking shelter with the door closed behind me as if I had really lived as if it had made any sense to go out as if I had actually heard the birds as if I had actually understood what is happening here and left the rest to. . . to what. . . to go out with me out the door at the wooden shack in Hunter's Point greet the dogs still alive that have not been poisoned past the old man lying on the kitchen floor or digging in the garden for his bottle to the front gate to go out with me down Kant St. on my bike. . . proud like a boy bringing the groceries home up the hill but now on Kant St. . . . passing the movie house marquee. . . a double feature "Bleibt Gesund" and "Achtet Aufeinander" starring. . . starring who. . . who are playing the leading roles. . . I turn to the street and see the face mask. . . the leading man. . . the leading lady. . . the straps like arms. . . and legs could be an animal decades ago. . . I'm driving a nursery school bus full of kids and suddenly a cat darts out from behind a parked car. . . I slam on the brakes and hit the cat and drive a few yards and look back in the mirror I see blood gushing out of the cat's neck. . . there is an animal shelter not far away. . . my father worked there years ago. . . he brought animals home trying to save them. . . I drove around the block. . . returned to the cat. . . jumped out of the van. . . took a T-shirt I had in the back. . . I had been sleeping in the van. . . grabbed the cat and wrapped the T-shirt around it. . . hurried it into the van. . . the kids began crying out. . . the cat bleeding and moving toward the back. . . I raced the van running stoplights and arrived at the entrance to the animal shelter. . . fell to my knees at the front desk with the cat in the T-shirt now completely soaked in blood. . . the kids I heard them screaming and I grabbed the cat and turned once again to the double feature and walked out the front gate to the car and locked the door you don't want to be sitting in a car when the door is not locked our neighbor was washing his light blue Mustang and those guys that had been drinking and had a knife. . . it was in all the papers. . . never saw him or his wife again get the rifle said my father and where are my bullets and my mother hid the bullets but it is the first day at school and nothing but nightmares wake up and it is just a science fiction movie and now I am ten or eleven years old again and I reach for my school clothes still wrapped in plastic that my mother and my brothers and I got at the Emporium downtown Market Street. . . and take the pins out of the shirt and wake up in the old wooden shack for the first day at Pelton Junior High School. . . and the auditorium is full of black children and just a handful of white children from the shipyards. . . the kids whose parents are in the military. . . the barracks up on the hills where the Japanese were forced to leave and the black families came from the Deep South. . . the rocks thrown through the windows and the kids jumping the fence or circling me on my way back from school. . . I know what I have to do. . . I have to avoid the joggers I have to avoid breathing that is what I will do I will not breathe a word to anyone I will keep to myself I will observe life through the peephole in our apartment and now we have a system with twine to lower and raise items from the open window and my wife creates nature images outside our door where there is only a wall to project our nightmares and dreams. . . to be out with me is not to be out to be out with me is to be inside the beat-up Rambler station wagon I bought from my friend for 50 dollars and with my books and the key in the ignition because at any moment I may have to start the car and go where I can be left alone and where can I be left alone when I have no place to live if I am not living in a cheap hotel room and wait 'til there are no sounds in the hallway because you don't want to meet your fellow residents and they don't want to meet you. . . but if you go out with me then come with me into the past or walk up or down the steps did you hear something get back in the apartment did you see something but I have found the best route to take that the kids don't know about. . . I go past the wrecking yard to the train tracks and place Lincoln pennies on the rails and watch the train roar out of the tunnel and then I go past the pie factory and look for pies they toss in the garbage can and then up the hill to Pelton Junior High School and the kids walking together in the Schloss Park count them. . . four of them. . . what are they doing? Call the police. . . my hands behind my back. . . fists in my face. . . a swarm of bodies in front of me stay away from them kids stay away from the school yard get into the library where I repaired the binding on books and where I discovered new worlds where I could be alone so go out with me for fresh air or for some sun or to listen to the birds.

MASKS AND GUNS:
MAKING MASKS IN AMERICA,
SOUTHWEST PANDEMIC PANIC, AND
GUNS IN AN OPEN-CARRY STATE
Aimee Parkison

There are chords in the hearts of the most reckless which cannot be touched without emotion. Even with the utterly lost, to whom life and death are equally jests, there are matters of which no jest can be made.
> —Poe's "The Masque of the Red Death"

Every time we leave the house, Death walks among us, one of us, in disguise, so we never really know who or where Death is, though we fear he is near us, coming for us, in the guise of an acquaintance, a friend, a lover; or a family member, colleague, fellow shopper, citizen, immigrant, woman, man, child, law breaker, rich person, poor person, Republican, Democrat, Christian, atheist, young or old. Death could look like anyone, even you or me. Death could enter any house, church, school, or business, invited or uninvited, an intruder, an esteemed guest, a member of the family. Any one of us could be Death to another, without even knowing.

That's why today, after reading Poe's "The Masque of the Red Death," I'll be making masks for me and my husband.

Poe published "The Masque of the Red Death" in May of 1842, 178 years ago, but never have the events of its plot (people attempting to avoid a dangerous plague and wearing masks in social isolation) felt so current. Sadly, never have the chilling logic of its theme felt so prophetic and terrifyingly relevant—that Death is inevitable and inescapable because even if we attempt to lock ourselves away in our houses and wear masks at any gathering, Death will find us.

Nevertheless, today, like Poe's characters of 178 years ago, those of us who most want to escape Death go about wearing and making masks and locking ourselves in our houses, to keep Death away from ourselves and our loved ones and to protect our neighbors. I haven't seen my family in many months, though we all live near each other, because we're afraid we might infect each other, though we are all without symptoms. I have only left the house to gather supplies like food and cleaning products, and when I'm out of the house I see strangers, some wearing masks and some wearing guns.

Here in Oklahoma, we're living "The Masque of the Red Death" with guns, since as of November 1, 2019, Oklahoma no longer requires a permit for a person to legally carry a concealed or open firearm in public if that person is twenty-one years of age or older. Adults can carry guns in public, openly or concealed, without a background check or training. So, here in Oklahoma, now that the pandemic has reached the public, we are walking in a land of masked faces and guns.

Perhaps from far away, to a stranger from a not-so-distant past, when we leave our houses we appear like little kids walking our neighborhood streets with masks and guns, playing cops and robbers. If only this were a game in the usual sense of the word, where the good guys and the bad guys were easily recognizable because the robbers wore masks, it would be so simple. What fun we would have—those of us who grew up playing with toy guns and delighting in wearing masks and costumes to hide our faces and transform us into characters. Today, the masks aren't costumes and the guns aren't toys and no one is happy or playing. Everyone fears each other and the very air we breathe. In particular, it often seems those who wear masks fear those who wear guns and those who wear guns are annoyed by those who wear masks, perhaps because those who wear masks are a reminder that we all should be afraid, even in middle America, even in small-town Oklahoma, where life is supposed to be safe in the slow lane of the Bible Belt.

Here in the Bible Belt, we used to only cover our faces for parties on Halloween. Now, some of us wear masks every time we leave the house, hiding our mouths and noses, not our eyes, from friends, family, acquaintances, and strangers. Masks are a form of disguise but also of protection: sometimes they protect the wearer and sometimes they protect those around us. Wearing a disguise suggests we have something to hide and a reason to hide from others. Many believe the virus is a conspiracy, that it's just a glorified version of the flu or an exaggeration by a government wanting to steal freedom from its citizens. Those of us who believe the virus is real try to stay at home to save lives, but when we can't stay at home, the masks come out. The masks make us delirious because it's hard to breathe in them. Our breath fogs our glasses. Have you ever tried to smile at someone through a mask, or even talk? The words come out garbled, especially now that we have to stand at least six feet apart.

We fear each other's breath but we also fear showing fear. For a very short while, we were required to wear masks before entering public places, but then employees were threatened for asking customers to socially distance or put on a mask before entering stores and restaurants. Just hours after implementing the face-covering emergency order on May 1, the mayor of my small college town amended the order to "encourage" but not require face masks. The reason for this quick amendment? Employees asking patrons to wear masks were threatened with violence, verbal abuse, and firearms, since some citizens thought that the order about wearing masks was a violation of their constitutional rights and their freedoms as US citizens. These threats occurred only three hours after the order requiring people to wear a mask in crowded public spaces to slow the spread of the virus was first implemented. Employees at McDonalds were shot, another bashed on the head, for telling customers the dining room was

110

closed due to social distancing.

Now, whenever I go to Walmart, I sit in the car, waiting with mask in hand, just watching people enter and leave the building to see how many are wearing masks and how many are wearing guns. Some guns are holstered and others are shoved into back pockets. People are watching each other for various reasons, mostly to see who is wearing masks and who is wearing guns. Typically, those who wear masks don't carry guns and those who carry guns don't wear masks. Don't ask me why. It's hard to explain. Refusing to wear a mask and carrying a gun is supposed to represent the ultimate freedom. Those who wear a mask are thought to be sensitive or sick or repressive, as if they have something to fear and something to hide. For many who want to simply get on with the business of living, those who wear masks are the ultimate threat, since the mask wearers remind us that the virus is everywhere in the air we breathe, in our breath, that we are all a threat to each other. Ironically, those who wear guns also believe we are all a threat to each other and are claiming to protect themselves and others by carrying the gun, just as those who wear a mask are trying to protect themselves and others by wearing the mask. The difference, though, is that the mask wearers think the threat is the virus while the gun wearers think the threat is the reaction to the virus. Either way, the threat is inside us all, and we are divided on how we think it is best to tackle it—with masks or with guns.

Every time I leave the house, I know I'm a guest at a masquerade where Death walks, an uninvited guest. I fear if I don't wear a mask someone might get sick from my breath, though I have no symptoms. I also fear if I wear a mask I might make someone angry enough to use their gun on me. Only weeks ago, our government said no one needed to wear masks, that wearing masks could make the threat of the virus worse. At the same time, masks were selling like hotcakes going out of style everywhere they were for sale and the public was asked not to buy masks, to leave them for the health care professionals. My sister, who is a nurse, has to wear the same disposable paper mask for days at the hospital, where each nurse has a plastic bag with her name to store a reused mask that was made to be thrown away after one use. That one disposable mask now must last for days or weeks.

Now, the government is recommending that everyone in the general public wear a mask in public, and that people should make their own masks out of old T-shirts and scraps of material, like I'm doing. Wearing the mask is optional, though, unless your state government makes it a requirement. Here in Oklahoma, one thing has become clear: there are certain things certain people won't allow the government to tell them to do. One is give up their guns, another is stay home, and yet another is wear a mask.

As much as I fear the virus, I also fear for my husband, who is not white, walking into a gas station with a mask over his face. What if the cashier thinks he's a criminal and shoots him in "self-defense"? Oklahoma's Stand Your Ground law states that "A person who is not engaged in an unlawful activity and who is attacked in any other place where he or she has a right to be has no duty to retreat and has the right to stand his or her ground and meet force with force, including deadly force, if he or she reasonably believes it is necessary to do so to prevent death or great bodily harm to himself or herself or another *or* to prevent the commission of a forcible felony."

Stand Your Ground laws can quickly become a threat to public safety when almost everyone sees each other as a threat. Only months ago, anyone walking into a bank or restaurant or gas station wearing a mask was thought to be there to rob the place, and anyone who saw a masked adult in a public place feared that person was criminal and ducked to avoid being shot. Now everyone who respects the virus is wearing a mask like a criminal in a state full of guns that are allegedly for protection against criminals.

I'll never read "The Masque of the Red Death" the same way. In the past, though it has always been one of my favorite short stories, it always felt far away and abstract, like a beautiful gothic painting of a fairytale. Now, it feels like a prophetic warning about a new reality, a new world where we're living Poe's allegory. For many of us in the pandemic, the figurative world of Poe has become literal since we're guests of a masquerade, isolating ourselves from society in hopes of escaping Death.

In trying to keep myself and others safe by making masks, I realize I might also be making us unsafe because if the wrong people see us wearing masks in public they might want to shoot us because in obscuring some of our most human features— our mouths and noses—the masks are making it harder to communicate and making us less human to each other in public spaces where so many are heavily armed, while also reminding all of us that we are threats to each other, that any of us could be Death disguised, or disguising Death inside us, at any place or time.

Scissors, thread, fabric, elastic catching in the old Singer sewing machine I hadn't used in years: ten yards of elastic makes 25 masks. Five half-yard cuts of fabric is perfect for 25 masks, so I can make some for family and friends, leaving room for error. The cotton thread sings through the machine. Sewing masks for myself and my husband, I wonder if things will ever get back to normal.

What is normal now? What is normal ever again? I've come to the realization that there are some faces I might never see again, at least in person. I know that now, but if I don't make more masks for my loved ones to wear, there may be many more faces I'll never see, at least not in person. I should have known it long ago. Once, only criminals wore masks to banks, gas stations, grocery stores, and places that might be robbed. Now the law-abiding are wearing masks like criminals, just trying to buy food and supplies to stay alive. Isolated in our own houses, walled off, we remove our masks and let our naked faces breathe.

CORONA IN ISTANBUL
Zeynep Camuşcu

I have been sleeping. Midday naps to kill some time. Without a constant occupation, quarantine in times of Corona has meant that there's much more time to spend. From mid-March to May, we stayed at home as a family, but we weren't terribly concerned. The only thing that kept my physician father from going to work was his age, but that did not stop him working from home. With each patient he diagnosed with Covid-19, however, our anxiety grew.

Istanbul is a city with a strong connection to the sea. It only takes ten minutes to go to the seaside from my home, but during the quarantine, not only the seaside, but also the city's parks and gardens were forbidden grounds. Seeing my friends who live abroad relaxing in parks or at the riverside, I constantly felt jealous. I was angry, but on the other hand, I knew very well that keeping Istanbul's citizens away was a necessary precaution— you have no idea how deep the Turkish people's love for picnics is. An epidemic would never stop them from setting up their tables on the grass with a view of the famous Princes' Islands in the Marmara Sea.

The month of May not only brought a sense of habit, but also very hot weather. Watching the blue sky from the narrow windows of an apartment complex and envying the sea birds alighting on the adjacent roof, I started applying for master's programs, not knowing what to expect from the future. I needed my own space, so I took a deep breath and decided to explore the streets of the epidemic-ridden city. At first, I only walked around my neighborhood. Then I began stopping off at supermarkets for a bottle of milk or some ice cream. The mask and gloves. . . how to describe the burden? The small drops of sweat covering my mouth and my glasses fogging up with each and every breath. . . an unbearable level of stress that made me want to run home.

With the coming of June, we were forced to "normalize." Suddenly, the crowded Metrobus—a type of transportation unique to Istanbul, a mix of subway and bus that services most of the city—started to appear again. People reclaimed their jobs, the parks and the seaside were once again crowded, and no one seemed to care about the rules of social distancing anymore. The city regained its chaotic regularity—if this is the correct term. I started dreaming about unmasked people coming after me, and I woke up in fear. On my bike cycling through the recently reopened seaside, I wanted to tear off my mask, but it was prohibited and subject to a fine of 900 Turkish liras, about 130 dollars.

The normalization liberated the elderly, who had been forced to stay home for more than two months. To be honest, though, even the strict ban had been unable to stop them from going outside. Passing them in the street, I looked into their eyes, searching for signs of distress, but couldn't find any. I specifically remember one who was buying a big box of chocolate for the upcoming *Bayram* visitors—in normal times, it's common for people to visit their elderly relatives to celebrate a *Bayram* or holiday in Turkey, but I doubt much of that happened this year.

On TV, there have been ads praising the beauty of Turkey with images of pristine beaches and turquoise-colored water, mosques at sunset, and archaeological sites to encourage people to support domestic tourism and keep the broken economy alive. To add to this, private companies keep running ads emphasizing "the power and the unity" of the Turkish people. If I hadn't already heard the voices of people on the street complaining about the insecurity of their jobs, rising inflation, and the high cost of living in the big city, I might have believed them. But I did not. What I've seen over the past several months has been a troubled city and its people, who suddenly, without warning, found themselves in the Covid nightmare.

It was not that long ago that I was sitting in their place, those poor souls sweating through the university entrance exam. Like every June, millions of people waited for their children in front of school doors. This time, it was a festival of masks; a festival some children were brought to in ambulances.

And now? We are looking for a new house. I can hear you asking "in the middle of a pandemic?" Maybe not a wise choice, but it's our own. Did you know that the city district I live in, Kadiköy, is itself already the size of Amsterdam? That's how big the city is, and no part of it is like any other. Trying to find a house in this city feels like trying to find a grain of salt in a kilo package, and no one can guarantee that you won't run into unpleasant surprises. Home owners greet us with masks on, a bottle of cologne on their hands. We are wearing our shoe covers and smell the strong odor of alcohol in the cologne. The viruses are killed, we are happy. Old furniture and old people in new houses, family pictures attached to mirrors and smelly kitchens. In each house, we try to imagine living there, and in each house I search for a corner to put my book shelves.

These days, I am working toward getting my driver's license. I take private driving lessons and navigate the car as if I were about to operate on someone: gloves on both hands and with a mask on. Fear seems to have vanished, and even the rising number of people coming down with the virus does not cause enough pain. The city is still pretty much alive, but I am not sure about its inhabitants.

WRITING AGAINST THE VIRUS

UNCERTAINTY EVER AFTER
Jon Roemer

I spend too much time thinking about uncertainty. As a writer and editor, I think about what pulls a story forward. Will our heroine lose everything, will our hero make it home safe. It's a state that I enjoy—reveling in not knowing what's next. I make the space to do it, to engage in imagining horrible loss.

But this week, after several weeks, uncertainty has run out of fun. The path ahead feels too urgent for speculation, for the work of a novel. Should novels even be a priority right now?

I know the proper answer. Imaginative work is how we change, how we find new directions. But it's happening so fast. What feels monumental this morning will get outdone tomorrow night. The uncertainty of an invisible virus has crashed into the certainty of George Floyd's moral cause, which has fiercely pivoted to the uncertainty of remedies. It's very hard to say how this year will end, except as a measure of how we care about each other.

Since the start of our Coronavirus troubles, I've been watching how writers express their expectations. A week before George Floyd was killed, I listened to two clever and famous poets talk about the impact of Covid-19, how its disruption will usher in a new era, ending racism, homophobia, and patriarchy, along with capitalism's rapid collapse. A very bright outlook. In fact, I thought they were being funny, and I laughed with my dog. But when I looked at the screen again, their smiles were kind of wry, like they knew it was wishful thinking, but maybe only kind of. Like right now, maybe, who can really say.

The next week, following Floyd's killing, I got Roxane Gay's take, in an essay explaining that a new path to equality is not on its way. "Eventually, doctors will find a Coronavirus vaccine, but black people will continue to wait, despite the futility of hope, for a cure for racism." That's very different from the radical poets. Gay isn't so rosy; she doesn't think we can imagine our way out of this mess.

And then this week, Anna Deavere Smith called herself a hope-a-holic. Smith's theater piece *Twilight* reflected on the Rodney King riots, and as she's done before, she called on writers and artists to grow our moral imagination. With a wincing look at a TV anchor, she described our imagination as "not as robust as it can be."

Well, ouch. But also, yes.

In my family—white folks with roots in the Midwest—I have a niece in Denver who yearns to join the protests but is continuing her family's pandemic confinement. Another, now in Tampa, is out and about, juggling her work, her daughter, her wife and their church events. Yet another has been to Ozark family reunions and flown across the country to reunite with her dad, who's been isolating alone for weeks. Here in California, my boyfriend owns a bar shut down by pandemic restrictions, while protests against police have blocked doctors from treating his father's heart condition. On a recent group call with Silicon Valley consultants, I heard one after another welcoming the idea of career counseling, looking for exit strategies, while my sister works in health tech in a new job that's bustling. I could pull them into a novel in a Dos Passos maneuver, starting with the counterpoint of POC communities. But this slice of life could quickly feel naive. Given the pace of change, the catastrophe coming next week, it could quickly get dated, reading painfully oblivious to the new disasters still on their way.

Less than a year ago, I published a novel crafted around a moment in time, aiming to capture the pressures re-shaping San Francisco. My focus was on the neighborhood, how proximity has lost its potential for identity, and how modern urban life can be so solitary it can skew our measure of ourselves and reality.

The same pressures are still here, but new ones have piled on, and the book's relevance, as always, is in the hands of the reader. I also wrote it with a very open ending, wanting the protagonist to arrive at a new awareness but still reside in the same place, with a lot of the same problems. That was important to me, to dramatize a recognition of shared responsibilities.

It's not autobiographical—the narrator is even more of a buffoon than me. But I think that's the condition I'm trying to describe today: my anxiety around a lack of movement, which is mandated here in this phase of the pandemic, and my fear of a failed imagination, which even the sharpest poets and writers are facing.

Late February/early March felt like a horror movie, the fast, almost tidy way the pandemic was unfolding and the way cable news filled an expository role. It looked like a Soderbergh split-screen concoction, like *Contagion* on replay from a decade ago. Until the spectacle got repetitive, the numbers got close to home, and angry people started filling my streets.

It's important, I think, that it felt like a movie, like it's a story we know already, even if the actual lived experience has been entirely new and challenging. Because that means we're up to speed—a writer and an editor has already anticipated our uncertainties—so we at least know the common wisdom, and we'll be able to move quickly.

But *writing* quickly hasn't always been my thing, and now more than ever, it's probably smart to work without expectations, without a sense of an ending. I'm listening, taking notes, moving things around, because new thinking sometimes comes from rearranging old ideas. I'm still interested in the tension between individual and communal obligations, I'm still looking to greater minds, and I'm still hoping for a time when uncertainty feels a lot less perilous.

AFTER GINGER
Alice Stephens

Isamu Noguchi found it was easier to get himself into an internment camp than it was to get out.

Confined at home these past months due to the Coronavirus, I think often of the Japanese and Japanese Americans who were interned during World War II.

After five years of research and writing, I had recently completed a historical fiction novel based on the visionary artist Isamu Noguchi's internment in Arizona when the news emerged of a deadly new disease in China. Oblivious to the import of the news and proud of my effort, I began querying agents.

As an East Coast resident, Noguchi was exempt from Roosevelt's Executive Order 9066. Nonetheless, he felt it his civic and patriotic duty to express solidarity with his fellow American-born Nisei and their immigrant Issei parents, voluntarily interning himself with the loftiest of intentions: to teach the latter how to love democracy and to instill pride in the former in Japan's rich cultural legacy. However, he quickly discovered that he was in over his head, and almost as soon as he entered the camp, he sought to leave.

As someone who had always succeeded in living outside the strictures of his race, Noguchi did not face the same challenges or bear the burdens of his fellow internees. They had been forced to abandon homes, businesses, crops, pets, and their worldly possessions—to say nothing of their sense of belonging and identity—to be herded like so much livestock into flimsy wooden barracks hastily built in America's most desolate hinterlands for an unknown period of time. Stripped of their basic human rights, they had no idea what the future held. To many, it must have seemed like their lives, and futures, had been stolen from them.

Though I had immersed myself for several years in the history, studies, and anecdotes of Noguchi's internment camp, it is only now in lockdown that I think I understand the extent of their suffering, anxiety, and fear.

Comfortably sheltered in a suburban, three-bedroom house, with easy access to nature walks and gourmet take-out, I can't compare my situation to theirs. And yet, some days I'm almost incapacitated by malaise. On the really bad days, that malaise putrefies into dread and horror that weigh upon me like a lead apron, mimicking the symptoms of the disease I'm so desperately trying to avoid: shortness of breath, hot flushes, headaches.

Meanwhile, outside my lockdown bubble, the nation is in accelerated meltdown. Facts, prudence, and common sense have been abandoned for fiction, wild speculation, and magical thinking. The person who is supposed to be leading us through the biggest national crisis in a generation muses on live television about injecting disinfectants into the body and steers lucrative contracts to his cronies. One moment he advises adhering to the precautionary measures of his public health experts, and the next he praises gun-toting white people who storm state capitols for their inalienable right to get a fashy haircut and a swastika tattoo. Grocery store clerks and gig workers are lauded as heroes as they reap poverty-level wages, while the stock market soared the same day that a record number filed for unemployment.

The anti-Axis hatred that flourished after Pearl Harbor was largely directed at the Japanese. Though Executive Order 9066 was directed at "any and all persons" as "the appropriate military commander may determine," it was only the Japanese and their American descendants who were interned; immigrants from Germany and Italy faced no such curtailment of their civil rights. The particular physiognomy of the Japanese made them easy to spot and easy to persecute. (To escape the rampant prejudice, some Chinese Americans resorted to wearing buttons and signs proclaiming they were Chinese.) Newspapers, none more so than those owned by William Randolph Hearst, were instrumental in ratcheting up the anti-Japanese sentiment, while war posters and other propaganda, including cartoons by Dr. Seuss, portrayed the Japanese as slant-eyed, snub-nosed, bucktoothed hordes, or slavering, long-nailed monsters with blood dripping from their fangs.

Seeking to distract the public from their own egregious missteps, Trump and his lackeys insist on calling the novel Coronavirus 2019 the "China virus" and the "Kung flu." Taking up Hearst's racist mantle, Rupert Murdoch—who owns *The New York Post*, the *Wall Street Journal*, the *Times* of London, and Fox News—oversees a news empire that spreads specious and hateful anti-Asian rhetoric. Since March, incidents of harassment, bullying, and violence against Asians and Asian Americans have soared, including the stabbing of a Burmese man and his children, two and six years old, in Texas.

I am fortunate enough to live in one of the most diverse areas in the country, if not the planet, and despite my Asian heritage, I have not experienced any virus-related harassment, but the anecdotes from friends are heartbreaking. Almost 150 years after the Chinese Exclusion Act of 1882, Asian Americans are still deemed to be menacing outsiders intent on destroying all that is good and true.

Noguchi wasn't one to sit still, even while languishing in a concentration camp. He produced blueprints for landscape improvements, trekked into the desert to gather weather-carved knobs of ironwood and other bits and bobs of nature's bounty, tried (unsuccessfully, due to objections by the War Relocation Authority) to arrange for academic lectures and lead workshops, schemed to get art commissions, and kept up copious correspondences. But he only produced one piece of art, a pink

Georgia marble bust of Ginger Rogers, which now resides in the National Portrait Gallery, where I saw it on display along with a letter Noguchi had written to Rogers from internment, sparking the inspiration for my novel.

It's not one of his best works, nor even one of his best busts (I am partial to those of George Gershwin and Buckminster Fuller, neither of which are in stone). No one would look at it and exclaim, "Ginger Rogers!" Her hair was styled in an unfortunate pompadour for a movie role, her neck is impossibly long. No matter, the face draws you in. Each angle reveals a different Ginger. Straight on, she's not beautiful, but she's strong, with a forthright, intelligent gaze, her full mouth curved ever so slightly into a knowing smile. In profile, she's cool and aloof, unaware of her own charisma; at three-quarters, she's ambitious and just a little high-strung. Truly, it is an act of genius to show the many different facets of a subject in just one work.

Before internment, Noguchi had been making his living carving busts for the rich and famous. After Ginger, he would never do such overtly representational work again. In the camp, Noguchi had been forced to face deep-seated questions of his identity and his purpose as an artist. He vowed to leave behind the political and the representational, transforming into an astonishingly versatile and prolific abstract expressionist who also designed everything from coffee tables and lamps to courtyards and landscapes.

I'd been querying agents at full throttle for a month before lockdown began. Publishing is a notoriously fickle business and I've already had two agents. When I was an as-yet-unpublished author, the response rate to my queries was encouraging. This time, the lack of interest was palpable, and I don't know if it's the subject of my novel, the fact that I'm considered washed up as a non-bestselling debut novelist, or a combination of the two. And when New York, the epicenter of publishing, became the epicenter of the Coronavirus in the US, my querying, like my life, came to a standstill.

Globally, the toll of Coronavirus is as yet incalculable. I tick through the countries where I have lived for a view on how the virus is being (mis)managed around the world.

- The country of my birth, South Korea, has successfully contained the spread and returned to a semblance of normal life. A small nation, it learned the lessons of previous respiratory illness outbreaks and was prepared with medical equipment, the laboratory capacity to produce enough tests for the population, and public health steps like rigorous contact tracing.

- Small, landlocked, and relatively prosperous Botswana is on lockdown. As of May 11, there were 24 confirmed cases, eleven recoveries, and one death. The government recently made face masks compulsory in public.

- Like many authoritarian states, Egypt is censoring news stories and engaging in political repression under the cover of the pandemic. Government statistics on the spread and toll are not reliable.

- With one of the highest death tolls in Europe, Spain has recently released citizens from an extremely strict seven-week lockdown.

- After initially bungling their response by suppressing reports and threatening doctors, China, where the virus originated, has managed to triumph over Coronavirus through draconian quarantine methods and cell phone tracking. Due to government censorship, many details about the virus' spread, including the real death toll, remain unclear. Isolated flare-ups are still being reported across the country even as Disneyland re-opened in Shanghai.

- Under the repressive rule of Erdoğan, Turkey is claiming that the disease is being beaten by hydroxychloroquine, a favorite panacea of autocratic leaders. (After our own aspiring autocrat relentlessly flogged the drug as a miracle cure, the FDA was forced to release a statement cautioning against the use of the drug outside of a clinical setting.)

- Japan is struggling with a resurgence of the virus after prematurely lifting lockdown.

In less developed nations, prevention could be deadlier than the disease itself. Migrant workers, off whose backs the whole world prospers, are suddenly without work, and many are forced to return on foot to home villages far from where they earn a living. Crowded living conditions and lack of running water make social distancing and hand-washing impossible, and there is no government safety net available to them. So far, the world's most impoverished nations seem to have avoided the brunt of Coronavirus, but the first wave has yet to crest.

There will be a second wave in the fall, we are told. It will be more deadly. Perhaps, if no vaccine has been developed, there will be a third wave in the winter, as there was with the 1918 flu pandemic.

For many of the Japanese and Japanese American internees during World War II, the world outside the camp was more dangerous than inside, despite the primitive housing, harsh conditions, and pitifully low-paying jobs. Like the interned, I yearn to return to normal, but know that there will be no normal to return to. And like them, I can't tell if I'm at a crossroads or a cul-de-sac.

The US government realized very quickly that the internment camps were a mistake, and began to relocate as many of the interned as were eligible and willing to go: students who found colleges willing to take them, laborers recruited for factory and farm work, men finally allowed to join the armed forces. After six months of internment and a series of increasingly desperate appeals, Noguchi finally gained permission for temporary furlough. He hightailed it out of there, later saying in his autobiography, "So far as I know, I am still only temporarily at large."

PERPETUUM MOBILE

Alexander Graeff
Translated by Mark Kanak

I used to complain about my long-distance relationship. I wrote heartwarming letters full of longing and "what if" speculations— once I even wrote a story titled "Empty." That's how I often felt after our encounters, empty. Our professions prevented us from visiting each other every weekend. Worse still: the damned job was the reason he'd moved away in the first place.

These days, with travel not permitted, the memory of the self-imposed ups and downs of our encounter, of the journeys from A to B for the sake of love, fades [*Von A nach B der Liebe wegen (from A to B for the sake of love)* is a line in the song *Perpetuum Mobile* by Einstürzende Neubauten, from the album of the same name (2004)]. Today, when leaving the apartment is forbidden and you're stopped by the police and asked for the reason behind your short walk to the last late-night shop in the neighborhood that's open and hasn't yet gone bankrupt; or to the supermarket to maybe get some gluten-free pasta—normal pasta is always sold out immediately: today the memory of the times we visited each other, which were electric, charged with all kinds of expectation, fades. And yet they were always meant to be the most beautiful and intimate weekends ever.

Today, with so much prohibited, we no longer ask ourselves when we'll be able to see each other on the weekend again. The crisis, the quarantine, the pandemic have compelled me and many others in long-distance relationships to give up, along with most businesses or shops that don't have a multi-million-dollar corporation or government aid (or both) behind them. Relationships only seem to exist in the form of traditional nuclear families, with a mom, dad, and child who live together in one place and at a single address.

Patriarchy is in bloom, or it manifests itself in the same way it always did before the crisis; only those who refuse to conform and are patronizingly tolerated by those in power endeavor to lovingly obscure it. Now, it's the people heroically facing the crisis who are the *real* men: the doers, the machine operators, an army of virologists, health ministers, press spokesmen, and crisis managers that keep the machine running. The women and the rest remain invisible in some analogue space, in nursing, in hospitals, buying groceries, or simply in quarantine—much like us, the dreamers, the pussies who write letters to each other.

In the midst of the crisis, all that remains are my memories of him, whom I love all the more now since we've been separated for so long, something I've only recently grown aware of. The relationship is fading, but the love is growing. Absurd. Once again, I write letters to him. This time they're sober, they aren't heartwarming, but full of a hope that I haven't yet given up on. My hope corresponds to the length of the lockdown. I follow every official announcement with keen interest, watch every press conference, and study the pandemic dashboards every morning.

Even the selfies he sends me give me hope. Especially the ones where he looks happy. His beard's gotten really long since I last saw him. I send him selfies, too. Responding to the last photo, he only said that I looked relaxed, despite my ridiculous hair. My hair grows fast, too fast, and distorts the picture I would like him to remember me by. Add a hoodie, gloves, and a protective mask, and you've got yourself a bona fide post-apocalyptic Coronapunk.

I've put on weight, too. Not enough exercise, too much junk food. I now prepare three quarantine meals a day. Even though certain products are often no longer available because I simply can't manage to stand in line outside the supermarket at

8 a.m. in full protective gear, most basic foods are not yet lacking. Rice, potatoes, canned goods, bread, tea, wine, and beer are all still available. I also notice that I buy completely different things than the majority tends to. Margarine, for example, is always sold out rather quickly, whereas soy-based margarine is available for quite a while. Meat—there's almost only poultry left—sells out and is hoarded quickly; fish, on the other hand, remains on sale for a relatively long time. For breakfast I make myself a cheese sandwich with cucumber and eat an egg every day. In order to save coffee, I drink only one cup in the morning, and throughout the day mainly tea.

There's lunch now, too. Often gluten-free pasta with tomato or tuna fish sauce. I haven't really eaten lunch anymore since I moved out of my parents' house when I was twenty. In the evening a tray of French fries with ketchup or vegetable casserole or red curry with coconut milk. I suspect that there'd still be frozen French fries and ketchup even after a nuclear war between competing health agencies in Europe.

Now *that's* a notion born of crisis, and I certainly wouldn't swear on it—but it does seem there are and always will be enough French fries and ketchup to go around. I often have crisis-induced thoughts. I ask myself: can it get any worse? Will the curfew become even stricter? When will the strikes against the healthcare system become more violent? When will the looting begin? Enough of that.

Throughout the day I drink—as a prophylactic measure— at least two liters of tea. Alternating between sage, fennel, and Earl Grey. In the evening my stomach gurgles from all the liquid I've consumed. According to the health authorities, the virus can only really be fought with tea. There's still no vaccine or medication for the disease. Which means: drink a lot of fluids, don't smoke, stay at home and rest. I am resting to escape from a hyper-acidic society. And smoking more than ever.

My work lies untouched. What I used to complain about

in my relationship has now become irrelevant, light as air. It's the same for him. Neither of our professions are systemically relevant. After the first few weeks when we were, as at the supermarkets, busy standing in a virtual queue to apply for an aid package, doing paperwork, making lists of lost income, cutting costs, things have calmed down again. A bit of a break from the money worries. A sense of uncertainty remains.

Since then, there's been plenty of time for completely different activities: for example, spending a day watching films and reports on Anneliese Michel's exorcism; or watching a scary number of fantasy and science fiction series; or producing my own videos with me reading crisis poetry in a particularly dramatic way; or watching the videos of colleagues reading their own texts—in polar bear costumes, in their underwear, together with newly-hatched chicks, while drinking beer and looking like crinkly, creepy characters due to an overloaded network.

At some point, then, my stomach became hyper-acidic. It was just too much coffee, definitely too much wine, and too many fries with ketchup. I went on a diet for a week. Just carrots and rice. And water. Then I drank cosmopolitans two nights in a row. I just had to. Cranberry juice was finally back on the shelves. My last letter was devoid of hope. So far there has been no reply.

I'm dreaming like mad. About this letter. His reaction to my dwindling hope. In my dream, he wrote to me about his youth. He's dreaming a lot right now, too. We both dream about being young, about the agony of growing up and what we had to leave behind to become adults. I dream that he's dreaming. That sounds crazy, because it feels like the negation of a negation and makes the dream something *positive*.

In one dream, I, that is, he, was in the oldest temple in the world. Somewhere in Turkey. A priest sprinkled his blood on the faithful—there were eight, including me—and each was given a 12,000-year-old skull, which we then worked on with sharp stone wedges. Following the priest's instructions, we were to carve characters into the skulls in order to unlock the secret of the human brain.

In another dream, I see my father, that is, his father, trying to carefully detach the upper part of a cabinet display case together with the porcelain figurines inside from the lower part and set it aside. The lifting bit succeeds, the putting down less so. Everything in it slides and bangs against the glass doors, they open and all the stuff tumbles out and shatters into a thousand pieces. The father curses and scolds, and all he makes clear is that he's never really learned to be careful, to be cautious, to be gentle. And however hard he tries, in the end he destroys the delicate, filigree porcelain figures. Our relationship is like one of these porcelain figurines, we break into pieces with all the lifting and the setting down, because we have never really learned to be gentle.

Gentleness is not required in a crisis. Only the machine operators keep moving, and with them the digital machines, the dashboards, the video conferences, the live streaming. They're not losing any energy, but my relationship is—even the letters don't seem to help. And neither do the dreams.

Dreams are just virtual encounters with myself, I think. They only become positive *mathematically*, when he dreams in this other place, at night in his bed. They say the same as the image of his face on my screen: more about me than about him.

Like that, or something like that.

WINDOWS
Beverly Gologorsky

The comfort of the couch is an unexpected joy. The early dusk enters the room to brighten the lamplight. Nothing new in the way of decoration has been added, so most everything within sight is at least half my age. Objects long held, whether paintings, photos, worn chairs, even the plants along the windowsill, feel dearer at my age than they once did. What strange mood is this?

Perhaps it's the result of too many hours alone. Going into my fourth week of self-isolation, I can't help but wonder when the dearness of home will begin to feel like a cage. Recently widowed, I turned eighty not that long ago, and being alone can be difficult. At my age and with asthma, the new virus has made me an endangered species.

I can't go outdoors, which makes me grateful to be a writer. What keeps me working every day is life. Why else start a new book, which will take forever to complete? As long as the work itself is there to get on with, my earthly being has purpose. When I leave the computer, I'm done for today, but only for today.

The apartment is quiet, too quiet. In the silence, I think about my younger years when I wasn't alone. Then sure I knew so much, I only now understand there was still everything to learn.

I pour a glass of wine and sit at the kitchen window. Bodily insults come and go at my age, so the Coronavirus feels less like a threat than a fact. I fix my sight on two people walking their dogs, keeping social distance, although the dogs strain at the leashes to reach each other. It's begun to rain and an unflattering light casts a gray, smoggy coat over the city rooftops.

I remember the winters in Maine at our old farmhouse near the water with their pristine, invigorating frost. Now, the winters offer only the danger of slipping on ice, how unfair. Youth wasted on the young, then age wasted on the body. Bummer.

Taking the wine to the living room, the only other room beside the bedroom, I flip through the pages of *The New Yorker*, but my mind is on this weird new level of survival that can't be ignored. It's the uncertainty, of course; everyone is experiencing it now, but at my age uncertainty is familiar, and so perhaps not as anxiety-producing as it might be to younger people whose lives are still being planned.

For me the future is all in a day. It's best to respond to a wish as it arises and not bank it for later use. Interestingly, to recognize that reality is a relief. To no longer worry or think or wonder about what may or may not be coming, there's the relief. And for now, I watch as life occurs outside my windows.

POEMS IN TIMES OF CORONA
Scott Martingell

WEDNESDAY, APRIL 1, 2020

I'm definitely getting tracked and docile
But random celebrities
Reminding me I'm home
Is not my idea of soma.

Systemic response
Is kicking in amongst the primates
Creating new vectors
Of chronic frustration, chains of volcanoes at home.

I'm hustling for work
Trying not to avoid
The noticeable shuffle
As e-learning packages survey the kids.

I need to get on the screen
See if a meme's turned up
Sharpen those pencils
And color-code my plastic bags.

FRIDAY, APRIL 3, 2020

The ones who're resilient, I've only now realized
(of course) are the alkie sociophobes
the OCD-ers hoovering their palaces
just above your ceiling at night.

It's not a great change
if you work from home
and don't equate life with movement.

We're not seeing a great deal new
in terms of the day-to-day;
maybe a few writers starting to squirm

as they come to terms
with their cul-de-sac of ironic distance.
No place to hide, now—ha.

TUESDAY, APRIL 7, 2020

My no doubt selfless striving
To keep the Italian vintners above water
(like a Saint Mark's Square trattoria
As a docking-denied cruise ship
Pulls away with her skeleton crew
To try her luck in Istria)

Is becoming more frayed by the day.
Hospitals of nightingales
Sing thee to thy rest
Scan the shelves for sewing kits
(like we need more needles at the end of the day).
I'm training my vast unusable lens
On keeping alcohol away from the front end of the week.

And a deputy PM, blinking like a raven,
Addresses a shrink-wrapped mike,
Saying "We" when he means "I. . ."

I hope, Dear Leader, you regain some measure
Of bonhomie when this has passed.
Perhaps there'll be some comfort to be had,
Even by Scots, from buffoonery.

THURSDAY, APRIL 9, 2020

Who's this slapdash that did anglistik and wants the gig?
I'm gonna translate what the flick I want
And if *you* can't be bothered to fossick around for synonyms
Why should I?

You're just shouting in another room
I can hear you going through your travails
Cutting your toenails

While I'm a camp follower of Heidi Klum's cohort
Measuring out the weeks with "Leider. . ."
Maintaining insignificance in the light of key workers

Resisting the urge to feel heroic
(the woman below with her windows unopened
and her boys somewhere, silent, unheard)

But what can I say?
There's kids here, shouting, and adults,
Working their passage through isolate grief.

I. FRIDAY, APRIL 10, 2020

Well, that industry's gone and this one's on its knees
And cruise ships for a generation and this thing's written like
    dreams

Hitchhikers on the hard shoulder for hours
And people in porn can't even rub shoulders
Street magicians are repurposing tricks
And Zoom masseurs are nudging out online shiatsu.
The trick to get out of Moria is to be under twelve and alone
While I stay paid, translating Negotiationsprozessen as
     negotiations,
Chasing up refunds and e-funds.
This is how I write when the news is on
Glancing across at Goya.
I'm an analogue age that remembers
The time before archive footage was slowed

II. TUESDAY, APRIL 14, 2020

B-listers are telling me the world is round
And I should keep my distance (would that I could)
From Trump going postal.
If you can't say anything that's not on the news—
No Kuhnian comments, slicing the cake elsewise,
Citing *The Ambassadors'* stretched-out skull
As reasons for a certain ambivalent stance
Towards the expert with a nice line in testing—
Then hold your noise; I'm just scoping your bookshelves.
Your spines are mine to judge, you muppets.

TUESDAY, APRIL 21, 2020

Wouldn't it be slick if oil were useless
And the Newcastle takeover never took place?
Sovereign wealth funds grounded the world over
Fleets of consultants suddenly stuck.

We're going thru that age-old editing process—internal
    combustion,
Soft-power sheiks rethinking the execution of minors,
Oligarchs with nowhere to shop,
Going the way of adverbs in a first draft.

That thing *Apollo 13* landed on
Taking her red pen to us.
Meanwhile, the park's getting battered
The grass can't take us—over-use.

The dogs are rolling around, and the days;
That's why I'm coughing
My morning chats with the birds
Are bringing me home dust-ridden
The backs of my hands caked and cracking

It's not so much the soap but the epidermal erosion
That makes me wish I could bleed for key workers
Whose hands-on, proactive, charlatan government
Masks its failings and waits on paperwork.

TUESDAY, APRIL 28, 2020

There's no connection—or none I see—
That links the cold fact of solitude
(As it wells up in your bones)
With the actuality of others.

I have graphs to prove this.
Some show intersections, areas of common touch;
A few are shaded where variables bleed.
In some, a hint of contour
Delineates the prevailing mood.

There are swings and tendencies
And, beyond the line of the farthest axis,
Shapes emerge, and discerning eyes.

I hope I haven't bogged you down
In overly technical explanation
But we should definitely prepare for parabolas.
The experts are all of a mind on this.

THURSDAY, APRIL 30, 2020

Like a fool, I ticked "non-perforated"
For my *V for Vendetta* Amazon mask.
Hyperventilation's a luxury,
I think, as I join the basket queue.

Luckily, my phone can tell me exactly
Where the May Day parades will be trending this year.
Maybe you'll see it as progress
When the airport closes
And you don't have to get up at four
To serve red-eye coffee to strangers.

I need a bailout
But not half as much as these reps
Whose job it was to release energy
From all that sunlight tucked into trees
Millions of years ago.

I need to bail out
From these half-suited, pencil-skirt dæmons
Buffering in front of their bookshelves (I've got my eye on
    your spines)
A bike going nowhere in your background.

So here's to the grandparents freed from the burden
Of having to take care of our brats.
A line of rusting 737s
And the echolocation of bats.

TO COVID, WITH LOVE

EXCERPTS FROM ANOTHER LOVE DISCOURSE
Edie Meidav

TO CIRCUMSCRIBE

Here in the time of the great panic, people retreated to their bunkers, the people of the past come forward. Yesterday we found a path at an odd road, named as if after a bad blues song, like Coffinnail Cove: *I'm going there to find my beloved.* But this was true; at the mouth of the trail, a cheery older man approached, unheeding and wanting to hand us a card about a book he wrote. He no longer cared for construction; he cared for spreading his name out on the waters. His wife looked on skeptically, as if often she had seen him needing to have his writing recognized. He was of an older generation and equivalently skeptical about death.

While this east coast forest was so splendid in its understanding of how death could cohabit with life. Branches fell to climb upward. A bark prince sat on his pillow inside one hollow trunk and regarded us with some idealism from inside a moss-covered pelt.

I am beginning to cohabit with this beau, no longer so new. We are no longer rank amateurs, we are known to each other, microbes merge. The father of my children is rightly skeptical about who comes in and out of this house. The house represents the heart. Is it wrong that I wish more light to enter it than what I knew before?

TO BE ENGULFED

Take this as our first premise—we begin with fear.

To be hauled out of whatever is safe and comfortable is

what you encounter starting this screed.

Also let us consider the premise of the womb. For our purposes here: my first memory of a mother, carrying me down a narrow corridor toward a gust of cold air. Maybe there was a chain hanging by the door, the first bling meant to protect those inside, but who cares about any of that when memory itself is always that narrow corridor: it reinscribes itself in the brain backward from a premise.

And where does second memory live, where does anyone place it, how much does not get remembered?

Early truths: the need of others, whether tyrant or mothers, can squash. Safety is to be found away; in the unblue light of outside; exile.

More first lessons: the egg of my seventeen-year-old daughter lived in my mother's body when I too was born, my girlchild with her birthday February 3, a day before her grandmother's on February 4. This will be daughter's first birthday without her grandmother, that first home. Less than a year ago I essentially set fire to the world as I had known it; a divorce; three moves; it has been a year of cutting.

Is it possible to learn about love only through absence?

ADORABLE

Early on in the relation with X, I kept looking at the marks on my hands and body and thinking: how can I be loved? Would it be silly, he said, if you were all that you were and I let a few lines keep me from that? When you have been my dream since I was young?

The thing we fear with age difference is that we exist on tilted timelines, that one of us will skid into an unlike metaphysical vista, that the core wound—of being fundamentally unlovable, of being bad—will be revealed. Calvinism would say the lack of grace would become evident. Judaism would say that everything depends on works, not faith: hence the melodies that sang through my prior marriage, as in the scene of *Fiddler on the Roof.* Do I love you, they sing to each other. Bound by peasant work, as if they are fulfilling a dictate given them from a view they did not quite own.

I keep calling him adorable, which is truly a word I never used before. What I mean by this: he lives to be loved, he is like a wise avatar of love dropped to earth, he seems always to be able to see the world from the prospect of the fire tower.

Years ago in upstate New York when I had met but didn't know him, after my father died, I would walk alone in the woods up to a fire tower, and believe I saw and felt my father, a lover of the evanescent and sublime up in the trees' frond and fringe. Once a dog got caught up in the fire tower; humans claimed dominion over forest, domesticated dogs, and sought to prevent fire, the excrescence of egoism: the poor dog met at the vertex and vortex of these claims.

How sad to get caught in another's manifest destiny, as was the case with first nations who every year were celebrated with turkey hand-outlines by misguided tour guides in my kids' public schools: reverent older white men would appear, triumphant and defaming in their feather headdresses belonging to no tribe.

But to love is to agree, as if a folie à deux, that you are each other's manifest destiny, some other power led you to drop the veils of civilization, your animal natures are revealed, there is no path, fire tower, or howling dog, there is only eros and mortality.

Hence, adorable. We have these brief spans; might as well love. Your portal opens and there is the loved one.

ANXIETY

Why is it some women seem to know how to keep their physical space so orderly? I knew you were neglected, my husband said, I could see it on you, the little girl in you. So many mates have seen this little girl. When the genius therapist asks me to do what a friend who helped me through the bleak years in upstate New York asked me to do, to imagine my current self cradling my inner child, I could not. That particular exercise was always so hard: you must become the adult knowing how to love. Part of the problem with this whole love and intimacy thing was that it was so fraught: I hungered for it, I had *disorganized attachment style*—the great combo platter, anxiety and avoidance. Craving connection, working hard for it, but then ending up afraid of being engulfed by others' needs and narcissism, that hard dance. I knew myself most fully as I would stride out from my college boyfriend's tiny dorm room, with its curated LPs, discarded burger wrappers, the teen-boy funk of it all and out into the bracing cool of another New England morning, and before had known myself most fully even at sixteen, with a 26-year-old beau living in my brother's room and my pleasure in writing a sonnet railing against the lure of domesticity. I would be in bed with him thinking: okay, now what, how does anyone make this time matter? When you are born into a system in which you feel you must earn your keep, when you must work for love, when you find yourself near those who challenge the idea of love, your system goes a little haywire.

Last semester of college, music boy gone, I had a ground-floor studio apartment with no grillework or furniture, only a stove and sea of clothes often floorward. Easter break, two men fiddled at the window, silhouettes. I woke as if an anxious clerk in a Schwartz story and sprinted down the hall. High, maybe, my burglars took nothing, but stability shook: no room of my own could be safe. That same semester, ringing a friend's doorbell, I was held up at knifepoint in the lobby. This friend was my consolation buddy: we lay in bed and talked as friends, a guy so raised on Manhattan mores, his speeches about money, power, and a science-diet poodle became one.

The night I was held up in his lobby, I shivered. Don't blame us, the woman said, holding the knife at my throat, we're just black motherfuckers. Don't worry, I said, knowing an odd love for her, feeling the societal screw-up of it all, I get it—just let me have that computer disk from the backpack. Later, though I was at the police station and maybe drove through the city streets, I lacked the heart to identify anyone. Though perhaps I did see something of her in one woman—and not yet knowing I have the tendency toward face-blindness, prosopagnosia, meaning that someone needs to give me a tiny verbal cue so that I know them—I stayed silent.

For both attacks, I blamed myself: men broke in because I was messy, or had not protected my space, and fortunately they jarred me awake. The woman held a knife at my throat because the system was broken. In both cases, I believed I deserved the fear. And what about the people who were demonstrably loved by their mothers, whose mothers were present, who found themselves worthy enough to move through the physical world and create boundaries?

My eyes filled with images, and though I was a painter through most of college, I could not manage the stapling of canvases, and looked askance at a future art-world star crawling with his back smeared with Vaseline on the ground next to me in one of our classes: how did his act of shamelessness work as art, why did it matter?

The truth is so much of art comes from anxiety and how we use or fend it off.

It was not just the Romantics who felt we create art to order the vast chaos of the sublime. The bowerbird arranges its nonessential art and mystifies scientists. The infant plays with her food. Genet loves the smell of his bespattered bedsheets. We seek to create some kind of mark, we matter, we mattered.

A killer I knew as a child lay on a beach next to my friend and me when we were thirteen and scooped up some sand: you see why God created woman first? He was her father, she his daughter, yet she lived in that welcoming home my parents gave us. To create her own home of mobility, she used elaborate creams or rituals of self-care in order to mother herself, and nowadays across a social media platform, her face gleams at me with the smile of a twenty-year-old, as if outside time.

Do people who are well-mothered not wake with this little corkscrew of anxiety? Does the world not look like a slippery place? Do they feel the press of objects near and around them differently? There is a Giacometti image I love: a man in a room, every point on the contour of his being touching a corner of the room.

Which is why it is such a pleasure, on this particular morning, to rise and have as my background the composition my new love performed across the continent—I hear only its livestream, now a deadstream, but one with its sonic particles stirring me awake. In the concert hall, his warm grace welcomes everyone and he mentions the promise of snacks afterward. I am stirred not just by the music but by the fact of his authentic ease, warm congeniality, and understanding about what a moment needs, because he, like many of us, early on learned the unsafety of the outer world in which one must perform.

And so we have this emotional congruity, which I first discovered when we were on a beach, for a day, he visiting for a neuropsychology conference with his mother in California the day before I took the substance—that 15-minute trip which changed my life—which made me see the world as having two choices: the technicolor overburdened struggle or the solitary void, blessed by the ancient caryatid with translucent wings, an amethyst.

Reader, I chose the void.

And from that choice, the pleasure emerged.

ANNULMENT

The oddest part of encountering a person's sexuality after
years of having been with a different person is that it is like
a garden with a wholly different door and key, as if one were
indeed Alice having fallen. You see that, ah, they like to linger
under this mushroom and then they like to suddenly take flight
after this toadstool and then you are sitting at a long table and
prating about this and that which really has nothing to do with
anything allowed at any former table, and in fact the table is not
even a table as such, it is floating over Towlsley Canyon near Los
Angeles, hovering, and then you see two deer stop and eye you
as if they understand who you are in the great mating dance, you
feel a part of nature with this person in the way that another
mate might have been more a part of cities.

But then there is this to remember: this new beau with his
back which you rode behind on a bicycle in Berlin at night, a
city he knew, and you had arrived somewhere you had not even
dreamed possible.

It is not that long misery creates joy.

Of course there had been joy, and by declaring the annulment
and divorce, it was as if you acceded to some master narrative
which said yes, there was no joy, now this is the new script—as
psychologists say, you script your life anew. Of course there is
grief about the promise of other joy seedlings, now abandoned.

But this thing that happened a few days ago, doing yoga
in an overheated bedroom at the parsonage when suddenly a
part of my body looked as unfamiliar to me as the concept of
a crested butte—what, anyway, is a crested butte?—this is what
happens now too. You remember parts of yourself and thus the
whole body of your family moves in new ways. And then time
will not stop its hungry march, it severs the unneeded parts and
keeps on seeking.

WAITING

She lay down in her allotted five minutes in the women's gathering and bravely removed her hospital-color bra to show her hospital-created breasts, decided she didn't want the nipple made from some other cut-off part of her that would rub inside her clothes, said there was one brave little neuron that had made its way, asked us to touch her breasts here, saying symmetry is very important to me, touch me on one side then switch, the ten women gathered for the weekend, her longtime friend asking, if I press here, can you feel it. I had never felt younger or more immature than burrowing in next to my large friend, feeling the animalcave warmth of her, unable to touch her breasts. Feeling not the prohibition against touching a woman but a kind of gentle recoil, related to this: women who had asked to see me naked and I had recoiled, or who had touched me in ways I had not wanted. Women with bodies like the one who first invaded my own repelled me, I couldn't help it, if they had a certain flop and overextension, I had to flee. How does one rework that neural pathway? Just touch my periphery, I had said, when it was my turn in the retreat, sing, anything. You are held by a river, you are safe, one started, and another began singing a song that means a lot to me, or at least it sounded like the song, b'shem hashem, in the name of the name, this angel is near you, that angel is near you.

And the woman who shared my bedroom that morning had played a video of a man singing I am blessed by the help of a thousand angels, softening my way to you. She overachieves; she pushes; I understand her exactly. Yet when it came my turn to dance something about my interior, I didn't know how to soften my head; if the spot between my eyebrows stopped its current overfunctioning, everything would collapse: my greatest myth. One sage said long ago we should each have two pockets, each with a slip of paper. One slip says: I am but dust and ashes. On the other: The world was created for me alone, and the secret of living has to do with knowing when it is best for you to reach for either, or both.

HEART

One of the most painful parts of writing is revealing oneself. This should be obvious but it is not. When I was young, I had a relative who consistently read my diary. I can't help it, this relative said, your writing is so good. And there was the rub. The first reader to like my work had already violated my internal space in more than a few ways.

Later there was a first teacher whose eyepatch made him a swaggering pirate of literature, who said with his friends they talked of agents and the like, but said: write what you don't know! Another teacher traveled the world and sometimes his work creaked under the weight of his research. When I worked as a waitress in a garden restaurant off the boardwalk south of Santa Monica, a man used to come in, a lawyer, who said: how does a young writer manage to write, work, and live life? I don't know, I said with rueful excitement, curious about the next adventure. In that period I moved three times over eighteen months.

One of the problems being you could not hide your face. You had the opposite of a poker face. Even if people sometimes misinterpreted your resting face to be that unfortunate sort, believing you were exhausted or annoyed by something which, in fact, you were truly enjoying, in this case you truly disliked one customer at the restaurant, showing unhid distaste at a pimp-looking producer who did not treat his mate well, and then your manager, an older man with a mournful handlebar mustache who had been a Kinsey sex subject in the '70s, that was his claim to fame, took you aside and said, so sorry, we're going to have to let you go.

And then there was the publication of some work and a relative of yours was disturbed: you dishonor the memory of the dead, I am used to seeing you as magnanimous, do not write about me or my family.

The revelation of the inner bad self: this is what writing can do too.

For years, the worst thing you had done was read the journal pages of a second beau and told him. But he had read your journal: this was in your twenties. His comment: it is amazing to see how your interior is so confident. That is the rub of writing; you observe and have faith in what the eye knows.

FULFILLMENT

It is the time of the great shutdown and a blizzard falls on the land. People rediscover touch and slowness, there is dread and gold, raised flowerbeds are ordered. At night in the messy parsonage, they sit on the couch covered with cat hair and they make up songs which they decide to send out on the airwaves. As if to sing is to be seen.

COMPASSION

I had three beings depending on me and now I have a beau, renters, animals. I stand and nod listening to another man talk about the physical universe to me. You must grade the land if you want to put in your writer's shed. You must have someone come and take out all the dead trees. At noon, your friend wants you to do a daily meditation with her: you breathe in the black pain of others and breathe out light. Right now your throat is scratchy, your land ungraded, your seminar book unread, your own book unwrit, and to breathe in suffering goes against the tiredness of afternoon.

TO UNDERSTAND

The dream was of going to the megahealth grocery and then a moment comes in which blackout curtain flaps are pulled down. The store employees have become police. The one checking the sanitation has everyone line up, arms outstretched. You don't want to touch someone but now we are asked to do so. Disobediently, I see as if in a line dance I can circle the line toward the entrance. Why don't we just leave? Why don't we just go to the parking lot? The anxiety is so great, the dream is its reward. Milton says: they also serve who only stand and wait. In our new time, they also serve who, rather than flee, just line up and obey in humility and compassion.

BEHAVIOR

That somebody starts to judge more. That another starts to feel vulnerable to judgment, as the openness of the branches to the wind start to be more solitary, without the human gaze. On the secret paths that thread along the rivers in the university town, the mix of those who inhabit nature changes. The nature now belongs to everyone and so the habits of the city come to the brink. For eons, humans knew the wisdom of the riverbanks. For the riverbanks had no need of the wisdom of humans or any understanding of eons. And now there are trucks hauling the province of the rivers to the mouths of those who forgot how to say thanks. The text from the husband is curt: we want to talk to you about social distancing. They don't want the beau to be around their son. This is not just bourgeois mores. This is old love rejecting the new.

CONNIVANCE

The dreams of that time start to drag you through your past with a willy-nilly intensity. Your dead mother speaks with her sister who ate herself to death. Because you are messy, a man thinks he can follow you into corners abandoned by the populace, a hotel with no one staying in it. Such has been the state of your joy. You return to a journal which you began two years earlier, and though you are in a new place, the hammock of your life conspires to swing in one direction: gratitude.

BODY
In the cold outside the body inside is hungry for that which it cannot have. And yet in the middle of the night the body next to you is so beautiful you make love to the idea of beauty itself without waking anyone or touching anything but the way the poisoned air rests astride your cheek, gazing at him.

DECLARATION
Families that look happy seem to flow inside a riverbank made up of common rites and assumptions, while other families act more like holograms in which everyone has a strong story projected onto everyone else and love must find its way among the rays.

In the morning you hid under the blanket in the room where your mother sequestered your late father before she shipped him in his last years out to a nursing home on the water's edge, the room in which another great-aunt, a great idealist, lived at the end of her life, a room of death which had chilled your beau so he was sneezing the next morning as you went to the Ethiopian buffet and you all got sick, you, him, your daughter, and you hid hearing another relative talk to the dog whom your daughter wants to steal and take home so that forever you can have a love bomb and be a savior.

DEDICATION

Everyone keeps asking: what does it mean to write in a time like this? Your students, friends, you ask this of yourself. Adam in the garden gave names to the garden. In the garden of chaos, is it important to gather names? You provide for your family through two means: packages from the megaboss lie outside, toasting in the sun or freezing. The new animals of the parsonage seem to understand this time as a confusion of inside and outside, and their interiors end up on blankets inside cages when they go in to the vet's, where you sit in a car while the semi-blanketed nurse lifts up gates and then comes back and smears the virus, which you are taught to think of as glitter, glitter spreading everywhere, all over your door and the interior of your car and your credit card. The rain pours down. She is a hero as are the cats, who just got shots to protect both of them from the penchant of one not to take the edict of being an indoor cat and instead to roam outside. Outside is where danger lives. The nearby students, quarantined, have a habit of blithely petting the cat. They don't want to stop. It is disappointing, one of them says. They like the outside penetrating in: of course, everyone wants to be loved. To be heard, to read and speak. While your class during this time feels like a front line of intimacy. Everything matters, you tell students, this is why you dedicate yourself to writing. The one album you listen to over and over is by Oophoi—*Behind the Wall of Sleep*—you play it as you and your friends write together in aeries around the world. You want to read one another and hide together and soon emerge: for this promise of literature we sing.

ROOMS AND CLARINETS
Clifford Thompson

Malcolm X has been on my mind lately. I'll get to that in a moment.

In my early and mid-teens, I played the clarinet, badly. I gave it up after that, and I don't even know where my old clarinet is. But I have another one now, given to me by a friend who found it in her apartment, left behind by a previous tenant; my friend thought of me as she herself was preparing to move out. The clarinet has mostly stayed in my closet, forgotten—until recently. Most evenings at seven, when the clapping and cheers begin for health care workers pushing on bravely in the face of Covid-19, I open my window and add to the din, trilling two notes, an open G and F sharp, until the clapping and shouting and banging wane, or until I get tired. It is in these moments, holding this sleek black instrument, that I think of Malcolm X, who is shown in a famous photograph standing at a window in his home, dressed in a suit and tie and holding a sleek black rifle. Each evening I chuckle at the absurdity of the comparison. Then I stop chuckling, and a sadness overtakes me.

Malcolm was thirty-nine when he was killed, in 1965. I am nearly two decades older than that now, but Malcolm will always feel like an elder. On the whole I have always been a bigger follower of Martin Luther King Jr. than of Malcolm X; I am a peaceful person by nature, and my wish, as laughably unfashionable as it is, is for people to get along when possible. But if King were my father, Malcolm would be the uncle whose visits I secretly couldn't wait for, the one who said so many things I absolutely disagreed with and so many others I would dismiss, I know deep down, at my peril. King's message and actions brought out the best in many of us, and it wasn't his fault if they also brought out the worst in many others. But there was something in Malcolm's message—something that kindled an often shaky pride and self-respect, something that spoke to a righteous anger—that touches a chord in most black people too, whether they'll say so or not, and many will, quite proudly. (It should be said that King was a more radical figure than many today take him for, and it is not acknowledged often, or often enough, that at the ends of their respective journeys, the two men were not all that far apart ideologically.)

I feel sad because I know Malcolm would feel sad if he could see us now—if he could see this peculiar moment in our journey, if he could see his warnings seemingly borne out. Malcolm dreamed of a separate nation for black people, scoffing at the idea that we could ever get a fair shake in this one, and the more time that passes, the harder it is to dismiss his view out of hand. Covid-19 is only the latest development that is bad for the country as a whole but worse for African-Americans. Of the nearly one hundred thousand Americans who have died from the virus, the number of blacks is disproportionate to the percentage of blacks in the nation. That is partly because many black people have preexisting health conditions and jobs that expose them to the public; that, in turn, is because people of color are often lower down on the economic totem pole, and the many reasons for *that* share a root cause, which is racism.

For many years now, more than seem possible to me, my wife and I have shared a two-bedroom apartment in Brooklyn. This is where we raised our children, who are now grown and living elsewhere. And this is where, for two and a half months and counting, we have spent nearly all of our waking hours and seen only each other. Until I was eighteen, I lived in the same house, but when I think of that house, what I picture is the view from my bedroom window of the one across the street; similarly, when I think of my current home, it is not my own face I see but my wife's, and she would probably say the same about me. I am black. My wife is white. We are sort of a microcosm of the country, or of what the country would be if its demographics were slightly different and its different groups cared more about one another.

We go quietly about our days. Much of my work pre-Corona was already done at home, so our current life has not been a huge adjustment for me that way. My wife's work has been more affected by her having to be here. She manages. We manage. I get up early and read and listen to music until she wakes up. We greet each other with tight hugs and then have coffee in bed. Then we mostly go to separate parts of the apartment, seeing each other occasionally, checking in over dinner about our respective days. Sometimes we watch movies together in the evenings. Comedies are great during this time. I can recommend, if you haven't seen it, Frank Oz's *Bowfinger*, with Steve Martin and Eddie Murphy—I hadn't heard my wife laugh like that in weeks. Other nights, she watches documentaries while I paint in the same room, an arrangement we both like. It's not ideal—I miss movies in a theater, book stores, bars, my local diners, the Y, art museums—but it's comfortable.

One of the strangest things about our routine, in fact, is how comfortable it is, in contrast to what we know has been happening outside, which of course is death on a fairly massive scale. The closest contact I've had with it are the times when I put on mask and gloves and go to the grocery store, which, during the period when New Yorkers were dying of Covid by the hundreds daily, made me feel like a character on a mission in a World War II movie.

And this weird disconnect parallels what I felt a lot of the time pre-Corona. I live in a very nice, very comfortable neighborhood where there are not a lot of people who look like me, while a lot of people who look like me are in prison— largely because of the so-called war on drugs, a manmade virus that targets people of color. It is not quite accurate to say that I haven't done anything about that or about other issues facing blacks—I've taken part in protests, I've made calls—but I've done it fitfully, while wondering if it does any good, if my puny and inconsistent efforts matter at all in the face of such enormity.

Like many people in this city where space is at such a premium, I sometimes have dreams—not fantasies: literal nighttime dreams—of finding another room in my apartment I didn't know was there. My wife brilliantly came up with something approaching a real-life answer to this. She placed a little table of ours beside a window in our bedroom; it would not have occurred to me that this little table could hold dinner plates for two, but it does (small ones), and sometimes now we dine there, with a view of brownstones and people and leafy trees, now that spring is here.

I like to think I might also find, not in my apartment but in myself, not rooms, but room—room for more contributions, room for thinking about other ways to make my voice heard. I have written about the issues close to my heart, which can feel like blowing notes into the wind. But perhaps that is the wrong way to think of it. Perhaps is it important to understand that the real enemy is despair, that it is better to find what one can do, with the knowledge that it may not make much difference, than to do nothing.

In the meantime, at seven most evenings, I blow my black horn, adding to the noise. I blow it for those brave health care workers. I blow for black and brown people in prison, too. And a few of those trills go out, though no one hearing them knows it, for Malcolm.

AROUND THE BEND
Saskia Vogel

Normalcy. It's all I wanted to return to. But during the last leg of a half-year-long book tour for my debut novel *Permission*, I was suddenly pregnant with my first child, flying into the path of Hurricane Dorian. My climate-change anxiety surging, I opened my laptop to work on the translation of Greta Thunberg and her family's latest book *Our House Is on Fire: Scenes of a Family and a Planet in Crisis*. The text boomed, *Save the planet: Stop flying!* I felt like a hypocrite. I questioned the sanity of bringing a child into this world. A child, so far just a smudge on a screen with a flickering heart. I spent my days managing waves of panic: its health, future, and well-being, ours. But as I entered my third trimester and Covid-19 was shifting our reality in Berlin, I felt oddly well-equipped for the crisis. I felt calm.

Weeks after sitting out the hurricane in Nova Scotia, I almost lost the baby. Measures were taken, but all anyone could really tell me was *We'll have to wait and see*. It had been the same the years my husband and I were trying. We'd been given so slim a chance of conceiving that we'd started to make peace with childlessness. As my pregnancy progressed, the doctors' answers to our questions remained unchanged. They could offer tests and statistics, I could slather my belly in oil to ward off stretch marks, but there were no guarantees. It was either going to happen or not. My therapist and I had been talking about this for years: how I needed to let go of my fantasy of control.

These lockdown days are much like my regular days—us working from home, preparing the house and ourselves for the baby, now relying on mail-order and limiting news—but saturated with unease. The world, the social body, is changing.

No one can say how it will be. Our fantasies about the baby's early life are moot. We'd wanted to bring the child into a loving hubbub of family and friends. Now, overseas visits from my parents and sisters are indefinitely on hold. Grandparents here in Berlin, over-70s, are in isolation. I think about the role smell plays in memory, touch as a communication. How will it impact the baby to have only us? (*For how long?*) I discipline myself to stop thinking about California as a point of arrival or departure, of seeing my family, my home. It's all I can do to keep the sadness in check. I'm trying not to think into the future. I do my best to prepare, but it's out of my control. The on-march of a child made this concept concrete.

For a long time I didn't think about the birth itself. My birthing plan had only ever been "get the baby out safely." The trust I have in the German system has helped me feel relatively secure even as the pandemic has progressed. But as our orientation meeting at the hospital drew near, it wasn't clear if my husband would be allowed to attend the birth. A fresh fear arose. I'd been thinking of birth as a medical procedure. I hadn't realized how deeply it was about us, the moment when baby makes three.

It was our first question for the midwife and the first truly satisfying answer. From an epidemiological perspective, she said, my husband and I are the same person, and so inextricable. We'd all be present for the dawn of our new life. Recovery was a different story. Five days alone in a hospital room I couldn't leave with only my newborn for company and nurses with differing opinions speaking to me through my car crash haze. I was sure I'd never see my family again. That the pandemic was already over, and they were conspiring to keep me here. It was the hormones talking. So this is what they mean when they talk about hormones, I thought in the light of a new day, having calmed myself down by narrating the night to myself as if it were a fiction.

Life back in the world was gentler for us than I imagined it would be. Though whenever I've met our Berlin family or a friend, an old feeling rises to the surface. A hypochondria from my single days: that there is no such thing as safe sex, only safer sex, and even if I imagine I've taken precautions, I can think of seventeen ways I could nonetheless have been infected. Having decided to become the same epidemiological person as my husband's mother, we move in with her in the countryside. At least one grandparent will get to have something like a normal time with their grandchild. At least our child will have nature for company, will see a horse, a raccoon, a deer, a fox, even if it's mostly just us. At night in bed we listen to the dormice running through the walls and his gentle moaning breaths.

In the cracks, hope springs. Things that should already have been done get done. This morning, the news that the Redskins have finally decided to ditch their name. I hope. I hope. I hope. I hope. I am hoping for the best. I am forever a believer that around the next bend we will arrive at the idea that a society structured around well-being for all is the only society worth building, and then will draw that future down from the sky.

My dad calls from Los Angeles and says he's heard that there's a legitimate way to get to Germany via Austria, which includes testing and quarantine. I feel parts of my mind light up, hope, want. And then risk. Mind the risk. As much as you want this, mind the risk. I promise to look into it, and I will, but I can't. I can't ask him to take this trip. I think about all that I have risked for fleeting pleasures, and if this time the risk would actually be worth it.

I sing to the baby and all the songs that come are songs of the West. I sing to the baby. The idea of a visit. The balance of risk and will. The awful thought: This is a thing I could make happen. It is within my control.

166

PAIN AND COPING
Christine Henneberg

Recently an old knee injury from my twenties flared up. The knee aches every time I walk down the few steps into the garage. In bed at night, I can feel it throbbing; it distracts me from the book I'm reading. I blame it on the fact that the pool is closed and I haven't been swimming. Instead I've been walking a lot—almost exclusively with the double stroller. I even went running a few times, for the first time in years. And I've been doing a lot of home exercise videos when I wake up at 4:30 in the morning, unable to fall back asleep. All of these things must have taken a toll on my already shredded cartilage.

My best friend, who also has a baby and a toddler at home, has been having pain in her lower back and hip ever since President's Day. Yesterday it got so bad that she called her doctor, and learned (over a video visit, without anyone to physically touch her and ask *Is this where it hurts?*) that she "probably has a herniated disk." She texted me: Now I just have to find out if this muscle relaxer the doctor prescribed is okay to take while breastfeeding.

I have been thinking about pain—both chronic and acute—as it relates to stress and isolation, and specifically the current "crisis." I've observed that my abortion patients have been having more pain during the procedure, even though I'm giving the same doses of moderate sedation that I always use (Fentanyl 100 mcg + Midazolam 2 mg). This combination is typically effective for most patients, but lately the medicines seem to hardly touch them. To the point that it seems like a pattern. There's always been variability. In the past, on any given day, I might joke to the nurse that we got a "bad batch" of Fentanyl, because no

167

one seems quite as relaxed and comfortable as I would like. And then other days, everyone seems perfectly calm, almost serene, with exactly the same medicines. But there haven't been any days like that since the beginning of the Coronavirus pandemic. I just keep hearing patients cry and tell me it hurts, watching their hands clutching the sides of the table while I work as fast as I can, trying to finish.

I have also noticed another pattern, which is an increasing tendency for women to apologize during and after their procedures. This might be directly related to the observation that they seem to be feeling more pain, because one of the things patients apologize for (and this has always been true) is crying or moving around on the table, or in some other way involuntarily expressing discomfort or sadness during the procedure. But lately, especially the past two weeks, it has been remarkable.

A few patients come to mind.

The first woman was barely pregnant, maybe five weeks. I told her there was a chance her pregnancy would be too small for my instruments to reach, or that even if I did get it out, it might be too small for me to see, and I might need her to come back in a few days for some blood work, "to make sure your pregnancy hormone level is going down." I made a downward sloping line in the air with my hand as I said this, as I always do when talking to women with such early pregnancies.

This obviously made her anxious. She explained that she was a sheriff's deputy, and she worked "weird hours" at the county jail. She wouldn't be able to return for a blood draw for at least a week. I told her that wasn't ideal, but would probably be okay. But she kept asking how likely I thought it was that she would need that second appointment. I couldn't give her a definite answer. I could see that what she was nervous about was the idea of not being done today, of walking out of here possibly still pregnant.

"I will do my very best to make sure you're done today," I

said. "I promise."

She was tall, with big shoulders and long legs. She looked like a woman who could hold her own among police officers and inmates. She wore no makeup. Her blonde hair was pulled back in a tight ponytail like a softball player. It was almost hard for me to imagine that she was pregnant. I suppose this was because it was hard to picture her surrendering her body, making herself available and vulnerable to a man, which (a limitation of my own imagination and experience) is the only way I have of conceptualizing penile, penetrative intercourse.

She asked me about the para-cervical block. "Is it a shot?"

"It's an injection," I said. "Of lidocaine."

"But is there a needle involved."

Yes, I admitted, there was a needle.

"Oh Jesus."

When I gave the first injection, she jumped. Her bottom lifted higher off the table than any woman I've ever seen. She begged me not to give the second dose, so I didn't. "It's not absolutely necessary," I said.

She didn't have an easy time with the rest of the procedure, either. I kept having to remind her to hold still. At one point I stood up to talk to her, reassure her, coax her back down on the table, closer to me. She was biting her knuckles; she had half her hand in her mouth. Around it she whispered, "Shit. Okay. I'm sorry."

"It's okay," I said. "It's hard."

Afterwards in the lab, I could see that I had definitely gotten the entire pregnancy. It was tiny, but it was complete. I went back into the room. She was still pressing her eyes and lips together. I was happy to tell her the good news, thinking she would be relieved and grateful. But she just nodded, almost imperceptibly, and said. "God, that was painful. And I screamed like a bitch. I'm sorry."

"You were brave," I said. "It was really hard."

169

"Shit," she whispered. "Shit. I'm sorry."

The second woman I'm thinking of was a former heroin and meth abuser, now in a methadone program. In retrospect, I should have offered her a double dose of fentanyl right from the beginning. She was wincing and writhing even when I placed the speculum. I did give her a second dose soon after that, but it was too late—or maybe nothing would have helped her. By the end she was sobbing, these big, groaning sobs that reminded me of a child crying out for her mother. I often think about addiction and pain as being related to our most childlike state, the part inside each of us that has no real way to cope at all, can only cry out helplessly and wait to be held and comforted by someone—or something—entirely external to us. Possibly (this is just my unformed but, I think, empathic idea), abandonment and abuse are related to this also. Where does a person turn whose experience, as a child, was of loneliness, fear, even suffering at the hands of the adults who were supposed to comfort them?

This woman embodied that childlike helplessness. The way she sobbed, her mouth wide open, all her white teeth showing, tears and mucus streaming from her eyes and nose. In between sobs she said over and over, "I'm sorry! I'm sorry! I'm sorry!"

I thought: She isn't even here in this room right now. I am the immediate cause of her pain. But the pain has become its own force. It has lifted her up and carried her somewhere else, far away, where far worse things are being done to her. "I'm sorry! I'm sorry! I'm sorry!"

My patients, who are screened at the door for Coronavirus symptoms—no one with a cough, fever, or sore throat is allowed inside for an abortion—all seem to have developed some strange underlying affliction, something that started at exactly the same time as the Novel Coronavirus pandemic.

Even stranger: I have come down with this affliction, too.

When the world stopped and the paid (read: male) economy ground to a halt, a weight fell upon us, the women. Specifically, the mothers. For me, the weight has fallen on my knee. I feel it lifting and carrying two 25-lb bodies all day, and pushing the double stroller anytime I want to leave the house—because I cannot leave the house without taking my two children with me. For my friend, the weight fell on her back. She's spent much of the past three weeks horizontal, lying on a heating pad on the floor, while her children sit and stand beside her, their little arms outstretched.

For my patients, the weight has fallen on a place that is both embodied and disembodied. It is located inside their uteruses but also, bizarrely and unfairly, somewhere else, somewhere untouchable.

As this virus was swirling in its invisible droplets around the globe, clinging to tongues and nose hairs and corneas, lurking on airplane trays and car doors and in the fingernail crevices of nursing home aides, men continued to insert their penises into women's vaginas, as they have always done. Now these women are my patients, as they have always been. And the burden falls on them, as it always has, and always will.

And the men in their Big White Buildings—in the halls of the Capitol and the benches of the high courts and the pulpits of mega-churches—have the audacity to call abortion "non-essential" healthcare.

The third woman was young, seventeen, and had a technically very difficult procedure. She was 14 weeks and 5 days, with a tight and tortuous cervix. The calvarium was way up at the fundus and I could tell it was going to be hard to get it out. She was very anxious and nauseated. About halfway through the dilation we had to stop for a long time so she could throw up. That's always terrible. Whenever that happens, I agonize about whether to take the speculum out or leave it in. I never know how long her vomiting will last. I don't want to have to remove and reinsert the speculum, and re-grasp the cervix with the tenaculum, etc. if I don't have to. But in this case I should have removed it.

She just kept puking. Each time, the force of it lifted her hips off the table, her feet still wide in the stirrups, her vaginal walls clamping around the speculum, which stuck out of her body like a weapon. In between heaves, she would spit weakly into the emesis bag and mumble, "I'm sorry. I'm sorry."

Afterwards in the recovery room, she looked somewhat better. I was relieved, as I always am in those cases, to see her dressed and reclined in the armchair, her eyes closed, a heating pad over her belly. Her mother, who under normal circumstances would have been allowed to sit at her side during the procedure, was waiting in the parking lot, an unlikely but possible vector of infection barred from inside the clinic doors.

I touched her knee and her eyes opened.

"How are you? How's your pain?"

"Better, thanks." She grimaced, not a look of physical pain, but of apology. "I'm sorry. I feel like I was a bad patient."

"No. Don't. You weren't," I said. "It's hard."

"Yeah," she said. "But. I just couldn't. . . I feel like I was all over the place."

Why do women apologize when we feel pain? A simple answer is that our pain means someone else must care for us, so we cannot do the work of caring for others. But why should isolation enhance our pain and our compulsion to apologize for it? I do not have an answer. With my drugs, my words, my swift and gentle touch, I am trying desperately to treat this affliction—until the Coronavirus pandemic is over, or, as we are beginning to talk about more and more these days, until we can all learn to live with it. A chilling thought, as I touched this young woman's cheek, still damp with sweat, over the edge of her mask.

I told her she'd done beautifully, and that she was strong and brave. But I could tell nothing I said would make a difference. She was living in a story where she had failed: failed by getting pregnant, by needing to come in for an abortion—Now! Of all times! When everyone else was able to stay comfortably and safely at home!—and then by not even being able to gracefully and stoically handle the pain that she so surely deserved. I imagined these were her thoughts. I felt certain of it. I've seen enough women go through this. I've heard enough of them talk, under the effects of drugs that, even if ineffective against the pain, make them forget what they've said, forget that anyone was there to listen.

SOMETHING NEW
Caille Millner

A few weeks before my city issued a shelter-in-place order, I gave birth to my first child. While I was learning how to be a mother, the Coronavirus pandemic was decimating economies and cleaving communities. It was disproportionately killing Black Americans and laying bare the brutal costs of the country's collective unwillingness to invest in everything from basic social goods to public spirit.

The week before my city was scheduled to begin the process of lifting its shelter-in-place order, it instituted a curfew to try and control what began as protests against the killing of George Floyd in Minneapolis and that age-old American menace, the wanton destruction of Black life by agents of the state. Within days the protests had morphed into the century's largest multi-racial indictment of the institutions and ideas that have failed to provide even a semblance of opportunity to Black people—and, increasingly, everyone else.

In other words, I have spent the past few months welcoming an infant into a world order that is rightfully under attack. In large part, it is under attack because it's failed to protect my child and all who resemble her. It's sobering, but not surprising, that the same people who are likeliest to face death by disease due to official neglect have chosen to risk their own lives by taking to the streets against their deaths by official violence. Those with the least to lose are the best equipped to lead.

While the people are protesting in the streets and dying in the hospital corridors, my days are quiet. I feed the baby, change the baby, play with the baby, and sing the baby to sleep. Over and over again. Initially, I was racked with guilt over my embrace of constancy and repetition while the old structures crumble outside and so many brave people fight to expand the world's imagination. But repetition offers a spiritual dimension for those who are patient enough to listen for it. The baby is my mantra and the repetition is my love.

This is especially true for Black mothers, who must undergo an additional series of repetitions with their children. Over and over again we must explain police violence. Over and over again we must tell them of the burdens they will face and the worry they must carry. When we've finished with each of these explanations, we embrace them, over and over again, because we know the world will not. Creating an atmosphere of love amidst this repetition of violence and fear is one of the impossible tasks Black mothers are called on to do, and I knew it would come for me eventually. But I was astonished that it had come so soon.

During the first few days of protest, repetition was what saved me. The hardest moments were when I was nursing, because that was when I had short blocks of time to scroll through the news of teargassed protesters and murderous demands from the highest levels of government. To distract myself from this terror, I started listening to John Coltrane's "A Love Supreme."

I don't know much about jazz. I picked the album because I wanted to hear something pleasant, without a lot of lyrics. But what few lyrics they are! At the beginning of the album, Coltrane chants "a love supreme," over and over again. Like me—like Black America—he's stuck in repetition.

Then he begins his famous improvisation, or at least what seems to be his famous improvisation. It's actually the same riff, played in all twelve possible keys. Coltrane is repeating the same thing over and over again. He is creating his mantra. With repetition comes the possibility of transformation. With repetition comes the possible breakthrough of love.

Once I recognized the pattern Coltrane had laid out, I

was able to hear something different from the streets. These were not the protests of 1968 or 1992 or even 2015. Instead of dissipating, the protests grew larger. The usual propaganda was employed about order and looters, but somehow it had lost some of its strength. Instead of being undermined, the protests attracted more age groups, more races, more solidarity, and more imagination.

The repetition of despair had opened a crack for something new to seep through. You might even call it love.

No one knows what will happen next. Historical precedents aren't comforting: the backlash that usually follows racial uprising has a grim repetition of its own.

But the past few weeks have reminded me that every awakening creates space for new possibilities. Led, once again, by its most hated and disenfranchised people, the country has been handed yet another chance to remake its broken republic. The demand that has risen yet again from the streets is what Coltrane might recognize as the sound of love.

INVISIBLE DANGER

THE BLUE VIAL
Mui Poopoksakul

I found it on May 19, I told the detective.

Coming home from the post office and waiting for the elevator, I checked our mail as usual. Nothing but a vial with blue liquid. I couldn't be bothered with whatever free sample someone had dropped in our mailbox and chose to ignore it.

The next day, again grabbing our mail on my way in, I decided to pick up the blue vial because I wasn't going to leave junk in our letterbox forever. It was a test tube in form—round-bottomed and made of clear glass, just like the ones from high-school chemistry, except it was almost as skinny as a pencil and nearly as long, and had a cap, the specifics of which I now can't recall. The liquid it contained had the color and clarity of blue Listerine. As I stared at the label taped neatly around the tube, without yet having had time to develop any particular reaction, I heard the building's front door swing open. I looked up—my husband was stopping home after a court hearing.

"Look at this. It says 'Sars 19' with some Chinese characters," I said to him.

He blinked and walked over.

"Should we call the police?" It seemed something one would say, and the words felt recited as they came out of my mouth.

"Yes, I think so."

Climbing the stairs to our apartment, we discussed the possibility of bioterrorism—that was the first thought that came to mind. I remembered the period immediately after 9/11 when, in New York City, where I was living at the time, opening your mail was a fraught exercise: white powder had been turning up in envelopes sent to offices around the city. But more likely, this blue substance was harmless, and what we were faced with was a prank. Still, legally speaking, a reasonable person ought to be able to foresee that the vial, labeled as it was, would have the effect of creating fear in the recipient. The sending of it, therefore, constituted a threat, a crime, so yes, we would call the police. It would be a good hour before the thought crossed my mind that this could be a racist act, but as soon as I verbalized it, I could no longer shake the idea, and neither could my husband.

I messaged a Singaporean friend, a fellow translator, attaching a close-up of the blue vial. "Help! Someone put this in our mailbox. Is this Chinese? If so, what does it say?" I was still Panglossian enough at that point not to write off the possibility that the characters might spell out "prevention against" or something equally benign, even benevolent; the blue liquid did remind me of my over-fragranced hand sanitizer, also blue, though paler. "Very strange," my friend wrote back, "It says 'stellar corona'—is this some kind of weird wordplay?" I didn't understand. The character used for "corona," she explained, was not the one for corona the virus but corona as in the gaseous outer layer of the sun. Was this a punning racist or a Google Translate job? I opened up Google Translate, typed in "corona" and tried translating from English and German into both traditional and simplified Chinese. The right-hand box showed two characters each time, none of the language pairs producing the one I was expecting. Only weeks later, upon a college roommate's suggestion that I try an "off-brand" online translator, would I figure out that the text on the vial was indeed in all likelihood a machine-generated translation: the German program DeepL, popular among professionals, spat out a match.

When my husband called the Mitte precinct, the officer on the phone sounded blasé until my husband told him, "My wife's Asian." Still, nothing would be done unless we filed a report online, something in writing. Within an hour after we pressed "submit," two police officers rang our buzzer. As we led them to the mailboxes, the handcuffs dangling from their belts clacked together and I felt as if I were on a crime TV show—I had never been in such close proximity to real handcuffs. On the scene, there was not much to investigate. I told the officers about the circumstances of my discovery of the blue vial and relayed to them the information from my friend about the Chinese characters, and the police took the evidence away in a Ziploc bag. I sorely regretted handling the tube with several fingers and turning it in my hands: I had probably smudged whatever fingerprints the culprit had left.

•

Earlier that month, we had finally ordered curtains. When we moved into our new home last August, there had been so much to do to make the place livable that I simply let the sun singe my skin or avoided the street side of the apartment altogether. Then fall came, and then winter, and curtains became simply a matter of privacy and not urgency. Now May was a quarter over and we had been inside the apartment twenty-three and a half hours a day because of the stay-at-home order, and as summer approached, I was determined to acquire curtains, at least for my home office.

They arrived, but much to my frustration, the package had been brought to the post office. It was nearly five feet long because of the rods, but I didn't realize this until the postal worker had already scanned the package. One look at her face and I knew asking the post office to hang onto it wasn't going to be an option. So I was determined to get it home—a twelve-minute walk away—somehow. The sight of me struggling with a package almost as large as my frame, though in fact it probably didn't weigh more than ten kilos, must have been laughable, pitiable. Strangers smiled, made faces with widened eyes; several volunteered to lend a hand. Halfway back, sweating and red-faced, I finally accepted the help of a woman who offered to roll the box atop her bike to my destination.

In front of my building, I thanked the generous woman profusely and kicked my box inside. "My faith in humanity is restored. Like, ten people offered to help me on my way home," I texted my husband. I praised humanity but felt a boost to my own sense of self: I appeared to strangers like someone worthy their kindness. I felt good and worn out when the front door clamped shut behind me. And then I opened my letterbox and noted something blue.

•

Since the start of the pandemic, much has been made about how Covid-19 would change the way we live for a long time to come. I was skeptical about whether it would rewire me, especially as my husband and I were already reverting to our old ways in the meal department, cooking less and less as the weeks passed by. But one instance of collateral damage from the virus would end up altering my perception of how I moved about in the world. In the days following my discovery of the blue vial, I kept picturing myself walking down the block, my face not a face, but reduced to a label. I was on guard taking the S-Bahn in broad daylight.

Still, the blue vial was no random attack like the ones we'd read and heard about happening to people of Asian descent on trains and in other public spaces in various countries in the West. In a way, it was less frightening because I hadn't been threatened with physical violence, but in another way, it was more sinister because I had been specifically targeted. The perpetrator knew who I was, knew my name and where I lived. Who would do this? Who could do this? The culprit had, or somehow had gained, access to our building's mailboxes, which are inside the locked front door. This fact narrowed the likely pool of suspects: the neighbors, building-management employees, mail carriers, delivery workers, possibly someone from the block who had been observing me. While it wasn't exactly difficult to ring up a resident in the building and make up some excuse to be buzzed in, this last group was less probable than the others because the culprit was able to match my face to my last name. I have a Thai name, but Thai names often aren't obviously Asian to the uninitiated. What if the vial had never been meant for me? I did have a neighbor whose equally long last name contained similar letters, and on more than one occasion, his mail had wound up in our mailbox. But he was a white German, making the Chinese characters harder to explain. I was loath to point fingers at our neighbors in the building, and fearful of the consequences of going down that route whether it proved right or not, so I came up with theory after theory, only to dismiss them as too longshot.

•

A week or so after the local police's visit, my husband and I received summonses to give witness statements at the *Landeskriminalamt*. The State Office of Criminal Investigation had taken up our case, likely because they believed it to be a potential hate crime. And they likely reacted so quickly because of the case of a Korean couple featured in a front-page spread of the *Süddeutsche* newspaper, published just days before and detailing the rise in anti-Asian racism in Germany in the wake of the virus. Met with police inaction after they had been harassed on the U-Bahn, the couple had sought the help of the South Korean Embassy, prompting investigative progress. My husband was convinced that we were direct beneficiaries of the Korean couple's proactiveness.

I took pictures of the *Süddeutsche* article in six rectangular sections and sent it to two Asian friends in Berlin. "If something happens to you, you should report it to the police. We'd only be helping one another," I wrote to them. I meant it, I was pursuing my case to the fullest extent of the law, but I knew it was a big ask. I, too, was weary of the process, of making the incident into a major, meaningful, consuming drama. How much easier was it to see the blue vial as a blip, as some little bad thing that happened and that required no more thought as long as nothing of the sort happened again? Optimism goes a long way toward making life livable, and what story did I want to tell myself I was living?

We put up a flyer in the entryway of our building, notifying the neighbors of the incident, asking them for any tips, and making known to any potential culprit that we had reported the matter to the police. We'd intended to leave the flyer up for exactly seven days, but before the week was up, our notice had been torn down. The sight of the four remaining corners, still taped to the wall, made me shudder, but upon reflection I suspected a real estate agent I'd spotted showing the apartment across the hall an hour before the flyer's disappearance.

We weren't holding our breaths for anyone to come forward with information. Everyone I told the story to said the perpetrator surely lived in the building. I ran through the units in my mind: five residential floors with two apartments each, and two commercial spaces on the ground level. Who did we know? Who appeared friendly and who not? Everyone in the building seemed to enjoy the anonymity of city living, so there was only so much detective work we could do before we entered awkward or insane territory. Funny how in our time of social distancing, I had never wanted to learn more about my neighbors than I did now. Eventually, I brought up the obvious, which was that our downstairs neighbor had complained, via a typed note, at the start of the lockdown that we "STOMPED"—yes, she used all caps—and it was giving her migraines. Naturally, we were annoyed. I found it hard to imagine that you could have a neighbor more pussyfooted than me—I'm small and prone to cracked, even bleeding heels that have trained me to land softly. But my husband quickly shut down the thought: her complaint, though aggravating, was within the range of normal gripes among neighbors, and to accuse someone of racism based on that letter was unfair and irresponsible. I agreed and felt guilty for having harbored despicable thoughts.

At the interview, the friendly, teddy-bear-of-a-man detective informed me the blue liquid had been analyzed, and it was innocuous—rubbing alcohol, ironically. No fingerprints had been lifted because the vial was still held up at the Robert Koch Institute, which had yet to test the blue dye. My hope deflated. How many people were the police going to allow to handle the tube before they tried to extract fingerprints? I began to feel that in pursuing the case, I was making a point only to myself and to this detective before me, who probably had homicide cases to solve.

"Anything else you'd like to add?" he asked me.

"Well—" I bit my tongue, reminding myself of the vow of silence I had taken on the downstairs neighbor.

The detective led me back to the lobby and swapped me for my husband. Mask on, I took out Shirley Jackson's *The Lottery and Other Stories*, from which I'd been reading at random. As if fate itself wanted to offer a tip, I flipped to "Trial by Combat": Emily Johnson, a young army wife staying in a rooming house, has her handkerchiefs and other trinkets stolen and suspects Mrs. Allen from the room immediately below hers. Emily takes matters into her own hands but finds herself powerless to confront the petty thief when she develops a creeping feeling that she is faced with the ghost of her own future who might be looking to reclaim mementos of her past—Mrs. Allen, whose late husband was also in the army, occupies a room strikingly similar to Emily's own, giving the two women a sense of intimacy in each other's personal space. My downstairs neighbor, too, probably lived in an apartment with the same layout as mine. Did she also work from home while her husband went out to the office each day? Did she go to sleep when I went to sleep? Did she wonder the same about me, or did she already know this from the sound of my footsteps at night, walking around to my side of the bed?

185

Perhaps she could gather pieces of my life from the noises she heard, from every drop of an object, every drag of a chair. As for me, I had no such advantage—I'd never even laid eyes on this mysterious woman. Stop! I told myself and shut the book. Fate is just playing with me, that's all.

•

A month has passed since our interviews at the *Landeskriminalamt*. There's been no word from the detective. In the meantime, my husband has managed to lose my Shirley Jackson book and we've managed to install more curtains.

Last week, under the pretense of wanting to assess how our new curtains look from outside—a pretense I concocted only for my own sake—I went across the street and glanced up at my own windows, only to let my eyes wander to all the others. I saw no one.

MASKS AND GLOVES
Rebecca Chace

Today a man died in front of our building, or maybe he didn't. It's spring 2020 in Brooklyn, New York. Yesterday, the death count was only forty-six, the day before it was sixty-one. Up and down have replaced north and south on the compass. I opened our front door, masked and gloved, inhaling Pine Sol from the spray bottle we use on the door knob we share with other tenants. The man's body was collapsed against a small iron gate separating our line of garbage cans from the rest of the sidewalk. He was curled on his side and his exposed behind was facing us.

We were on our way to install an alarm on the door of my elderly mother's apartment, where she lives with twenty-four-hour caregivers working in shifts. My mother has Alzheimer's and she'd wandered out of the apartment the day before. She got downstairs and halfway down the block, no mask, no gloves, before her caregiver caught up with her. Where am I going? she asked. Home, said Pearl.

At eighty-six, with emphysema, if my mother gets the virus she will die.

My first thought when I saw the man in front of our doorway—what if he has the virus? My second thought—is he alive?

I've lived on this block for five years. My husband has lived here nearly twenty, but we will always be outsiders. White artists who moved into the neighborhood because it was what they could afford. Our street is a main artery toward the subway station. There's a needle exchange and drug counseling storefront around the corner, a halfway house, and two low-income housing buildings with a sign in the lobby forbidding anyone to enter except TENANTS AND THEIR GUESTS (as if this weren't true of all buildings). A large public housing project, two blocks away, has the word GARDENS optimistically included in its title. The tall, leafy trees swaying over the sidewalk in front of the house are often used as urinals, men lean against their forgiving trunks and drink a bottle from the liquor store across the street. But this man wasn't leaning or pissing anymore. He came to a stop right between the tree and the front door.

Walking over and past bodies on the street or subway platform is not new to me, practiced as a subjective form of heartlessness. Who do I give money to? Why don't I carry sandwiches to give out? When do I swipe someone into the subway? It depends on my mood, how much cash I have on me and how late I am, as much as anything else. Some people I can't walk past, some I'm afraid to touch. I haven't ridden the subway since mid-March. I'm employed and working from home, unlike many of the people on my block. The backside of the man with his pants falling off was brown and clean. Most of the people on my block are black or brown, so the fact that his body was clean was something I paid more attention to than his skin color, at first. He was clean, his clothing looked new and he was wearing shoes. This was the list of facts which made me assume that he wasn't homeless, though he could be an addict, come to the neighborhood to score, or a drunk sleeping it off.

How many of these assumptions am I willing to question?

How many make it possible for me to live in this city?

I turned my eyes away from him, pity mixed with revulsion at seeing someone too far gone to pull up his own pants. Of course I couldn't touch him. We called 911 and stayed six feet away, waiting for an ambulance to come. I could say that the six-foot distance was social distancing in the time of Corona, but that would be a lie. I would have kept my distance even if I wasn't afraid that he was carrying the virus. He wasn't moving, his eyes were closed, face pressed against the sidewalk, no mask or gloves. Was he still breathing? I couldn't tell.

I was born in this city, in a broken nation built on slavery, where black and brown people are dying in greater numbers from this virus than white people. I've been shopping and delivering groceries as part of a grassroots response to the pandemic, but I volunteer with an afterschool group, not the local needle exchange, because I'd rather spend time with children than junkies. Growing up here, I was taught that it was safer to step around fallen bodies.

I avoid thinking about it as I avoid the bodies of strangers.

Most of us move like minnows on the sidewalk, trying to maintain the six-foot distance, even with masks on. We step onto a stoop to let someone pass, or into the deserted street. How narrow is the sidewalk? Is she wearing a mask? Is she even looking? I give way to everyone, afraid of becoming a vector to my mother and afraid for myself. When a black man walks toward me, I nod as I step out of the way, feeling like an idiot, as if a nod can mitigate all the times white women have crossed the street as he walked toward them. Sometimes they nod back, sometimes they don't. This is New York, you get everything and you get nothing.

There has always been a virus that people are afraid to catch.

There are maps showing the demographics of who has left the city in plague time.

My mother's caregivers take the subway to come to her apartment in Manhattan. One of them lives in Brooklyn and one in the Bronx. They are both from Trinidad, and one of the questions the homecare agency asked me, trying to find a good match for us, was if my mother was racist. I'm sorry, they said, but we have to ask.

No was too simple an answer; so was yes.

Standing outside, waiting for the ambulance, another man rushed up, no mask, no gloves, and put his arms around the fallen man, calling him by name. We told him that we'd already called 911 but he pulled out his phone anyway, panicked. He kept hugging the man and talking into the phone to the dispatcher.

He was fine ten minutes ago—about forty years old—I was just coming back to get him. Wake up! Wake up!

We could hear the sirens heading to our address this time. Someone came out of the shop on Fourth Avenue. Does he need Narcan? We've got some in the shop. Do you know how to do it? Aren't you supposed to just shove it up their nose? I don't know. What's Narcan? It's for when you O.D. But how do we know—

The sirens got louder. Red and white lights disappearing in the cold spring sun.

The EMT jumped out of the ambulance wearing gloves and no mask. We kept talking about it later. Did you see? The ambulance guy wasn't wearing a mask. Do you think he has one? Maybe they ran out. He had gloves on. Yeah, but no mask. You think they're out of masks? We watched the medics bring a stretcher and move the man from our front gate into the ambulance. Do they put the dead into an ambulance?

I suppose they must.

What do I know of this man? He collapsed in front of my door in the middle of the day, someone knew him and we called an ambulance. It might not have been the virus, could have been an overdose, could have been a heart attack.

He might have made it through.

There is a woman who sits on the corner across from our building and screams for hours, harsh repeated cries. She's white and dresses like a young girl in a flimsy dress, sweatshirt and sneakers, but has the face of an old woman. She squats on the sidewalk, bare-legged, nursing a bottle with her red shopping cart next to her, plastic bags and bits of cloth fluttering from her wheeled metal companion. We heard from the local deli guy that she's not homeless, she has a room in the big hotel on Atlantic Avenue—which isn't really a hotel. There is nobody to call for her. The deli guy told us that when he calls the cops, they don't come. It's not the pandemic, they've never come when he calls.

Some days the whole city is screaming through the throat of this bare-legged woman, and I'm not proud of it, but after a while I put on my headphones.

She's still there, but it's been quieter on the corner for weeks now. The empty buses don't stop and the birds seem louder.

I want to thank the first responders, the delivery people and the birds.

I keep seeing him every time I open the door, his back curled like a question mark.

Wake up, man! Wake up! He was fine just ten minutes ago. I was coming to pick him up.

What was he wearing? A friend asked. What she meant was, did he look destitute? Was he bare-legged, cracked feet, ripped shirt, fly down?

He was dressed normally, pants and a sweatshirt. Oh, and he wasn't wearing a mask or gloves.

CODA

About midnight last night, fifty cops in riot gear ran down the street in front of my building, chasing protesters. In one week, the sound of ambulances in deserted streets has pivoted to the sound of chanting and police sirens. The virus doesn't matter since George Floyd was murdered. Fires burn, combusted by this forced compression of racism and death. In the streets where we stand and march, there is no distance between us now, though most of the protesters are masked and most of the police are not. One sign, magic-markered on cardboard: The Cops Will Kill Me Before Covid-19. We hand out bottles of water and cola—the cola is for the eyes in case of teargas and pepper spray. Last night, we brought our garbage bags back inside from the curb so they can't be used to start a fire. Even the corner store, which never closes, pulled down their metal shutters before dark. The sign with the rainbow on our front door, thanking first responders, sanitation workers, and delivery people already seems like a relic from another time.

Before going out to protest last night, I nailed a new sign to the tree in front of the building:

WHAT HAPPENS TO A DREAM DEFERRED?
DOES IT DRY UP LIKE A RAISIN IN THE SUN
OR DOES IT EXPLODE?
— LANGSTON HUGHES

By the time I came back, just as the first curfew imposed on this city since 1943 took effect, I saw that the sign was gone.

Maybe someone took it to the protest.

HOPE INTERRUPTED:
ORGAN TRANSPLANTATION IN THE MIDDLE OF A PANDEMIC

Tiffany Winters

Even under the best of circumstances, making it onto an organ transplant list is no easy feat. Simply needing an organ isn't quite enough; rather, you undergo a battery of tests, procedures, and consultations over a series of weeks to prove you are not only healthy enough to survive a transplant, but also have insurance approval to foot the massive bills—and a support network to carry you through the recovery process.

The older you are, the more likely you are to have other "comorbidities" that could complicate a transplant. So when my mother made the liver transplant list at the age of 71 this past June, it was little short of a miracle. In addition to the routine tests, she had to undergo a heart catheterization and a frailty assessment and made a special visit to meet with the lead transplant surgeon, which was not part of the process for younger patients. We knew her age would work against her—they'd told us that at the very beginning—but they'd said if she cleared every test, that meant she'd proven she could not only survive a transplant, but thrive during the recovery process and live many happy years thereafter.

But age wasn't the only factor at odds with my mother's chances: she began the evaluation process awash with grief, mere hours after my father passed away. And then the reports started coming in: cases of Covid-19 had been confirmed in the U.S., and we were in the middle of a global pandemic. She was tucked away into relative isolation and ushered out only for appointments, many of which required she travel halfway across

Indiana and wear a mask for hours at a time. Appointments were delayed, user errors meant she had to repeat tests, and at one point she had to go to a crowded lab to be tested for Covid-19, just to make sure she was clear of the virus before a procedure—never mind that going for the test put her at risk for the very thing they wanted to rule out. But she did it all, never missing an appointment, even as she carried the incredible burden of quarantine-induced loneliness. It weighed her down and visibly slowed her gait, but she refused to give up. She re-focused her energy and continued to move forward, sometimes through tears, her objective remarkably clear: "I just love you all so much," she would say. "And I want to watch my grandchildren grow up."

And so she passed test after test and consult after consult until one day we got the call: they were adding her to the list, and they were optimistic they'd find a liver for her soon. A process that took five months had come to an end, and with it: we were rewarded with the glorious gift of hope. Like a pregnant woman eager for the birth of a child, she was advised to pack a bag and be ready.

•

For the first few weeks of the pandemic, my mother and mother-in-law quarantined together. My husband, daughter, and I took every possible precaution during that period, and—once in the clear—eventually started taking day trips to visit her, run errands, etc. During those rare visits, we kept our distance, wore masks, and maximized time outdoors. From there, we started taking longer trips and hatched an idea: let's buy our four-year-old daughter a kiddie pool to set up there. My mother, unlike us, has a beautiful backyard, and we could split our time between quarantining here in suburban Chicago and there, in rural Indiana—and then stay there for four solid weeks post-transplant, when she'd need 24/7 care while recovering. I imagined all these beautiful days outdoors, the small pool giving my dihydrogen monoxide-loving daughter a welcome distraction while her grandmother, someone who cherished her kids and grandkids above all earthly things, watched on.

•

Throughout this entire process, a recurring source of frustration for my sister and me, as well as our mother, was the politicization of mask-wearing and social distancing during such a precarious time. For us—and for much of Illinois, where masks were mandated as of May 1—wearing a mask and keeping our distance became a sign of respect for the most vulnerable members of society, my mother being one such person. We happily obliged with these and all other measures, forever focused on the end game: keeping my mother, and everyone else like her, alive. But social media painted a very different picture across state lines in Indiana. While I did see the occasional post from a handful of conservative friends that indicated their support for safety precautions, including masks, and their dismay that it had become a political issue, my newsfeed was otherwise full of dangerously false information, shared and re-shared at alarming rates. When legitimate news articles made an appearance, they were often outdated and presented to "discredit" more recent data. It was clear people were being hit with conflicting information from all directions, and the lack of a consistent authoritative voice led many to regard unsubstantiated memes as incontrovertible fact.

I held onto the hope that others would eventually grow to see wearing a mask as a simple way to protect others and no different than wearing a seatbelt or not smoking in public. But in the meantime, chaos was reigning and a big chunk of my home state was relenting to the staunchly anti-mask propaganda. Eventual visits to Indiana confirmed the more vehemently anti-mask posts weren't just online posturing but, rather, a terrifying reality. Even pharmacists in hotspot territory weren't masking up, but we still expected my mother's hospital—one of the largest networks in the region—to be an exception to what we were experiencing elsewhere in the state.

But no. When I accompanied my mother to her final evaluation appointment in June, we were shocked to realize that there was no way in or out of the building that didn't require us to walk through a confined space where the vast majority of visitors were not wearing masks. Once inside, we waited in a line where social distancing was lackadaisical at best, and it wasn't until they were at the front of the line that unmasked guests were directed to grab one from a community jar, invariably touching two to three others in the quest for their own. Beyond the front desk, an alarming number of people, visitors and employees alike, removed their masks. These weren't just quick breaths of fresh air, but rather sustained time without a mask in situations where staff interacted with patients: a lab technician who laughed heartily as she walked past us, a young man at the front desk who directed me to the wheelchairs, a receptionist who checked us into her department.

We had previously been told that this specific facility included wards dedicated to immunocompromised patients and, as such, didn't take on Covid-19 cases. That didn't mean everyone who entered their doors was in the clear, however, with many visitors coming into the building for miscellaneous lab work, imaging, physical therapy, etc. As such, we expected this location to be extra cautious in an effort to protect its most vulnerable patients, but as we worked our way through its halls, we experienced a very different reality. And in fact: on a future visit, I had no choice but to frequently interact with an unmasked nurse at the nurse's station. I'd consistently experienced better safety measures at my neighborhood Trader Joe's. But at this hospital, we felt increasingly anxious and vulnerable, as though all of our efforts to protect my mother were being undone by the political divide.

•

Less than two weeks after making the transplant list, my mom returned to the hospital to have retained fluid removed, a fairly routine visit for liver disease patients that involves both a paracentesis (an "abdominal tap" that drains fluid from around the stomach and other organs) as well as a hefty dose of diuretics to help re-direct additional fluid through her kidneys and out of her body through more natural means. Diuretics can significantly tax the kidneys, so doctors closely monitor kidney function during these stays. My mom had felt worlds better after a similar visit several weeks prior, and I didn't think much of it. I stayed 230 miles away in Chicago, planning to visit when she was discharged after what would surely be a three to five-day stay at most. But something went wrong. Her hemoglobin levels dropped after the first paracentesis, and her MELD score, which measures the severity of liver disease, increased by several points. They ruled out an internal bleed and she was subsequently moved up the transplant list—a "nationwide priority," we were told. And then two hours later: they had found her a liver.

It felt like every prayer under the sun had been answered, though I admit there was a bittersweet element: I never lost sight of the fact that our joy was countered by another family's torment. As happy as I was for us, my heart hurt for complete strangers. But as one hour ticked away, and then another, I grew increasingly concerned. Why was it taking so long for them to take her back? Aren't these procedures time-sensitive?

I was halfway to the hospital when I got the call: something was wrong, and they were cancelling her transplant. They remained optimistic that the problems could be corrected and that they would be able to find another liver for her. But the very next day, everything had worsened and their optimism turned cold. They said they didn't know what had happened, but gave us a jumbled smattering of details to explain why they'd called off the transplant: her kidneys were only functioning at 15%, which they didn't think was sufficient for someone her age to survive a liver transplant. And then they mentioned there was fluid in—and a "ground glass" pattern to—her lungs. "Wait a minute," I interrupted after they quickly moved on to something else. "That's what happens to lungs infected with Covid-19. Has she been tested?" My mind swirled back to one of my mother's nurses, who had recently confessed to me during a phone call that he refused to wear a mask anywhere outside of work, despite being entrusted with the care of one of the most vulnerable populations. "This whole thing has been blown out of proportion by the media," he'd said. "If you hear someone cough, just step back six feet. It's that simple."

They assured me she'd been tested and that her test was negative. They said they were acting under the assumption that she was fighting some sort of infection and had put her on a powerful course of antibiotics. But they also said her kidneys had suffered something similar to a heart attack, and they didn't expect her numbers to improve, even on dialysis. "How can you say things won't improve if you don't understand what's happening in the first place?" I asked over and over in a multitude of ways, their response always a variation of the same exasperating theme. When I hung up the phone, it hit me: aren't false negatives a known problem, particularly within the first few days of exposure to the Coronavirus? A quick search also revealed that kidney function is negatively impacted for up to 30% of patients hospitalized with Covid-19. I wanted my mother to be retested; my sister agreed and promptly called the nurse's station to put in the request. I was en route to Indiana later that evening when I spoke with one of the hepatologists who had been tending to my mother. He confirmed he saw the request, but he didn't think there was a need to test her again.

"But the transplant doctor described a ground glass pattern in her lungs. Isn't that typical with Covid-19?" I asked.

"It is," he said. "But that's not what I see what I look at the scan."

"OK, then what do you see?"

"At this point I really can't say."

•

The next morning, I was finally able to visit my mother in person. Due to restrictions tied to Covid-19, she was limited to one visitor per day, so I FaceTimed with my sister any time hospital staff entered our mother's room. And enter the room they did, with five to six doctors, nurses, and administrators coming in at any point and congregating around my mother's bed, their very numbers an indication that my mother's situation was dire. I quickly mastered the art of reading their expressions through the masks, the doctors' brow lines and vocal tones revealing both frowns and smirks with remarkable clarity.

My sister and I asked question after question, having spent the previous evening researching and conferring with friends in the medical field. Some of our mother's doctors patiently listened to our questions, were sympathetic, and seemed willing to do whatever might increase our mother's odds of surviving. But they also made it clear that the next steps were up to our mother and the nephrologist assigned to her case. When the kidney doctor came in a few minutes later, her attitude toward us was the polar opposite of the previous set of doctors—so much so, that it felt like they were playing the medical equivalent of good cop / bad cop. She was curt and uncaring and visibly upset that, in the absence of receiving any answers, we had taken it upon ourselves to search for them. That same doctor unapologetically painted a very grotesque picture for our mother, describing in graphic detail the unavoidable path that awaited her if she chose anything other than going home on hospice. And sadly, that doctor was the last, and loudest, clinical voice our mother heard on the matter. Her narrative was this: there was no hope, and my mom could either go on dialysis in the ICU and stay there until she died a miserable lonely death—or she could go home to spend her remaining days with family. So she asked to go home.

●

I was packing up her hospital room when they delivered yet another blow: they told us she might not be able to go home after all, as her blood pressure had dropped too low. And despite our mother requesting pain medicine, they continued to hold off because it could further lower her blood pressure—until all of a sudden they changed their minds on all of the above. They said they'd be sending her home despite the low blood pressure, gave her two doses of Fentanyl separated by two hours (when I expressed concern, they assured me it was a small dose), and then loaded her onto an ambulance gurney within a minute of that second dose. She was conscious and coherent when the ambulance drivers pushed the gurney into a staff elevator, and I said "I love you; I'll see you at home." "I love you too," she said, raising her head ever so slightly so she could see me over the gurney. And with that: the doors closed, and I hurried to my car.

●

My mother arrived home unconscious, her chest rising and falling with every labored breath. And yet, even still, we recalled our father spending days in hospice and remained hopeful she would wake up. We set about decorating the room she'd chosen; she'd specifically requested to be in a room with a television, in large part because the doctor's description of a utopian hospice death implied she'd have days to reminisce with family, tie up loose ends and, yes, even watch some of her favorite programs. We filled the room with photos of family, fresh flowers, and her grandchildren's artwork. As my sister and I came and went, my husband grabbed a guitar, sat down next to my mother, and started playing some of her favorite songs. She never woke up. She was home for less than two hours when she stopped breathing and our devastation began.

•

Even through our hurt, our anger, and our anguish, we had the bureaucracy of death to tend to: arrangements, wills, and the like, a horrible intrusion into our grief when all we wanted was to sit and cry. Our mother had made it clear she didn't want to ever be the reason someone else contracted Covid-19, and funerals are "super-spreader events." How do we respect her wishes and still celebrate her life? How do we ensure the safety of the people she cared so deeply about and still find closure?

I couldn't take a single step forward because my mind was racing with the emotional whiplash of the recent past. I wanted answers; I wanted to understand what had caused my mother's sudden and rapid decline, but her doctors gave us none of that. Rather, as we discussed each of the possibilities my sister and I had researched, and the doctors dismissed them one by one, we felt the need to justify our questions by reminding them that our mother's condition, although serious, was nevertheless stable when she arrived at the hospital for a routine procedure just a few days earlier. They had demanded we make impossible decisions; they seemed to think that "here is where we are" was a sufficient answer to a family repeatedly asking them: "Yes, but how did we get here?"

We were taunted by the turmoil of not knowing. What if there had been an undisclosed error with her paracentesis—did they introduce an infection, or inadvertently puncture something? Was this Covid-19 or another underlying infection due to cross-contamination in a hospital setting? They seemed cagey when I asked to see which meds my mom was on—could this have been an accidental overdose or an allergy to a medication they'd prescribed, or was it all in my imagination? Did they ultimately decide to discharge her, despite her dangerously low blood pressure, because we were asking too many questions? Or perhaps no one was to blame, and everything that had happened to my mother was merely an anomaly of the disease, an unpredictable but possible conclusion to any non-alcoholic cirrhosis patients' life.

•

I was lost in thought when I heard a tiny voice cut through my mind's chatter: "Can we still set up my pool?" My daughter only recently turned four, and though she is old enough to know, love, and miss her grandmother, she is too young to fully grasp the finality of death.

I admit I had reconsidered. This small, inflatable pool was initially a symbol of hope but had suddenly become one of devastation. I wanted to throw it into a pyre and burn it, giving it, and all my optimism, their last rites. But then I looked at my daughter, herself lost and confused and struggling to understand why Grandma will never come home again, and I obliged.

And so she swims while I write an obituary. She dives for rings while I sort through papers. She laughs and giggles as I look to the sky, and we both ask the age-old question:

"Mom, are you watching?"

FLATTENING THE CURVE
Aydin Behnam and John Casquarelli

You must believe me. I had never done anything like this before. Yes, it was his first time coming to my unit. It was my fault. I started it all. I read it in an old book I found in the attic and I mentioned it to him. The book said that it used to be an old custom. I'm so stupid! I should have known better. He had a way of obsessing over things. Of course, he took the idea and ran with it. Yes, of course I regret it. I'm sorry I ever put the idea in his head. Now I realize it was not a responsible thing to do. Yes, I regret what we did.

Regret is an old brownstone on Bleecker Street,
rent past due, wiping the stale beer from my chin
with the same arm that I damaged in an old rugby match
when I believed competition was a noble act.
What I remember from my childhood are
whispers between raindrops, voices once believed
to be tornadoes, spiraling from notebooks to typewriters
to an unknown technology in an unknown corner
of someone else's universe.

He said he ordered it off the Internet. There we were, facing each other, standing under the parasitic plant that hung from the ceiling. The silence between us made my ears ring. I could hear myself swallowing my warm saliva. I ran my tongue along the inside of my teeth, then my lips. They felt scorching hot. Outside, the snow landed slowly on the windowsill. He turned up the volume on the live stream of the countdown. The presenter's jubilant tone made me even more nervous. The ball was about to drop.

Cousin Ray lost his light on East 17th Street
after coughing in staccato. Ambulances whiz by
in a music of fireworks and denials.
What you once were, you'll be again.
This is our great lie, our nostalgic slideshow
amid the great boom of our collected ignorance.

I thought I heard a humming outside the window. I jumped. He noticed me eyeing the windows and the door. He assured me there was nothing to worry about. He said he had hacked the Proximity Protocol partition of his subdermal microchip implant and compromised its frequency with a VPN jamming signal. He also said he had paid off a third-party cross-sectional data dumper to breach the Ministry's surveillance network and fill out a phantom Mobility Transparency Permit Form. He said we had at least a thirty-minute window.

"Nothing sits on nothing in a nothing of
many nothings a nothing king." Corso's vision
in the silent, dark night of his mindfield.
The embodiment of a tangerine kleptocrat who likely
never read a stanza or an obituary.
I often refer to the U.S. as a perilous miasma

I trusted him. He was my first. . . the first guy to see me. . . to see me without my PPE. I felt naked without my mask on, but he knew how to make me feel safe, you know. I covered my mouth with my hands, but he held my fingers and pulled them off my face. . . and I let him. The countdown had started: Nine, Eight, Seven, I felt a tingle enter through my shoulder and travel down to my belly button as he brushed my skin with his fingers. Six, Five, Four, I never knew I could smell someone's scent through my mouth. Does that even make sense? Three, his lips were about to touch mine. Would they be as soft as I imagined them? Two, my whole body twitched and then eased up again. I felt like a jumpy kitten. . . One, Happy New Year. The soundbite of a pre-recorded cheer poured out of the speakers.

> *Hunger and filtered masks replace side-glances,*
> *laughter, maraschino cherry, velvet allegories,*
> *and Keats's beauty obliterating all consideration.*
> *Times Square, glitter of consumerism, midnight song*
> *in the year of contamination, when our faces become weapons.*
> *The doorway pours secrecy on the dying page.*
> *The doorway is a makeshift field hospital in Central Park.*
> *The doorway leads to tossed latex gloves and cotton swabs*
> *on the BMT Broadway Line. The doorway is the final*
> *snowfall on my fleeting youth, the chill that embraces me*
> *under the waxing crescent moon.*

The last thing I remember is seeing a flashing LED light past his face, behind him, outside the window and recognizing the hum of the surveillance drone. The P-SWAT team kicked the door off its hinges. There was a flash and a bang. My ears whistled painfully. I held my head in my hands and squatted. I couldn't breathe. The room filled with smoke. I saw the shadows of masked men sweep me onto the ground. "On your knees," they shouted. "Show me your hands, your hands!" I heard a pop, pop, pop. Everything slowed down. I saw the beer can flatten with a crunch under a shiny boot and sputter yellow froth onto the carpet. As the intruder drove his knee to the back of my head, slapped the handcuffs on my wrists, and led me to the door, the ringing in my ears died down. Auld Lang Syne blared out of the speakers, bathing the boot-trodden room and the swinging mistletoe in red and blue light.

THE FALLOUT

MILITARIZING THE POLICE
Roxana Robinson

In 1990, after the fall of the Soviet Union and the Iron Curtain, the United States no longer needed a powerful physical military presence in Europe. Congress passed legislation allowing the Department of Defense to release six billion dollars' worth of surplus military equipment to our local police departments across the country. This consignment included tanks, MRAPS (mine-resistant vehicles), assault rifles, grenade launchers, and bayonets.

Americans love technology, and there were many in law enforcement who welcomed the exciting new equipment. The South wanted it more than the North did. New York State, with a population of about 20 million people, has received about $26 million worth of equipment, slightly over a dollar's worth per person. Texas, which has about 30 million people, has received nearly $200 million dollars' worth of equipment, over six times that much per person. South Carolina, with a population of about five million people, has received $62 million dollars' worth, about twelve times New York's share. Georgia, which has ten million people, has received $88 million dollars' worth of equipment.

It wasn't only the South that was interested, though. Between 1980 and 2000, the number of SWAT teams (Special Weapons and Tactics) increased by 1500% throughout the country. This is despite the fact that we rarely need such highly trained teams carrying high-caliber military weapons. Most civilian crime is carried out by small numbers of people, not trained for combat.

But the increase in SWAT teams is part of the seismic shift caused by militarization. Arming police like combat soldiers put them in closer alignment with the military and distanced them from the civilian community. A combat-ready force, carrying lethal hi-tech military weapons, presumes a mission based on making war, not keeping the peace. This newly armed police force was prepared for the battlefield, and for confrontation with the enemy. But who was the enemy?

The "Black Lives Matter" movement has arisen in response to racist behavior by the police. For decades the Black community has reported such behavior, but the claims were often based on anecdotal evidence, and as such were often denied or ignored. Now cell phones and videos have made such incidents a matter of public record and public outrage. The response has been a massive inter-racial outcry against such unconscionable behavior. One result has been a call for the defunding or even the outright abolishment of police forces.

We want to abolish racist behavior, but we may not want to abolish the institution of the police. There will always be some kind of disturbance to the peace, and it's a good idea to have someone trained to maintain it. But questions remain: what is a "disturbance"? And what is "peace"? Whom do the police defend? Whom do they attack? Whom do they serve? What is criminal behavior? Sometimes the answers are obvious, sometimes not. Our own history of peacekeeping is complicated, and, like the history of our country, race plays an important part in it.

In the United States, peacekeeping forces date back to the 1600s, though they differed according to region. In the Carolinas, armed white men, volunteers, established slave patrols to enforce the idea that human beings were property. Anyone with dark skin who disagreed, or appeared to disagree, was considered a criminal. At that early moment, the idea of criminality and race became conjoined. These patrols expanded throughout the South, establishing a pattern of armed white men monitoring the activity of unarmed Black men. (During slavery, it was illegal for Black men to carry guns.) In Appalachia, in the next century, vigilante groups were formed, armed civilians who imposed rough justice on their neighbors. Lynching arose from this sort of activity: local men taking the law into their own hands, applying punishment as they saw fit.

In the North, during that same period, the approach to peacekeeping was very different. In cities, unarmed citizens volunteered for Night Watch, walking the streets to keep them safe. It wasn't until two hundred years later, during the mid-nineteenth century, that professional police forces were established. Debate arose over uniforms and guns, but the big question concerned the use of force.

Violence was already a pattern in the American South; its roots lay in slavery. Violence is fundamental to the institution. Since 1619, Southern whites were continually at risk of a rebellion from the powerful Black community around them. Their response was preventative violence, physical violence of every sort, imposed by whips, chains, ropes, shackles, and guns. Always guns. Violence became deeply embedded in Southern culture.

Though the North had strong economic ties to slavery, the institution itself was less present there. Northern farming was modest in scale and mixed in production; there were no vast cotton plantations that would require hundreds of laborers. There were far fewer enslaved people in the North, and violence did not become central to the culture. In 1878, Massachusetts, Vermont, and New Hampshire each reported one murder; South Carolina reported 128. The murders were committed by both races: violence had become a reflexive response in the South.

In the late nineteenth century, armed police began to be used for larger social issues, not just individual disputes. The question of whom they served became more important: was it the public or the powerful?

As cities grew and industrialization changed the social norms, working conditions became exploitative on a large scale.

Workers began to stage protests, and police were called in to restore the peace. They were ordered to quell the "riots," as they were called, though they could also be called labor disputes, or protests against inhumane working conditions. Here the police were called in by the company-owners and encouraged to use brutal force. It seemed that those police forces felt an allegiance to the powerful, not to the protesters.

Politics often played a powerful and opaque part in the role of the police. In the late nineteenth and early twentieth century, corruption was rampant in many American cities. Corrupt politicians worked hand-in-glove with both police and criminals, all covertly engaged in racketeering and other illegal activities. Because police chiefs were appointed, not elected, politicians used their power to control the police, and the powerful could count on protection. During Prohibition there was an explosion of criminal behavior and a continued involvement with corrupt police.

So for a time it seemed that the answer to the question of who the police were working for was the powerful. In any case, they were always working for the establishment.

Police were called to respond to civil rights marches, anti-war protests, and anti-racism protests. It's the job of protesters to disturb the peace; it's the job of police to restore it.

Conflicts between protesters and police are part of the long debate, constantly evolving, that's essential to a democratic society, a conversation between the people and the establishment, or the government. The people are entitled to protest peacefully; they are not entitled to become violent. But what if no one listens unless they become violent? What if outraged protesters have their own tendencies toward violence? The police are required to restore order, but how should they do it? Whose side are they on?

What should their role be?

American police forces rely far more on guns than do many

212

of our allies. Traditionally, English policemen did not carry guns, only nightsticks, and the country has always enjoyed a low rate of violent crime. It's only recently that they've begun carrying guns, and then only when violence is believed to be a part of an incident.

Countries who send out unarmed policemen are the UK, Ireland, New Zealand, Norway, and Iceland. Other developed countries, and our allies, allow police to carry guns, but they use different training methods and rarely use lethal force. In 2018, there were 11 deaths resulting from police in Germany. In France there were no deaths from police. In the UK there were three. In the US, in 2015, there were 1,022.

All American policemen carry guns, and the presence of firearms changes the nature of every encounter. Everyone knows, and the police know, that they hold the final and absolute response.

There is a practical reason for American police to carry guns: American civilians carry guns. 46% of all guns in private hands around the world, 400 million of them, are owned by Americans. This mad American commitment to firearms also has its roots in slavery and racism.

After the Civil War, when Black freedmen received the right to vote and hold office, white Southerners opposed it. Northern troops were sent down to enforce the new laws. They were not welcome, and after a while they were recalled. States created their own militias to enforce the laws. These official bodies were comprised in theory of both Blacks and whites, but, since white Southerners refused to serve with Blacks, the militias became de facto Black. This meant that Black men were given the official right to carry guns. This was more than Southern whites were willing to tolerate, and ten years after the War, a group of them decided they'd had enough of Reconstruction. They began a new era which they called "Redemption." Former Confederate General Cary wrote a letter urging his fellow white Southerners to unite against the Black freedmen who wanted to vote. He used plain terms:

"Determine if necessary to kill every white radical in the country—every mulatto radical leader—every negro leader, [and establish] a thorough military organization in order to intimidate the negro. . ."

Southern white men responded with vigor. They set up their own paramilitary armed forces, often led by Confederate veterans. They were called gun clubs, but they were really based on the old Slave Patrols. They were made up of the same people, angry white men, and they had the same intentions, the violent suppression of Black people.

One of the first incidents of Redemption took place in Hamburg, South Carolina, an all-Black town. Two white men tried to interrupt a Fourth of July parade led by the Black town militia. The Black men were accused of threatening the whites, and they were all called in to court by a Black magistrate. The local paramilitary group was called the Sweetwater Saber Club, named after a church. It was made up of white plantation owners, and was some 70-strong. Members were ordered to appear at the hearing and make trouble, and they followed these orders. By the end of that night they had killed seven Black men. Some were members of the militia; some were civilians, shot in the street, or captured and executed.

My great-grandfather was Frank Dawson, then the editor of the *Charleston News & Courier*. He was outraged by this incident, though he was a Confederate officer himself. He wrote that it was disgraceful behavior, breaking the code of military honor and shooting prisoners like rabbits. "Their only crime, we fear, lay in being black and carrying arms."

The belief that white civilians had the right to carry arms was founded in the South, first in order to create the infamous Slave Patrols, to establish control over enslaved people, and then later, after the Civil War, in response to the fact that Black freedmen were officially ordered to carry arms for the government. White men took up their own arms out of outrage at what they saw as insolence. They claimed that the government gave them the right to do so, but they were really just continuing the old Slave Patrols. The Second Amendment specifies the right to "A well-regulated militia": this was intended to protect the country from foreign forces. It didn't mean that unregulated civilians could murder each other.

But white Southerners felt they were under siege from armed Black freedmen. What stuck in the craw of the white men at Hamburg was the fact that Black freedmen refused to hand over their guns to an ex-Confederate general. White men were not going to stand for that. Following General Cary's plan, they instituted a policy of violent intimidation of Black freedmen, including vote-suppression, massacres, and lynchings. And so began the Jim Crow era.

Now the idea of gun ownership has expanded into unthinkable proportions, and mass hysteria erupts at the mere suggestion of any sort of gun control. Hundreds of thousands of Americans own handguns and assault weapons, weapons unsuited for anything but armed combat against human beings. This situation does not exist in any other developed country, all of which have strict gun control regulations. England has a long tradition of game-shooting, but it has very strict laws about weapons. If you own a shotgun, it must be kept locked in a closet, and available for the local constabulary to examine at all times. English law does not permit the ownership of military-style assault weapons, or of handguns.

But in America almost anyone can own any sort of gun, and so we have 40,000 gun-related deaths a year. It is true that it's people who cause deaths, but these 40,000 cases are caused by people with guns. Is it any wonder that our policemen are armed? It would be madness to send out unarmed policemen to deal with terrorists wielding automatic weapons. The existence of so many weapons puts policemen and women on an adrenaline-charged alert. At any moment they know they may die by gunshot, which makes them more likely to fire first.

Gun control would, of course, greatly reduce this lethal chaos, but our hysterical resistance makes it impossible. Instead of imposing gun control, we ratchet up the arming of the police, which today has reached military proportions.

Weapons have always made it easier to kill, not just physically but psychologically. Starting with the longbows at Agincourt, the more distance between you and your target, the easier it is to destroy him. Looking someone in the eyes as he walks toward you, both of you unarmed, engages your understanding of him as a human being. Even if you kill him, you will carry with you forever the knowledge of his life, the awareness of his particular humanity. Whereas inside a tank, or even an MRAP, you are cut off from your surroundings. You feel insulated from the people you are engaging with. They are outside, you are safe inside. You can't see their humanity. This is all the more true for someone dropping a bomb from an airplane, or causing a drone to drop a bomb, sitting safe in a base in Florida: it removes you one thousandfold from the reality of killing. The easier it is physically to kill, and the further removed you are from your target, the easier it becomes psychologically to perform the lethal feat.

Studies in military psychology show that soldiers resist shooting people who look like them—who could be them. They are more ready to shoot people who look different from them—people who represent the Other. Racism, then, has made certain wars easier to fight. And racism makes identification simple: anyone who looks different is the enemy.

Militarization of the police has made the use of lethal force increasingly likely. Riot gear, which hides your face and distances you from other humans, and which protects you from their actions, makes violence more likely. Combat training, which creates muscle memory for lethal action, makes violence more likely. Battlefield strategy, which makes every stranger an enemy, makes violence more likely. Using a "No-Knock Warrant," and using a battering ram to break down a door without warning is a combat tactic, used in enemy territory. This kind of action is deadly on every level, psychological as well as physical. It destroys the trust that should exist between the police force and the community it's supposed to serve.

But changing police culture, or even monitoring it, is difficult. The police community is tribal, insular, and self-protective. Powerful police unions are highly effective lobbyists, spending millions of dollars to present their needs to Congress and rejecting attempts to establish accountability among their members.

The civilian population plays a part here, too: police forces are a manifestation of our communal culture, and we're a violent nation. This trait comes from our racist past and our history of slavery, with its violence directed toward people of color. From our racist past we've created a culture of civilian gun-wielding, a strain of madness that is somehow entwined with a belief in American manhood. From our racist past we derive a tendency to see people of color as the enemy. All these things combine to create a tinderbox within the police culture, a firestorm waiting to erupt.

Perhaps we are now seeing the eruption, in the national protest movement of Black Lives Matter, in which thousands of protestors from across the racial divide and across the country march, chant, hold signs, and demand an end to this racist violence.

The demand for the abolishment of the police force would require a new way to maintain the peace. One community that has made such a radical shift is Camden, New Jersey. Seven years ago, the city was one of the most violent and crime-ridden in the country, rife with drugs, shootings, and police corruption. It was the corruption that made reform seem impossible. Lawsuits brought against the police revealed widespread malfeasance: planted evidence, fabricated reports, and perjury. The city decided that it was beyond reform, and they dissolved the Camden Police Department. They let go of 400 people and started over.

The new organization, the Camden County Police Department, is based on the premise that the community owns the streets, and the police makes those streets safe. The department trains its officers seriously in de-escalation and it holds them strictly accountable for the use of force. The ethnic makeup of the force reflects that of the community. The trust of the citizens is paramount: on his first day on the job, each new officer knocks on the doors of his beat, introducing himself and asking how things can be improved. Police officers play basketball with residents, drive Mister Softee trucks, put on drive-in movies, and host neighborhood barbecues. In May, Camden County Police Chief Joseph Wysocki marched with the community in support of "Black Lives Matter."

Violent crime is down 42%.

Camden's efforts haven't entirely succeeded—the ethnic makeup of the police department doesn't yet completely reflect that of the community, and the city still struggles with poverty and related issues. But crime is down, and the feeling on the streets has changed. Citizens feel safe. The police department is dedicated to its original mission: keeping the peace. Tanks are not involved.

Streets should make up a neighborhood, not a battlefield. On a battlefield, every soldier is trained to use lethal force, and the more highly trained you are to use lethal force, the more likely you are to use it. And the more you rely on weapons, the less you use empathy. A warrior may choose weapons first, but an officer of the peace should choose empathy. He should understand that the community is made up of people like him, whether or not they look like him. He should know that it's not killing people that keeps the peace, but understanding them.

Militarizing the police force is pointless and dangerous; it makes citizens into enemies and it makes officers into invading forces. But it's not only our citizens who are at risk; our police officers are endangered by our gun-mad society. They confront armed and violent citizens on a routine traffic arrest; no other developed country permits this. Gun control is just as important to our national safety as monitoring our police departments: we need de-escalation on both sides. We need a willed retreat from our history of racism, violence, and institutional enforcement.

Police departments can be constructive, intelligent, helpful presences in our communities. Our towns and cities can remake them, using new models of accountability and cooperation. Remember that these public servants are not only officers of the law, they are Officers of the Peace. And that's what we need, peace officers. Fewer guns, more empathy.

SPEAKING OF WHICH:
WORK IN PROGRESS
Uche Nduka

1

they maced their faces multiple times they broke
their eyeglasses tenth ride of the Mounted Units
this is not just about prosecution these protestors
are fighting against domination by a bunch of jerks
there won't be peace if there is no justice they fund
the military the paramilitary more than the health
department they bail out corporate crooks they peddle
untested drugs for the pandemic they whip millions
of citizens with unemployment devastation of civil rights
they look for ways to neutralize justified anger they kicked
their legs kicked their ankles decked them threw gas at them
agent provocateurs arsonists anarchists you know what's going
on stop asking this is not a Mad Max movie

2

birds flew into protestors whose hands were still in the air
what about those discriminatory practices against blacks
cell phone videos as truth-tellers the school term is steaming
the city she takes off down the block makes for the road with
a backpack says she's done with quarantine/lockdown
they've for ages given the police the benefit of doubt there's
no dialogue to be had with a hate-monger how long will it take
to realize the evil of hateful disinformation rogue cops throwing
gasoline on fire seems it's too late to reach across the aisle they

purposely spew conspiracy theories for political gain they're not
being delusional when they manipulate voters when they throw
voters into political sewer consequences of the crime spree of
government the corruptions of the unequal transfer of wealth
that shop talk of trees rising stocks bail fees soldiers firing at
speeding cars a demagogue's domestic terrorism disastrous industry
survey rushed condolence call counterattack nothing to write home
about in the transition of power burnt churches defaced billboards
violated shrines graveyards shot up synagogues schools offices
cinemas nightclubs stay up to date with a broken clock

3

footprints say this country was built by black hands the
Washington Monument was built by Africans this skyline
says the White House was built by black people this nation
cannot survive the normalization of the police killing of citizens
of color hot take on obelisks full of hatred full of carnage will
they attempt to burn down history too some of their monuments
celebrate lynchings nothing to see here but nutjobs in glass boxes
in the land of the free it's a sin to be black I don't trust these cops
taking knees with protestors don't drink the bleach they call you
a spic as if that is who you are they call you nigger as if that is your
name the gaslighting by these enforcers of white supremacy
          is getting
to me right about now is this your favorite period drama
          another hour
to record the atrocities of the police in public spaces whose job
          was it
to operate the elevator after each killing politicians tell protestors to
calm down what a ruse lawsuits fly from one state to another
          they yell
about chalets credible threats a shootout lampoons the G7
          they claim

spray cans foment unrest a knee pressed into the neck of a man a
TV reporter on duty shot by police at night absentee ballot
        issues demonized
mail carriers a president inside a bunker muttering about
        thugs ominous
weapons getting even surrounded by sycophants toadies
        inflaming the
national trauma no quarter for anti-black racists zero tolerance
        for lynchers

4

closer to where the wind rose bragged devoured coitus interruptus
it's tiring to always rebuild the houses of my exasperation
        the pressure
the calamity waiting to be spoken through thrown bottles
        protests teargas
batons the scrutiny of the elixir of exile I take a knee I burn
        sage pepper spray
riot shields police cordon the trial begins each day stomping
        on the roof of
vehicles barricades fall gas masks appear police cars set on
        fire agitations
over the violent death of another black man police lines
        betray another
afternoon nasty clashes over racial profiling over justice denied
        this is taking an
unexpected turn how cool are the secret service officers in
        mufti curfews
they're shooting smoke canisters into crowds again property is
        more important
than people they say blocked traffic rubber bullets shit is about
        to really go

down they're ready to crack some skulls why are they
    provoking protestors
why are they pissing people off blood stains bodies brains

WHITE FANTASY:
LAURA INGALLS WILDER, COVID, AND THE MYTH OF SELF-SUFFICIENCY

Joan Marcus

I know I'm not the only one who used to have apocalypse fantasies, long ago, back before December of 2019. I keep seeing that split-screen meme on Facebook, on the left a picture of Mila Jovovich or some other badass in skin-tight assassin couture, on the right some poorly-dressed schlub—a cat in a Muppet onesie with a plate of cookies on her lap; Jeffrey Lebowski wandering the supermarket in bathrobe and boxers. The caption: "What I thought my apocalypse outfit would be vs. what it really is."

For me that meme rings painfully true. I never thought I'd be roving the ruined wastes with a buzz cut and an arm cannon, but I did think quite a lot about economic collapse and climate disasters and, yes, global pandemic—that more than anything. I thought about what I'd do if things ever got really bad, how the family and I would get by. I imagined holing up in my house and teaching my college classes remotely. I imagined growing and preserving my own food if supplies got scarce, digging wild ramps in the forest, shooting deer and raising hens. At the time I thought this was my way of easing free-floating anxiety—imagining the worst, then convincing myself I was a survivor. In retrospect I think it was a perverse form of entertainment.

Survival narratives are great fun. Often in January I find myself picking up one of my childhood favorites, Laura Ingalls Wilder's *The Long Winter*, a lightly fictionalized account of how the author's family survived the brutal winter of 1880–81 in Dakota Territory. Most years I read that book cover to cover. Winters are five months long here in upstate New York and you'd think I'd prefer sunnier fare, but Wilder's book is its own kind of escape. It lets me dream my grey world into something heroic, a narrative in which I, the scrappy pioneer, survive with nothing but mother wit and tenacity to help me through. I read about twisting hay into sticks when there's no more coal to burn, grinding seed wheat in a coffee mill for sourdough loaves, the storm howling and scouring the house so you can't even see your neighbors across the street. As though you're the only people on earth, you and your loved ones alone in your little pocket of endurance.

So much for life pre-Corona. Real isolation is a lot less fun than reading about it in a kids' book. Thankfully I'm not hungry—I consider myself fortunate—but like other fortunate people, I'm a bit of a zombie lately, working long days in a little house, not grinding wheat but locked to my screen twelve hours a day, dim and thick-headed, out of shape. "She felt beaten by the cold and the storms," Wilder says of the fourteen-year-old Laura. "She knew she was dull and stupid but she could not wake up." I'm rarely cold but I still feel dull, half-awake, beaten by tweet storms and the pulse of electronic info that scours my brain.

Meanwhile my students begin to suffer in much worse ways. Friends and family fall ill. Some die. Covid hits a nursing home in Massachusetts where one student works, killing twenty-two residents, including a woman she loved dearly. A friend of ours, a teacher in Queens, gets hit bad in March and hasn't fully recovered two months later. She may have permanent lung damage, this woman younger than I who was perfectly healthy before the virus got her. She was never hospitalized though. Could this be what they're calling mild illness? Jesus. My older daughter works at a fabric store cutting cloth for online orders and brings home free scraps. She sews masks with a pocket for a coffee filter and a nose bridge of milled sculpture wire. They are excellent masks but they make me panic a little, forever on the verge of a hot flash as I walk through the market, filter sucking against my face with every breath. Endurance, it turns out, is not my forte.

As a child I would fantasize about traveling back in time with a sack of rice for Laura Ingalls. It seemed cruel to me that her family should spend the whole day grinding wheat when rice can be boiled using melted snow. A rib roast or fat back would have been better appreciated I'm sure, but that didn't occur to me. My ambition was to introduce a new type of food and educate the Ingalls family in the joys of low-effort cooking. What a smug, late-twentieth-century girl I was, with my convenience foods and my fancy diphtheria vaccination. Then again, perhaps my impulse came from a better place. I was the grandchild of Jewish communists—my grandma remained one until her dying day. "There's always bread in the Soviet Union," she insisted. "No one starves." Why should the Ingallses suffer because their country lured them westward to a place where no one could reach them when times got bad? Why not correct those ills by bending spacetime and sharing my food?

The grown-up Laura would not have appreciated my impulse. She was no fan of government support programs, though her parents had benefitted from the Homestead Act that granted free land to settlers. Wilder despised FDR, saw his New Deal as the sort of interference that robs citizens of autonomy and turns them into whiny children. Her daughter, Rose Wilder Lane, a widely-published author who collaborated with Laura on her eight-book Little House series, was passionate on the subject. "We have a dictator," she opined in her journal; to a friend she confessed she'd like to "kill that traitor." Rose and Laura's proto-Libertarian ideals are dug deep in the pages of the Little House series. The books are full of references to "free and independent" farmers beholden to no one and nothing but the whims of nature. The message of *The Long Winter* is clear: no one but ourselves can save us. The trains will stop running and those men in Washington never really cared about us. We're alone in this fight but for family and good neighbors. But if we all work very hard, twist enough hay and grind enough wheat and have enough faith in ourselves and in God, we'll come out on the other side of this crisis better than before.

It's pure fantasy of course, this American myth of self-reliance. It's also, let's face it, unapologetically white. Much has been made of the racism in Wilder's books. In 2018 the American Library Association removed her name from a children's literature award due in part to her crass portrayals of indigenous peoples and people of color. Laura's mother's insistence that "the only good Indian is a dead Indian" isn't the worst of it. Her father disagreed, after all, and readers are meant to listen to Pa, who is wise and unafraid and clearly Laura's favorite parent. What's worse is the larger message about westward expansion her books send by including some things and leaving others out. Twice we hear about settlers being removed by soldiers for squatting on Indian lands—once when Laura's family has to leave the cabin they built on the Osage reservation, again when we hear the story of Laura's uncle Tom Quiner, who went looking for gold in the Black Hills and had to be marched out of there by soldiers. "Oh, Tom," Laura's mother exclaims. "Had you nothing at all to show for all that work and danger?" Tom left the Black Hills with nothing just as Ma and Pa left Osage territory with little more than what they'd brought in—their sturdy, well-built cabin with the precious glass windows, their plow and their crops, all left behind. The child reader feels the loss deeply, how sad it is when the government makes hard-working folks waste a true labor of love. That child might be forgiven for not understanding that these were the exceptions that proved the rule, that the Ingalls family's life in the west was supported by a systematic campaign of genocide.

Then there's the minstrel show in *Little Town on the Prairie*, in which the men on stage are referred to as "darkies." Horrible, true, though as a child that word meant nothing to me—it went right over my head that the show was a parody of black entertainers. I'm sure I *did* understand what I now see as one of the most troubling lines in the Little House series, when Almanzo Wilder, who would later become Laura's husband, decides during the Hard Winter to make a dangerous trek on the open prairie to find wheat. "I'm free, white, and twenty-one," he says when his brother tries to stop him. "Anyway, this is a free country and I'm free and independent. I do as I please." The word "white" here is entirely gratuitous—there's no narrative reason whatsoever for that word—and yet there it is. The freedom to take a big risk, go where you want, do what you want, be brave and manly and save a town from starvation, is apparently a white people thing. I have no idea how I processed this as a ten-year-old. I wouldn't want my own children reading that line without some adult there to provide critical perspective.

What would Laura, and especially Rose—she of the FDR assassination fantasies—think of our 45th president? Here's a man who fails to provide any substantive guidance through the worst health crisis in a generation, who tells states it's up to them to decide how and when to reopen, then tweets "Liberate Michigan," egging on armed protesters. You could say he's the Little House fantasy commander-in-chief, the way he encourages us to embrace risk for economic gain, rip off those masks and get a haircut and splash around in the Lake of the Ozarks all free and independent. Until June when, in response to civil unrest after the police murder of George Floyd, he threatens to mobilize the US military against American citizens, calling himself the "law and order" president. Then he starts sounding less like a Libertarian dreamboat and more like a dictator. Would Laura and Rose have minded? I certainly hope so, but I can't say for sure. Those men in Washington are a royal pain when they tell you how to run your farm but just fine when they clear the way for westward expansion. Certain types of violence—slavery, for instance—have always been necessary to the American myth of self-sufficiency.

If survival narratives are fun, it's only because they are finite. Books come to an end and winter gives up the ghost. "It can't beat us," Pa tells Laura. "It's got to quit sometime and we don't." Well. Here it is deep springtime, nearly summer. Wild irises bloom in the ditch behind my house and Covid's on the rise in twenty-one states. This is what happens when you don't have steady, proactive central leadership, when your president downplays the threat and testing is botched and tracking doesn't happen and you miss your chance to control the spread. We're in this for the long haul, with all manner of hardship headed our way.

Today in my small upstate city, a thousand of us march to the police station. I'm in my most comfortable pandemic outfit—oversized tee and elastic-waist harem pants, cotton mask with a good, thick filter—trailing in the back of the pack with other middle-aged folks where we can maintain distance. There's little risk here. The cops give us a wide berth. I don't see any police on the street at all, just a few cruisers at far intersections blocking traffic to make way for us. At least 70% of the protesters are white. As America hobbles toward apocalypse I am neither heroic nor self-reliant, just dazed with grief. We reach the station and take a knee for George Floyd. My breath feels oppressive under my mask, the cotton plastered to my mouth and nose. Deal with it, I tell myself. Suck it the hell up. Plenty of air is getting through that filter; no one's knee is on your neck. I feel the pavement hard under my shin. I just keep going.

AUTISM IN THE TIME OF COVID: GUILT, HISTORIES, AND THE VILLAGE
Barbara Fischkin

GUILT

The Covid test for my son came back positive. Great, I told myself, first you gave him autism, now the plague. Bruno Bettelheim's long debunked theory that cold mothers caused autism had come back to haunt me. Dan, 32, has been unable to speak since he was three and a half, a rare case of Childhood Disintegrative Disorder. Doctors told my husband and me to expect the worst. *This*, they said, was as severe as it gets on the autism spectrum. The worst did not happen. As an adult, Dan has an active life. Still, he is far from cured. Due to his lack of speech and other disability-related deficits, he cannot live by himself or go anywhere alone. He lived with us until he was 22 and then moved to a nearby group home. It is a beautiful, well-furnished house and he has his own large room. Still, it *is* a group home. I do not know what happened to our once normal child; nobody does.

Dan appears to be healthy now. He has been symptom-free for weeks. He has, ahead of time, lost the 20 pounds he usually sheds in summer when he surfs the ocean. He looks like himself again, tall and solid, fashionably balding with a Roman profile. There do not seem to be any Covid after-effects, as many others report. But. . . can a mother tell such a thing from a distance of six feet? As I finish writing this on June 1, I have not been able to touch my son or even stand in the same indoor room with him since March 17. Seventy-six days. After 49 days, my husband and I were permitted curbside visits with him. It is as if our son were a restaurant permitted to offer take-out, but not delivery. Neither one of us has ever not seen him for this long, even in our long-ago days as foreign correspondents.

His movements and his usual activities have been severely curtailed as part of Corona-related New York State emergency guidelines. I believe these guidelines create a false sense of safety and discriminate against the disabled who live in group homes. Modified house arrest, I call it. No visitors inside, except for the staff who care for him and a nurse who comes once a week. Dan cannot leave his group home or his yard to go any farther than a short neighborhood walk with one of the staffers who help him. The state says these restrictions are needed because autism and other developmental disabilities often come with behavioral outbursts and sensory overload. In short: the state does not think Dan will keep a mask on in public. It thinks he will run close to people and cause a fuss, otherwise known in the worst of autism jargon as a "behavior," or a "meltdown." How, I ask, is this behavior different from the general population? As Dan's guardians, my husband and I could take him for an outing to a park or home for a day or for an overnight, as we often have done. But we have been warned it could be a long time before he would be permitted to return to the corner house— The Francis Avenue House—which has been a home he has loved for a decade. It is also the place where he gets the help he needs—the help he would need if anything happened to us. We are healthy, but we are 65. One never knows. Unmasked people are now among the throngs of those protesting the police murder of George Floyd, some making far more than a fuss. I deeply condemn police brutality against people of color. If I could get close enough to Dan to use the communication methods that work for both of us, I am sure he would tell me the same. I know his politics—and how he loves the diverse staffers who help him get through life. He would go with me to a "Black Lives Matter" protest in a flash—and all of those on Long Island have generally been peaceful. If only I could take him without making his own challenging life even more insecure. Without jeopardizing his ability to return to his home.

I think back to the Skype calls I had with him when he was sick. He looked like a wilted, life-sized Raggedy Andy. When I remember him like this, I worry. He had late-onset autism, why not late-onset aftereffects? I worry about his mental well-being. Restrictions like the ones under which he now lives deepen his anxiety. He likes to be out and about. The two vans used by his house stand idle. Often, two of his three housemates—both of whom tested positive and are now recovered—take those walks with him. They speak more than Dan but still only very little. I know them and I know they all know what is going on. And that there is a missing piece. One of the "guys," as we call them, was taken home by his mother when the pandemic hit. In May, she wrote to me that he was asymptomatic, never sick, but was testing positive and could not return until he tests negative. He has been gone for more than three months. He misses the guys and they him. That they live generally in harmony is amazing, since they have such distinct personalities and preferences. At the bottom of their first-floor steps it says: "A house divided. Giants versus Jets." That may be the most benign of their differences.

Depending on the hour, Dan tolerates a mask or doesn't. Friends, along with people I only know from Facebook, have, with an abundance of kindness, sent him different ones to try. His success with some of these is due to the fact that the group home staffers—all dedicated and most reprehensibly underpaid—constantly remind him to keep them on and at times it becomes habit. He seems to like a simple bandana best, which is what his father wears.

Yes, we could have taken him home. Whenever I hear from the mother who did take her son home from the Francis Avenue House, the guilt returns. This mother sent me a message that in regard to her son, no one "would have done a better job taking care of him than me. No one can. I am his mother." Gulp.

HISTORIES

I write this from a mother's point of view. But Dan's battle with the virus terrified his father as much as it did me. My husband harbors a sentimentality that quickly morphs from humor to despair. One day, a few weeks after Dan recovered, he and I hiked at a park that is special to father and son. "I hope some tree doesn't throw a dirty old pair of underpants back at me," my husband said. Like so many with autism, Dan has had gut issues. My husband then looked into the woods and wiped away a tear. Since then he has applied to be a New York State Covid Tracking supervisor. He now works as a professional investigator. Driven by Dan, he is determined to find out what the medical experts don't know. Just before Passover and Easter, my husband brought a care package with chocolate matzoh and chocolate bunnies to Dan's group home and left it on the front step for him. He peered into a window, hoping to get a glimpse of Dan. He didn't, and it broke his heart.

Dan's full name is Daniel David Mulvaney. He is also known as Danny—and in adulthood, with affection, as: "Dan the Man." He was the baby to whom I, his Jewish mother, sang "Danny Boy" off-key to celebrate his father's Celtic roots. His Hebrew name is Dovid ben Yacov. His Irish name is Donal Mulvenna MacSeamus.

The story of Dan, as we know him now, began in 1990 in Hong Kong, back when my husband and I were foreign correspondents. I gave birth to Dan in Mexico City and we moved to Asia when he was 18 months old. By the time he was three, he spoke English communicatively, as well as words and phrases in Spanish, Cantonese, and Tagalog. Fortunately, we have the clunky old hardware from a video camera to prove this. If someone had told me this story before it happened to Dan, I would have thought they were nuts. My little boy had straight blonde hair, cut Buster Brown style, large brown eyes, and long eyelashes. And little legs with small muscles that startled me with their definition. He started to fall apart that autumn. He chewed his T-shirts to rags, developed ear infections, did not like to be around other children, apart from the baby brother he alternately adored and challenged, like any kid with a new sibling. Eventually, Dan needed hospitalization for a raging fever and dehydration. Even then he could speak. My husband had our son Jack in his arms and Dan said, "Put my baby brother on my bed." After recovering, he slowly began to lose his language. A run-of-the-mill British pediatrician in Hong Kong diagnosed "superior intelligence. . . he knows the world is a mess."

"Huh?" I said.

Back home on Long Island, Dan was tested, re-tested, and ultimately diagnosed. The team at the Yale Child Clinic predicted he would never recover, wear a diaper his entire life, and be institutionalized by the age of ten. Dan lived with us until he was 22, on Long Island, in California, and then back again on Long Island, in a house that's become the family base and where we still reside. Over the years, he's learned to swim, surf the ocean, farm, ice skate, play modified ice hockey, ride horses and groom them, and create abstract art. He also learned how to use a wheelbarrow, a lawnmower, a rototiller, a sewing machine thanks to a former art teacher, a simple loom thanks to his current one, an iPad—and the toilet. He has learned all this even though he still cannot speak more than a few words and then only if he tries very hard. That he needs an aide with him all the time does not tell the whole story. It is too passive. What he needs—and gets at his group home—is constant support and prompting. After he graduated with a "disability" degree from our local public high school, we jumped at the rare chance he had to move to the Francis Avenue House, in a leafy neighborhood in the inland hamlet of Baldwin. Dan jumped at the chance, too. I had always taught him "independence is the key." And although he would have that round-the-clock staff, he liked the idea of not being stuck with his parents for the rest of his life. To be honest, we were also tired. Dan has come a long way, but he was—and on occasion continues to be—a handful.

Doctors *have* suggested that Dan's autism was caused by a virus. Which one? None of them know. Pictures of the foul, red-crowned novel Coronavirus nauseate me. But at least I know what it looks like. On one of those Skype calls, when Dan was very sick, I assured him he was not "a political prisoner," but rather quarantined in his bedroom to keep other people from catching it. His receptive language has always been good, as if he'd lost his voice but not his ability to understand. He seems to get our family's dark and sarcastic humor, despite his regression. Once, when he was eight, my husband told him he had plumber's butt and he immediately pulled up his pants. On the "you-are-not-a-political-prisoner" day I studied Dan's face and saw his signature sardonic smile. I took this to mean he got the joke but didn't necessarily like it. Perhaps he was again considering the possibility that his mother can be a jerk. Good, I thought. How sick can he be?

"Danny," I said. "I know this is hard but you need to be isolated because the health of so many is at stake." His smile turned to a serious nod. He watches CNN and demonstrated that he understands—and cares. "You are being a good citizen," I said.

The truth: with these restrictions on him now, I am thinking he *is* a political prisoner. It hit me hard when Trump said he will order states to permit houses of worship to open. Thousands of people may be able to gather together, and my son can't take a ride in a group home van.

THE VILLAGE

With Covid, as with everything else in Dan's life, it takes a village. In good times and bad, the villagers appear in many forms.

Dan's speech therapist, Tammy Neumann, has worked with

him since high school. She is one of the most-enduring villagers, as is Dan's surfing teacher in Long Beach, Cliff Skudin. Among the newest is the food writer Sara Heegaard, who lives with Dan's brother Jack. "What kind of cake does Dan like?" she asked, as his birthday approached last September. Apart from being a consummate baker, Sara understands that speech is not the only way to express opinions and preferences. For Dan, this is crucial.

If I named *all* for whom I feel grateful, this would be an encyclopedia. It would start with his father and his brother, now a New York City Special Education public school teacher. It would include a panoply of relatives, friends, therapists, support staffers, farmers, and teachers who have worked and communed well with Dan over the years. The best of those who work with him, love him, and also love what they do. They presume his competence and work to give him more independence. Apart from family, many move on. Or we replace them.

Now, as our family navigates autism in the time of Covid, I think back to January 1, 2018 when Laura Curran was sworn in as our first female Nassau County Executive. Yes, I felt proud for women that day, confident that Curran, a former newspaper reporter and kindred spirit, would do a great job. Mostly, though, I exhaled with the familiar relief that helps me sleep at night. Someone from the village was now important, as well. Curran lives a few blocks away from Dan's group home. She always greets him and his housemates when she sees them in the neighborhood. She, too, calls them "the guys." This year she has deftly handled the pandemic in our county with leadership, clear, honest information, warmth, and grit. I did not contact Laura when Dan first tested positive. She seemed pretty busy. Still, she kept an eye out for the residents of The Francis Avenue House. "Saw the guys on a walk yesterday," she wrote us as the pandemic lessened. She also assured us that she had an advisory committee which, among so many other tasks, would look at how and when to help reopen the Oyster Bay farm where Dan and others with autism plant, raise, and harvest crops.

Like so many, our family did not imagine the pandemic would hit New York as it did, or that we would need the village, in whatever form it might take, more than ever. We should have known this on March 11 when the upcoming New York City St. Patrick's Day parade was cancelled for the first time since it began in 1762. An omen, if there ever was one. The parade, always held precisely on St. Patrick's Day, March 17, is special to Dan. When my parents died from natural causes during my pregnancy, Dan's paternal grandparents took over. They, too, have now passed away. But Dan heard their stories. He knew they came from a long line of hardworking Irish immigrants. He'd heard about roots in Northern Ireland, in Derry and in County Cork in the Irish Republic. He'd heard that in America, his relatives had become NYPD patrolmen and officers, public school teachers, and more. The grandfather Dan knew, a celebrated criminal attorney, was a regular at school meetings where we requested services for Dan. "I am here as grandpa, not as an attorney," he would say, but it had an effect. So did Dan's paternal grandmother, a doctorate-level special educator who called upon her coterie of expert friends to advocate for him.

It is for them that Dan marches in the parade every year. Despite the concentration deficits that come with autism, he always makes it up Fifth Avenue, wearing an Aran sweater, doing his distinctive jig or carrying a shillelagh without mishap. People who recognize he has autism shout "good job!" at him from the sidelines. Code words for "we know." With good-natured skepticism, Dan stops at St. Patrick's Cathedral each year to be blessed by one cardinal or archbishop or another, even though their prayers have never brought back his speech.

Thinking of this, in mid-March we foolishly worried more about the effect the parade cancellation would have on Dan than the oncoming pandemic. So we made him lunch at the Long Beach home of his childhood. There was Irish smoked salmon, one of Dan's favorites. Then we took our best shot at a distanced walk on the local boardwalk. Dan walked much faster than usual, as if he truly were in a quick-moving parade.

St. Patrick's Day was the last time I was able to get close enough to my son to touch him. The next day, the large agency which runs his group home—and whose actions and license are monitored by the New York State Office for People with Developmental Disabilities (OPWDD)—shut out everyone not essential. The round-the-clock group home staffers could come for their shifts, after having their temperatures taken and providing acceptable answers to questions regarding their exposure. Anyone who arrived with symptoms could not work until a physician deemed them free from illness for at least 14 days. Except for the staff and a nurse, it was: "Nobody In. Nobody Out." No therapists. No communication class from Tammy the speech therapist, no art teacher, no supervisors. No parents, siblings, guardians, or other visitors. No. No. No.

This sheltering in place also cut off my son's most effective avenues of communication. Since he was four, I have been using a technique called facilitated communication with him, in which he requires the trained touch of someone else to prompt him to choose on his own terms the letters he needs on a keyboard. Educators at two universities—Syracuse and Chapman—have validated his communication. Locally, speech therapist Tammy and I are the only ones trained to use this technique with Dan. With this support, he can express ideas. Tammy likes to pose stimulating questions. Months earlier she asked him: "Are women smarter than men?" With minimal sensory support from her—compared to earlier years—he typed, with characteristic mistakes: *"Men pretend to knolw more."* Sadder, as I look over his more recent pre-lockdown communiques is one which says: *"I maamaake day progfram fun. . . program old people."* This was right after he began to work at the nursing home, which was now as closed to the world as so many nursing homes were, as the

Francis Avenue House was as well.

Dan and his father and brother have their own often foolproof way of communication with Dan. I see it as a meeting of the Mulvaney male minds, a critical one. But that was shut off, too. Also, on his iPad Dan has an app called Proloquo2Go which he uses to point to phrases such as "I want," and then to photos of foods, activities and people. But none of the staff are trained to use this with him, although many try. Many also have a sixth sense that enables them to understand Dan. Some have been able to inspire him to say a few words—and even sing a few during a karaoke night. But would those staffers be on duty? Or sick or scared? And even if they were working, with an accelerated staff shortage would any of them have time?

It all sounded like a death knell, and indeed, a number of residents of group homes in the Nassau AHRC, the nonprofit that runs Dan's group home, and other similar agencies would die. Most, I believe, were elderly. All mourned by bereft staff, perhaps as much as they were mourned by relatives and friends. Fortunately, the guys all survived. I worried about a staffer named Cardinal who has an autistic son himself, and—as a very tall, thin black man—has enthusiastically marched with us in a few St. Patrick's Day parades to be there if Dan needs help.

On the morning of March 25, Liz, the group home manager, woke me early to tell me my son was very sick. I shook myself awake. I shook my husband awake. Dan was running fevers at heights he had not known since the childhood hospitalization that ultimately led to his regression into autism. What would be the end result of this? I insisted he be tested for the Coronavirus and emailed yet another member of the village, Dr. Mary Mulqueen. She is Danny's primary care physician and has known him for years. Before medical school, she was a counselor at Camp Loyaltown, the AHRC sleepaway camp. Mary, as I call her, or Doc Mary—when I remember to do so—told me the medical clinic on the grounds of the agency had very few kits.

She did not think she could corral one for Dan. She never lies to me. Still, I was determined. We had to know with what we were dealing, particularly since Dan cannot speak. I had an ace in the hole, albeit one that broke my heart. I called a "village elder," so to speak, the youthful Shaun Weathers, who is the AHRC's Senior Director of Program Operations. He also speaks the truth and gets things done, even when I also give him a hard time about some agency lapse or another. I told him that before we saw Dan on St. Patrick's Day, I had been in contact with someone who I since learned had tested positive. "This changes the picture," he said.

Dan was tested March 26 with positive results on March 27. Cardinal took care of him. Then he was sent home with symptoms.

Immediately I applied to the state for my husband and I to be tested. Two weeks later they called us to a tent at Jones Beach, where a doctor looking kindly behind his mask stuck a tube down our noses and into our throats. For about two seconds it hurt in a strange way. The next day the results came back negative. Gradually, as the country began to learn some of the Coronavirus's mysteries, so did we. We realized that all that negative test meant is that we did not have Covid-19 on the day we were tested. Did this mean I did not give Covid to my son? Or that I am an asymptomatic carrier? Or that we merely did not have the virus on the day we were tested? We still do not know. There was much talk at the beginning of this nightmare about someone like Dan having immunity. Now that is far from clear. Which test? Which vaccine? Whose plasma? Whose reinfection? These questions revolve through my mind as if the answers will provide the key to the survival of the planet. Maybe they will. Or won't. Children don't get Covid-19, and then, suddenly, a hundred in New York have something like it that makes them very ill. We wind up to answers and then wind down to knowing nothing. To me it sounds alarmingly like autism, where more than three decades after the numbers of affected children began to increase geometrically, all those questions linger.

The village shrank even more. More people called in sick. Liz, who was pregnant with her first child, finally agreed to stop working and retreat to her own, private apartment in the group home. She was "replaced" with a group manager who would do double duty—her own house a few minutes away had nine "guys." As Dan's sickness and fever prevailed, at least two staffers were doing too-long shifts at Francis Avenue. They were exhausted and told me so.

Then, a miracle occurred.

Victor Cabral arrived to help the staff at the house. We had not seen him in a long time. He had been working elsewhere at the AHRC. But in our lives, he is mythic. Like Doc Mary, he worked at the AHRC sleepaway camp Dan attended and also helped us at home before Dan moved to Francis Avenue. He is half Dan's size, but over the years he has moved effortlessly in response to any challenge Dan offered. And he still lets us tease him about the time we visited Dan at camp and Victor threw Jack, still a kid, in the pool. Jack had his new—and first—cellphone in the pocket of his jeans. Around the time Victor arrived at Francis Avenue, the agency seemed to be in a beyond-reality staff crisis. He came in and did the work of many people. I am not sure of the timing—because I could not be there—but Dan's two other housemates may have already been sick by then. Sick or active, it was work.

Crisis again. Victor had to leave to get to another group home that was in peril of being without any staff. He got there in time—and then came back to do more Francis Avenue shifts. I can't help thinking there was some inexplicable "magic" connected with Victor's presence. But after he arrived for what we knew would be a temporary stint and then left, staffing seemed to fall into place.

And slowly Dan got better. His fevers popped up and

down, but never as high as before. He had a cough for a while, then it too subsided. The day program, led from home by AHRC veteran Dorothy DeMarco, sprang into action. Two staffers went to work with the guys at the house, also risking their health. They baked. They got him back on Facebook and posted photos. He started practicing surf pop-ups in the basement, where he also learned some boxing. Angel, a staffer who has worked with Dan before, was there—and the familiarity calmed me further. In the yard, they played basketball. Soon they were permitted to take walks. The walks were too short. I complained. The walks got longer.

Soon my husband and I were able to make those curbside visits. The first was May 5. Cinco de Mayo. More magic. The three of us had celebrated it together in Mexico City, eight months after I'd given birth to Dan. Now, Dan came out of the front door, dutifully wearing a disposable mask and with the stunned look of a political prisoner wondering about his fate. In the best of scenarios, a bridge would appear on his street followed by a noir trade-off of detainees. Would Dan be permitted to go for a longer walk in exchange for five Russian spies? We had more visits, including one on Mother's Day. Now we go every Sunday at six, bringing him bags of treats. He stays on the steps, sometimes with prompts from an aide, and my husband and I stay on the sidewalk. That he can do this now is amazing, as a little boy with autism he often ran away. We've found him at the grocery store, on a boat parked in a neighbor's driveway, where he had found a bag of Cheez Doodles—and at the police station after they called and said, "he won't talk to us." That really happened.

I have written to OPWDD saying that if people can go to the beach, so can Dan. They still say that if I do there this is no telling when I can bring him back. A week and a half ago they told me they were working on it. As they work, I wait.

Cardinal is well enough to be back working a bit. I long to

see him again, back in his usual mode, a frenzy of activity and caring. Liz had her baby and although she is still on leave, she wheels the baby boy on the neighborhood streets and stops at the window of the living room in the guys' part of the house. Recently she stopped to sweetly remind Dan to be quiet in the night so the baby can sleep. The locked door to her apartment is down the hall from his room. Sometimes he makes noises of frustration at night and hits his head with his hands. It stopped for a while after Liz asked him to be quiet—and has only returned once or twice since.

Day Program Dorothy, it turns out, has experience with Proloquo2Go. The other day, one of her staffers at Francis Avenue told me on a Skype call that while using the app, Dan touched the words "I want" with total independence. When asked to finish the sentence, he went to the square that read "vacation."

He wants a vacation.

I'll bet he does.

LIVING BETWEEN TWO WORLDS
Cheryl Pearl Sucher

It was the middle of January and my Kiwi husband and I were packing for our annual holiday to our other home in New Zealand. The Covid-19 virus was wreaking havoc in Wuhan, China but seemed confined to that Asian province. However, in the short time between preparing to leave and the actual date of our departure, January 28, Wuhan was cut off from the world as the Chinese authorities prevented all forms of transportation from entering or leaving the city. While the number of those affected beyond Wuhan were still minimal—570 infected and 17 dead—we were concerned and consulted my cousin, who is an infectious disease specialist. He believed, as many then did, that Covid-19 would fade away like the last pandemic virus SARS, affecting most only as a bad flu. Both my husband and I were still working—my husband in Trenton, New Jersey, while I commuted a few days a week to my part-time job hosting author conversations and curating the cookbook and travel sections at McNally Jackson, an independent bookstore in downtown Manhattan.

I left for New Zealand a day before my husband, who gave me the single N-95 mask that we use when we work on the eternal renovation of our 1860 historic cottage. Since flying to New Zealand from New Jersey requires four flights totaling 24 hours, we usually divide our travel into two parts, staying overnight with close friends in California before boarding the fourteen-hour flight to Auckland. After landing in San Francisco, I called my husband to tell him that I had arrived safely. As California is the major American gateway for flights from China, he wanted to know if people in the airport were wearing face masks. I saw a few, but they seemed to be the exception and not the rule. "We're safe," I said, as I truly felt we were.

While on the plane from San Francisco to Auckland, we crossed the international Date Line, arriving in New Zealand two days after take-off. During my flight, the World Health Organization declared that the outbreak of Covid-19 was a global health emergency. On January 31, I landed in Auckland in inclement weather that brought torrential storms to the South Island, forcing many of the nation's heralded Great Walks to close indefinitely for the first time in years. The only obstacle I encountered during my long plane journey was when the plane from Auckland to Napier was diverted to Palmerston North due to squalls that wouldn't allow it to land. The pilot made that decision in the air, and so we flew north, where we collected our luggage and boarded a bus that was to add an additional three hours to my already lengthy journey. My husband landed the next day.

Our three weeks in New Zealand were bucolic. We were able to see friends and family and even escape to the South Island to spend a few days in Dunedin, where we had lived during the early years of our marriage. We rented an SUV and ventured through the luscious Ida Valley, visiting a few vineyards and discovering the set of Jane Campion's new film *The Power of the Dog*, built to resemble a mid-nineteenth-century Montana ranch. After blowing out a tire on the gravel roads, we came to rest as guests of friends at the famed Millbrook Golf Resort and visited nearby Arrowtown, a rehabilitated gold rush village. We strolled through Queenstown, the adventure capital of the Southern Hemisphere as well as the bolt-hole for American billionaires looking to build escape homes in the event of the apocalypse.

After a week's holiday, we flew north to Auckland to meet with family members before traveling home, learning only then that the American President had suspended entry into the US by any foreign nationals who had traveled to China during the previous fourteen days. By this date, 213 people had died and nearly 9,800 had been infected worldwide. But in New Zealand, the weather was still stunning, the scourge a distant malady even as both the US and New Zealand closed their ports to air travelers from China. As I entered the gate for my plane to San Francisco, Air New Zealand representatives checked my passport and asked if I had traveled to China during the previous two weeks. No one took my temperature, and other than swathing my hands in sanitizer, I buckled myself into my seat in anticipation of the fourteen-hour plane ride to San Francisco, my only worry being whether or not I had enough time to watch the entire first season of HBO's series *Succession*, a dramatization of the dynastic greed that seems to have gripped my homeland.

I landed in the United States on February 18, my husband having arrived a few days before me to go back to work in Trenton. The airports were packed with travelers and no one was wearing face masks or protective gear. It took a while for me to find my suitcase before calling an Uber to drive me home.

During my holiday, I hadn't even thought about the relative safety of New Zealand. But within a few weeks of our arrival home in New Jersey, the New Zealand Prime Minister, Jacinda Ardern, would shut down the country, prohibiting most international travel and domestic transportation, as well. She commanded the population of five million to remain within their intimate bubbles and because her leadership was firm but also compassionate, the country obeyed her singular lead. After six weeks of careful scrutiny, the Coronavirus appeared to be completely eradicated in Aotearoa, the Land of the Long White Cloud.

Our first few weeks back in the US were active but calm. There was an uptick in Coronavirus cases and illness clusters in the New York suburb of Westchester, as well as on cruise ships that were not allowed to land. However, as March began, the Coronavirus was already moving with the rapidity of a Los

Angeles wildfire. By March 9, there were 500 cases recorded in the United States and on March 11, the World Health Organization declared that the Coronavirus outbreak "could be considered a pandemic." That same day, the Italian Prime Minister ordered a lockdown of the Lombardy region. Photographs of overcrowded emergency rooms monitored by frontline medical professionals dressed like futuristic Abominable Snowmen appeared on the Instagram feeds of Italian colleagues, captioned by such dire warnings as "This is going to be you in two weeks." Harrowing photos of empty cathedrals stacked high with empty wooden coffins bracketed videos of quarantined Milanese apartment dwellers appearing on their balconies to applaud spontaneous vocal recitals. Dolphins were dancing in the Venetian canals bereft of gondolas and *vaporetti*. As native species reclaimed their natural habitats and Il Duomo in Florence emptied of its relentless crowds to allow the singer Andrea Bocelli to serenade the world on Easter Sunday by singing the melodic plaint of Schubert's *Ave Maria*, it seemed as if the planet were rebelling against our incessant abuses.

At home, the crowds on New Jersey Transit were dispersing. I had no difficulty claiming a seat during rush hour, and the teeming masses of commuters scrambling through the halls of Pennsylvania Station were starting to thin out. Cleaners were everywhere, as were the growing numbers of the homeless claiming their spots in the station's empty expanses. The subway was similarly devoid of the usual rush-hour crowds, but no one as yet was venturing forth dressed in personal protective gear. The bookstore was still open but our familiar neighborhood customers were starting to disappear, relocating to their vacation homesteads, replaced by tourists who were sheltering on their way back to their homelands. Some stores were voluntarily closing, as many of my colleagues seemed anxious about their commute and started to voluntarily furlough themselves for fear of infecting their families. The two American pastimes, baseball and basketball, were canceling games or postponing their seasons, and governors and mayors were debating whether to shut schools down before the annual spring break. Soon all theater productions and live concerts were called off, and within days, schools and everything but essential businesses were closed, the latter subjected to strict rules of social distancing. Now everyone was scrambling to find surgical masks and disposable gloves and going shopping for two weeks at a time, learning how to keep fit by taking virtual exercise classes and planning virtual cocktails with distant friends. It was Passover when the lockdown began, and we held our ritual seder on the computer, hosting friends and family from their individual bubbles. My friend celebrated her birthday in lockdown, Zooming in friends from as far away as South Africa and London. When we visited one another online, we began by asking everyone where they were, what they were doing, what was their lowest moment, and what was the best thing to happen to them during the quarantine. Most appreciated the fact that they were suddenly able to spend long hours with loved ones as the demands of their work and study days had often kept them far apart for long periods of time. We all remarked how it felt as though we were reliving the Passover plagues as boils, fires, and scourges ravaged our planet, but we similarly believed that through faith and love and virtual togetherness, we would make it through.

We didn't know how long our quarantine would last, nor who would survive it. During the first weeks, we made contact with relatives and friends all over the world, many of whom we hadn't seen or spoken to for a long time. There was an eerie resemblance to my experience of 9/11. Even though my husband and I were then living in Dunedin, New Zealand, I had gone home to my Manhattan apartment a few days before that tragic day to celebrate the Jewish New Year and visit my parents' graves, as was my custom. On the day, I was one of the few individuals whose Internet connection was still operative and thus was able to communicate with my New Zealand family as well as many anxious friends and family members eager to discover the whereabouts of their loved ones. After being turned away from the local Red Cross Center, where lines of individuals were waiting to donate blood for survivors who never appeared, I spent the day communicating with people near and far, learning of those who had escaped the Twin Towers on foot, or walked across the Brooklyn Bridge from their downtown offices, or traveled in minions uptown to cross to Queens or the Bronx, or to the ferry terminals to Staten Island and New Jersey. I was able to locate all the individuals who had not communicated with their loved ones; until very late that evening, that is, when I learned that the sister of a friend I was supposed to meet for drinks that night had been lost, as she worked for Cantor Fitzgerald on the 104th floor of the first tower to fall. After the initial shock, I reported to Radio New Zealand on the crisis from my Upper West Side apartment. On the first day international flights resumed, I flew home to Dunedin to the relief of my New Zealand friends and family and the hopes of my New York community.

The irony was, it was toward the end of that first week of quarantine that I learned of the illnesses and deaths of people close to me. The mother of a good friend, who had recently survived eighteen months of intensive cancer treatment, contracted Covid at the beginning of April. She was never intubated, but instead made comfortable. Her family agreed to move her from her adult living facility to hospice. She told everyone that she was done. My friend was living in Florida and her mother in New Jersey. She spent her mother's last days communicating with her on an iPad.

Soon afterwards, I learned that one of the few remaining friends of my parents' circle of survivors, a German woman who had converted to Judaism after meeting and marrying one of my father's closest friends and poker players, contracted the virus and died, overnight.

In the interim, Covid-19 cases have been completely eradicated in New Zealand, despite a recent hiccup where two visitors from the United Kingdom were released from quarantine on compassionate grounds without first being tested for the Coronavirus, and subsequently drove from Auckland to Wellington to meet with friends. They were then discovered to have the Coronavirus, and the Prime Minister, lauded all over the world for her empathy and firm action in closing the country down in time to save the lives of thousands, was not amused. She subsequently instructed the New Zealand Defense Forces to oversee the quarantine of new arrivals and audit the process. Regardless, the country has returned to its new normal. Shops have re-opened, as have restaurants and museums. One can actually go for a haircut or sit with friends at a bar and enjoy a cocktail. My husband and I are wondering why we are not there, knowing that we cannot return until we figure out how we will earn our livelihood, which was the reason we returned to the United States four years ago. For the moment, we are working from our home in New Jersey as the state prepares to open for the summer. I am writing and receiving unemployment until the bookstore opens to the public, while my husband maintains computer systems for the state. We are wondering if we will be able to return to New Zealand for our annual visit in March 2021. We have virtual chats with my elderly in-laws on a weekly basis, sharing gardening tips and praising New Zealand while assuring them that we are all right, that the recent protests against racial injustice and police brutality are the necessary steps toward establishing the true equality promised by our constitution. Friends offer to send us their PPE as they no longer need them. We tell them we are grateful for their concern, that we are well stocked, but for the time being we have to remain in place, mostly because there is no way to travel internationally except by private charters, but also because we have a job to do—supporting those fighting for social justice and civil rights.

We hold up New Zealand and its firm, compassionate leader as a beacon to the world, hoping to once again live safely and securely between our two worlds.

HOPE IN THE AGE OF COVID
Liesl Schillinger

When the news of the Covid-19 epidemic emerged from China in January, alongside shocking images of the residents of Wuhan (population 11 million), I felt a sense of alarm, but not, as yet, dread. Watching footage of hazmat-suited rescue workers delivering baskets of food to quarantined apartment dwellers—who pulled the baskets into their windows on ropes, like the woman who hauls her little dog up and down in *Rear Window*—I mostly was struck by how surreal everything looked. The crisis felt far away, outlandish, fictional, dystopian—it felt like something that couldn't happen here, in the United States; at least, not so gravely. Thinking of the recent SARS and Ebola epidemics, I told myself that, although they had been serious, they had been quashed pretty swiftly. Wouldn't that happen this time? But soon the virus started jumping continents; it spread to Europe, to the United States, then to Africa and South America. In late February, I still was able to read a catastrophist essay in *The New York Times* with a certain sense of detachment. The author, a science reporter, advocated a Wuhan-style reaction to the virus, wherever it landed. The headline read: "To Take On the Coronavirus, Go Medieval on It." Surely it won't come to that?, I thought. Two weeks later, New York went into lockdown.

My first refuge in any crisis is books. This has been true since I first learned to read and became, almost simultaneously, a reader and *re*-reader. Any favorite novel becomes a kind of Bible for me, which I mine for *sortes*. When something is out of balance in my life, I will choose a book, as if choosing a prescription, to steady my keel, guided by its stable vision and sure direction, its specific or general insights, and its cohesive portrait of humanity in turbulent times, smoothed by the writer's hindsight, empathy, and, sometimes, humor. Through writers like Trollope, Waugh, Tolstoy, Naipaul, Austen, I could disappear into other worlds whenever I wanted a break from mine. There's a line from the 1970 song by Melanie, "Look What They've Done to My Song, Ma," that has always resonated with me: "Wish I could find a good book to live in."

But in mid-March, as the gravity of the Covid-19 epidemic hit home, I turned to literature not for escape but for information on past precedent; to seek reassurance that a time of plague, like most vicissitudes, could be endured, and to see how that had been done in fiction's pages. Even the darkest of these novels gave me hope. I began by rereading Camus's *The Plague*, which startled me with its point-for-point parallels with the present-day American reaction to the crisis earlier this year: the reluctance of the public and of officialdom to admit the gravity of the situation. From there, I moved to something lighter—Kathleen Winsor's historical bodice-ripper *Forever Amber* (which I'd last read in junior high), in which the shrewd, lusty, lowborn heroine tends to her beloved Lord Bruce Carlton when he's stricken by plague during London's Black Death in the seventeenth century. (He survives.)

Knowing that the details of Winsor's chapters were drawn from other plague accounts, real and fictional, that I hadn't read, I ordered half a dozen novels and novellas concerning epidemics of one kind or another (some were allegorical), written from the fourteenth century to the twenty-first. There was Boccaccio's *Decameron* (plague); Daniel Defoe's *Journal of the Plague Year* (plague); Katherine Anne Porter's *Pale Horse, Pale Rider* (influenza); Thomas Mann's *Death in Venice* (cholera) and *Magic Mountain* (tuberculosis); José Saramago's *Blindness* (a plague of sudden blindness); and Ling Ma's *Severance* (late-capitalist zombies). I was not alone in this instinct: all these books quickly became bestsellers. It stirred and consoled me to see how many people also had the reflex of turning to literature as remedy and guide. It showed me that many millions of us were in this together, each in our separate shelters.

Picking up Defoe's novel about the Black Death in London (1665–66), which was informed in part by diaries kept by his uncle, I discovered a tactic, a strategy that the uncle had apparently adopted and which I immediately annexed. He had kept lists of the death counts in London parishes, charting the rise and fall of cases in the neighborhoods around him in order to navigate his imperiled city with a proper sense of the risks he might encounter on a given street. Defoe's uncle had chosen to stay in London during the Black Death (against the advice of his brother, Defoe's father). His business actually prospered that year (he was a saddler, a good profession to be in at a time when saddled horses were in demand). Almost one year in, the narrator repents his choice, saying, "Though providence seemed to direct my conduct to be otherwise, yet it is my opinion, and I must leave it as a prescription, viz., *that the best physic against the plague is to run away from it.*" (Italics his.)

I kept that in mind, but in New York City in March, April, and May of this year, I could not run away. I was trapped in the city because I have no car (nor horse and saddle), and public transportation was dangerous during those peak months. Still, following Defoe's lead, I began keeping a daily log of Covid statistics—international, national, and local—taking the figures from the online Johns Hopkins Coronavirus map. Updating those numbers each morning and organizing them into lists gave me a small but important sense of control. It made me feel like I was at least doing something. My first job in New York— which I held for fourteen years—was working as a fact checker at *The New Yorker*. That job had taught me that any situation, however complicated, could be made more straightforward, more reconcilable, if you nailed down the facts surrounding it. Determining the facts, and knowing how to fix them when they were wrong, made a story clearer and more valuable.

Checking facts is anxious work, but once you've accepted it as your duty, it gives you a sense of security. You learn that if you inform yourself on a subject, even a complicated one, you can avoid unpleasant surprises. And you also learn, from the scroll of history, that paths to progress often emerge, improbably, from the worst setbacks and blunders. No, you could not solve the calamities of the past or the confusions of the present, but you could at least understand them correctly. This gives you hope. In 1947, in his novel *The Plague*, Camus wrote of "the gradual loss of hope in a better future" that crushed the townspeople of Oran when plague shut their city down. I did not want to be crushed like the fictional inhabitants of Oran. Facts were my shield against loss of hope, my arsenal for the future.

On March 30, the day I began my Covid tally, I had only four categories: World, United States, New York State, and New York City. The sole statistic I tracked was the number of reported cases. Two weeks later, as the virus spread and the numbers climbed, I added nine countries to my watch list, plus half a dozen states and the three counties where my parents and brothers live. I also added another statistic to the chart: Deaths. By June 2, the day I piled my possessions into my dad's SUV and drove out of New York, the number of worldwide Covid-19 cases had risen from under 750,000 to more than six million; the number of cases in the U.S. had increased more than tenfold and was approaching two million; and New York State had more than 370,000 cases, of which about 200,000 came from my city.

That morning's tally showed me that numbers alone could not help me correctly understand America's post-Corona future, after all. That was because a pattern had emerged alongside the pandemic in this country: a pattern of setbacks and blunders of a kind I recognized from other nations and other centuries, which I had not expected to see in my own nation, in the twenty-first century. The American president and his administration had ignored the facts that the numbers proved; had ignored the advice of medical experts and epidemiologists; had failed to consider the consequences of past plagues; and had failed to implement a prudent national strategy to quell the epidemic. The reasons for their inaction (and in some cases, negative action) were ideological and had nothing to do with public safety. This meant, I saw, that the novel Coronavirus would proceed unchecked in America as long as it liked, indifferent to political considerations, pursuing its own multiplication and meeting no resistance. I thought then of what Daniel Defoe's narrator wrote with hindsight, in September of 1665, long into his city's epidemic: "the best physic against the plague is to run away from it."

It was that insight that took me, guiltily, out of New York City for two months. I worried that leaving was cowardly. But really, it was a case of proper judgment, shored up by facts and buttressed by literature. The virus was still present, and though New York in 2020, like London in 1665, had good government that kept the situation from becoming worse than it might have been, the virus was still present and spreading across the country. To revive my "hope in a better future," I needed to revive my spirits, my confidence, my hope. Books alone were no longer enough. A little before noon, my father and I drove out of my street, turned left on Second Avenue, and passed the boarded-up bars and bodegas (their windows had been smashed on previous days, reminding me of the "multitude of rogues" Defoe's narrator describes in plague-era London), turned right on Houston, passed the boarded-up Whole Foods, and headed straight for the Holland Tunnel, the car's windows rolled all the way down. Both of us wore masks; neither of us was sure I was not infectious, though I'd tested negative a few weeks earlier. It was the first time I'd been in a vehicle for ten weeks. I hadn't anticipated how exhilarating and liberating it would feel to be in motion, the wind in my hair, the city retreating behind me, the landscape rising and undulating, rivers streaking silver, the asphalt gray ribbon of American highway unrolling reliably ahead and behind, and then, as we neared Shenandoah County, farmsteads and barns, pastures, Angus cattle, hay bales, horses, hills.

We pulled into town around five pm. The sun was bright, the air languid; the leaves of the trees seemed to float. The car slowed, making its final turn, and eased onto our sleepy street lined with old Victorian houses wrapped in front porches and picket fences and ruffled with oak leaf hydrangea and day lilies. The hamlet where my parents live is cradled by two mountains in the Alleghenies: Massanutten, rising green and square-edged in the east, and North Mountain, darker and less distinct, in the west. Painted from above, the town would look like a Tolkien shire. Getting out of the car, I saw my mother on the porch, beaming and a little a-tilt (she has Parkinson's), flanked by her basset hounds, who were baying and hurling themselves at the porch gate with joy, eager to jump up on me. As I stepped over the gate and the dogs to greet her, I felt the invisible clamp loosen that had closed tightly around me for three months. I had not realized its presence until I felt its absence.

After two months in Virginia, I returned to New York for the month of August. In Virginia, grounded in stable and familiar surroundings, cocooned by my parents' educational idealism (they're both retired professors), I had recovered my self-assurance. Within a couple of weeks, I was teaching a summer school book club on plague literature (on Zoom, from a study up in the attic). Week by week, memories of the tensions of the past three months of isolation, agitation, and uncertainty faded, replaced by a renewed sense of determination and purpose. In retrospect, I think it was the "superstructure" of home that made this possible, restoring my faith that this country would outlast this plague, would endure, and might even get better. This idea of "superstructure" comes down to the idea that a conviction of solidity creates solidity—even when that conviction is based on illusion. "Superstructure," by this definition, is the social framework that gives a person the conviction that solid, supporting structures exist that will allow them to act with confidence and agency. My upbringing gave me that conviction, and later on, in Manhattan, so did my community. But for many in the mercantilist America of the last half century, where a devil-take-the-hindmost mindset has steadily eroded or removed protections for the majority of the population, such a conviction is increasingly hard to sustain, or to come by at all. The advent of Covid to America this year exposed all of the places across this country where this superstructure has crumbled, or failed to arise. In Virginia, at my parents' house, I had found it still intact. The idea of superstructure came to me as I was sitting with my parents in the family room one evening in July, watching old Monty Python sketches as the dogs sprawled on our laps, their chins on our knees. In one sketch, a husband and wife learn that the apartment block they live in wasn't built with bricks and mortar. It was erected through hypnosis, by a psychic named "El Mystico." A smug architect explains on a news report that such buildings are solid and safe "provided, of course, people believe in them." When the couple receives a note from the Council informing them that "if we ceased to believe in this building it would fall down," the building collapses. In much the same way, it occurred to me then, the superstructure that once undergirded many of this nation's cities and states, even the country as a whole, has gradually disintegrated, as the government (and the citizens who elect the government) have chosen to disbelieve its necessity. The solid building of the American state was falling down, like London Bridge in the song, and had been for some time. Corona didn't cause this; it just made it visible.

When you're fact checking a dark chapter of history, however desolate it may make you feel, you know that its brute moment has passed. The very fact that it is behind you, verifiably, makes you feel hopeful: at least it will not recur. But when you are inhabiting a dark chapter of this kind while it is actually occurring, and there is no end in sight, and you do not know its resolution, it is harder to feel hopeful. Fall is around the corner, schools are back in session, or soon will be (mostly online), and we are still very much within this brute moment. Today, the first day of the last week in August, the global number of Covid cases stands at 23,500,000, with more than 800,000 deaths. The United States now leads the world in the number of Covid infections—almost 5,000,000, nearly a fifth of the world's total cases. This country is being ravaged simultaneously by Covid, a rogue president, political polarization, systemic racism, and mass unemployment. A new president may or may not be elected in November, but hope alone is not enough to light a way forward. One day, the fact checkers of the future, reviewing the narratives of this prolonged national crisis, may find hope in having it behind them. But what motivates and encourages me at this moment is not so much "hope" as a fierce belief in the importance of persevering; of insisting that the conviction of solidity in this society must be made more real, not more illusory, for more people. The values of the superstructure that sustain me and that uphold democracy—humanity, education, justice, fairness, decency—must be not only believed in, but stubbornly defended, at an individual and familial level, and finally, society-wide, if a hopeful new chapter is to begin. Camus wrote as much: "It may seem a ridiculous idea, but the only way to fight the plague is with decency." Hope is not the sole, nor the most important, component of the persevering spirit that is required if all of us are to move forward. But hope is the spark that keeps the engine of progress going. Its counterpart, despair, gets us nowhere. As Camus's Dr. Rieux observed in Oran, "The habit of despair is worse than despair itself."

AFTERWORD
David Dario Winner

The works in this anthology were written as our world was turning upside down. By the time it sees publication, the US presidential election will be behind us and we'll be either breathing a sigh of relief or anxiously glued to our screens as the results are contested via legal or other means. We will likely see violence. We may also be in the depths of a second Covid wave. If one white male septuagenarian wins, some semblance of science and sanity may protect us. If the other does, writers (and we are all writers one way or another) may power down their laptops in despair. In any case, these particular pieces of writing can serve as a record and reminder of a very strange period in all our lives.

Throughout the spring and summer of 2020, as we endured months of anxiety and Coronavirus-related restrictions, pressure mounted and helped fuel a mood of anger and frustration with the US government's grossly inadequate reaction. People of color, many of whom are employed in the so-called "essential" professions, were disproportionately affected by the virus. When a Minnesotan police officer pinned George Floyd down in a knee-on-neck hold for seven minutes and forty-six seconds, killing him before the eyes and cameras of horrified onlookers, the age-old anger at racial injustice merged with a free-floating Coronavirus volatility to fuel the remarkably peaceful and disciplined BLM protests that, unlike the beaches and bars of Florida and California, did not seem to lead to spikes in Covid. The majority of those who gave up their distancing protocols to protest were spared.

The works in *Writing the Virus* are vastly different, but they all touch on that complicated calculus called "distancing." An existential alteration of human contact. In Brooklyn, where I live, some friends did protest, but others limit themselves to talking on the phone or walking in parks while wearing masks. Each person or "pod" has its own manner of transacting risk. Beyond the rift between the Trumpian Corona-liberators, who wish to dance mask-less amidst teeming crowds, and those who hang on Dr. Fauci's every word, there are levels within levels of responses to the possibility of contagion. By the time this book goes to print, our freedom to choose how to respond to the threat, along with so much else, including the right to demand that safety standards are upheld and potential vaccines proceed through the proper trials before being administered to a large section of the public, may be in danger.

We can only base our decisions on our understanding of the virus. Yet its basic nature seems to change constantly as we learn more about its modes of transmission and its symptomatology. Each individual who contracts SARS-CoV-2 seems to experience the illness in a way that's at least partly unique. And each society or nation develops its own mythology—vodka cures in Belarus, bleach in the United States, chloroquine in Brazil—as if the virus were attacking socio-political organisms as well as human ones. Long-standing evils get activated—racial violence in the United States, fascist sentiments in Germany, mistreatment of the indigenous in the Brazilian rainforest—while commonly-held conspiracy theories grow more and more outlandish. George Floyd is alive somewhere. Liberal mayors are responding to George Soros-sponsored "looting" with dangerous gentility. Even those of us not prone to populist notions of "fake news" sometimes don't know what to believe. The past four years have seen a steady erosion in public trust in the solidity and reliability of the information researched, fact-checked, and published by reputable journalists, and it's become more and more essential to adhere to and actively defend objective fact. But apart from basic medical science—that anyone who has ever taken an antibiotic should surely believe—the closest thing to "truth" may be our own individual thoughts and experiences and our intuitive understanding of what is happening to us. This volume relays a wide variety of these experiences from a very particular moment in time.

David Winner
Senior Editor, StatORec
Brooklyn

CONTRIBUTORS

AYDIN BEHNAM

Aydin Behnam is an Iranian-Canadian writer and English instructor who currently lives in Istanbul and teaches English at Koç University. He holds a Ph.D. in English Literature and writes poetry and short stories. He has recently completed his first novel. Aydin is also a photographer, a comedy buff, and a podcaster.

JOAN JULIET BUCK

Joan Juliet Buck has been interpreting Europe for Americans and vice versa since 1972 in *The Observer*, *Vogue*, *Vanity Fair*, *The New Yorker*, *Traveler*, and others. A 1980 MacDowell Colony fellow and the author of two novels, her 2017 memoir *The Price of Illusion* details an expatriate's quest for firm ground. For seven years the editor-in-chief of French *Vogue*, she has played Marguerite Duras onstage, Meryl Streep's nemesis on film, and Calista Flockhart's mother on television.

ZEYNEP CAMUŞCU

Zeynep Camuşcu studied history, media, and visual arts at Koç University Istanbul. In 2016, she spent the summer as an intern at Koç University Press. She has also worked for the *Lethe Literary and Art Journal* as art editor and chief designer. Camuşcu currently studies 1960s Turkish cinema and plans to pursue a career in academia. She is currently an editorial assistant at *StatORec*.

JOHN CASQUARELLI

John Casquarelli is the author of two full-length collections: *On Equilibrium of Song* (Overpass Books, 2011) and *Lavender* (Authorspress, 2014). He is a Lecturer of Academic

Writing at Koç Üniversitesi in Istanbul, as well as the Managing Editor for *Lethe Literary and Art Journal*. His work has appeared in numerous journals and anthologies.

REBECCA CHACE

Rebecca Chace is the author of *Leaving Rock Harbor, Capture the Flag, Chautauqua Summer, June Sparrow*, and *The Million Dollar Penny*. She has written for the *New York Times Magazine, New York Times Sunday Book Review*, the *Huffington Post*, the *LA Review of Books, Guernica Magazine, Lit Hub*, NPR's *All Things Considered*, and other publications.

STEVEN CHESLIK-DEMEYER

Steven Cheslik-DeMeyer has been telling stories for over three decades as a writer, composer, performer, and filmmaker beginning in the New York downtown theater and music scenes of the 1980s and 1990s and culminating in his current work as a musical theater writer.

BARBARA FISCHKIN

Barbara Fischkin is the author of three books of narrative non-fiction and satiric fiction and is currently writing an autism-related historical novel titled *The Digger Resistance*, some of it set in what was once an Eastern European shtetl. She holds an inter-disciplinary Master of Liberal Studies Degree in "Autism Past and Present," is a writer for City University of New York's Office of Communications and Marketing, and is a member of the CUNY Disability Scholars Group. As an international journalist, Fischkin covered stories in Latin America, Asia, and Europe and wrote for major publications including *Newsday*, where she was on staff, the *New Yorker*, and the *New York Times*, among many others.

BEVERLY GOLOGORSKY

Beverly Gologorsky, born 1939 in New York, is the author of three novels; her fourth, *Can You See the Wind?*, will be published in spring 2021. Her most recent book, *Every Body Has a Story*, was published in 2018. Gologorsky's novels have been *New York Times* Notable Books of the Year and have received starred reviews in *Publishers Weekly* and distinctions in the Discover Great New Writers Program, the *Los Angeles Times*, and Indie Next Pick. Her essays have been published widely. "What Does Poverty Feel Like" and "To Be Sick and Not Rich" were published in *TomDispatch*, *Huffington Post*, *Salon*, *The Nation*, et al. Gologorsky's contribution to the feminist movement is noted in *Feminists Who Changed America*, ed. Barbara Love. Gologorsky also edited two political journals: *VietReport* and *Leviathan*.

CHRISTIAN VON DER GOLTZ

Christian von der Goltz is a jazz pianist and composer based in Berlin. Recent recordings include the CD of his sextet *cvdg projekt* (Rudi Mahall, Henrik Walsdorff, Martin Klingeberg, Christian von der Goltz, Jan Roder, and Kay Luebke), titled *paradise*. He has been working on a novel for the past several years.

ALEXANDER GRAEFF

Alexander Graeff, Ph.D., is a writer and philosopher who lives in Berlin and Greifswald. He also works as an editor, curator, and lecturer and has published numerous philosophical texts and pieces of fiction. His prose and poetry are occasionally surreal, and he frequently mixes literary forms. Graeff is the head of the literature program at the *Brotfabrik Berlin*. In the *Queer Media Society*, he is committed to increasing the visibility of queer biographies and stories in the literary establishment.

CHRISTINE HENNEBERG

Christine Henneberg is a writer and a practicing physician in California. Her essays have been published in *The New York Times*, *Slate*, *HuffPost*, and multiple medical journals.

WILLIAM CODY MAHER

William Cody Maher, born in San Francisco in 1950, is an American writer and performance artist living in Berlin. He has lived and performed his work i.a. in Berlin, Zurich, Paris, and Moscow with various poets including Dmitri Prigov, Lev Rubenstein, Ted Joans, Jan Faktor, and others. From 2001 to 2008 he collaborated with dancer Tony Rizzi and members of the William Forsythe Ballet Company in Frankfurt as performer and writer; in 2010 he traveled to America with the photographer Signe Mähler, where they shot "Down Southern Roads," a documentary road movie through America's troubled South. Recent works include a collaboration with the jazz musician Jochen Seiterle on the CD "Blind Date with Love" (Fixcel Records, 2016) and the literary works "The Return" (Moloko Print Verlag, 2020) and "Venetian Blinds" (Peter Engstler Verlag, 2016).

JOAN MARCUS

Essays and stories by Joan Marcus appear in *The Sun*, *Fourth Genre*, *The Georgia Review*, *Alaska Quarterly Review*, *The Smart Set*, *The Laurel Review*, *Gulf Coast*, and elsewhere. She is a two-time winner of the Constance Saltonstall grant for upstate New York writers. She lives in Ithaca, NY and teaches fiction and narrative nonfiction at Ithaca College.

MC JABBER

MC Jabber (Scott Martingell), born in South London in 1966, performs as a singer and poet. He won the first UK National Poetry Slam in 1995, the first Glastonbury Festival Poetry Slam in 1996, and the International SLAM! Revue in 2006. From 1999 to 2008 he was a vocalist in the Danish band Blue Foundation, with tracks featured on "Miami Vice" and the Billboard #1, Grammy-nominated soundtrack to "Twilight." He lives in Berlin.

EDIE MEIDAV

Called "an American original," Edie Meidav is the author of *Kingdom of the Young*, novels including *Lola, California* (FSG) and *Crawl Space* (FSG), and the coedited anthology *Strange Attractors*. She is on the permanent faculty at the UMass Amherst MFA program.

CAILLE MILLNER

Caille Millner is the author of *The Golden Road: Notes on My Gentrification* (Penguin Press). Her short fiction has appeared in *The Southern Review, Zyzzyva*, and *Best American Short Stories 2016*. Her essays have appeared in *Michigan Quarterly Review* and *The Paris Review Daily*.

UCHE NDUKA

Uche Nduka was born in Nigeria to a Christian family. Raised bilingual in Igbo and English, he earned his BA from the University of Nigeria and his MFA from Long Island University, Brooklyn. He left Nigeria in 1994 and settled in Germany after winning a fellowship from the Goethe Institute. He lived in Germany and Holland for the next decade and emigrated to the United States in 2007. Nduka is the author of *Nine East* (2013), *Ijele* (2012), and *eel on reef* (2007). Earlier collections include *Heart's Field* (2005), *If Only the Night* (2002), *Chiaroscuro* (1997), which won the Association of Nigerian Authors Poetry Prize, *The Bremen Poems* (1995), *Second Act* (1994), and *Flower Child* (1988). *Belltime Letters* (2000) is a collection of prose. His forthcoming book *Facing You* will be published in September 2020 by City Lights.

AIMEE PARKISON
Aimee Parkison is the author *Girl Zoo* (with Carol Guess), *Refrigerated Music for a Gleaming Woman, Woman with Dark Horses, The Innocent Party,* and *The Petals of Your Eyes.* Parkison has won an FC2 Catherine Doctorow Innovative Fiction Prize and a Christopher Isherwood Fellowship. She teaches at Oklahoma State University.

MUI POOPOKSAKUL
Mui Poopoksakul is a lawyer-turned-translator with a special interest in contemporary Thai literature. Her translations include three story collections: *The Sad Part Was* and *Moving Parts,* both by Prabda Yoon, and *Arid Dreams* by Duanwad Pimwana. She is also the translator of the novel *Bright* by Pimwana. Mui lives in Berlin, Germany.

ROXANA ROBINSON
Roxana Robinson, a novelist and biographer, is the author of *Sparta* and most recently of *Dawson's Fall,* which investigates the moral consequences of slavery and charts the path of its fell legacies, racism, and violence. Her work has appeared in *The Atlantic, The New Yorker, The Washington Post, The Wall Street Journal,* and *Vogue,* among other publications.

JON ROEMER
Jon Roemer is the publisher and senior editor at Outpost19 Books and author of the novel *Five Windows.* His writing has appeared at *The Millions, KGB Lit, The Writer, OZY, San Francisco Chronicle Book Review, 3:AM* and elsewhere. His public speaking includes the Editors' Picks panel at Library Journal's Day of Dialogue and Northwestern University's guest lecture program. He is queer and based in San Francisco.

JOSEPH SALVATORE

Joseph Salvatore is the author of the story collection *To Assume a Pleasing Shape*, published by BOA Editions, and the co-author of the college textbook *Understanding English Grammar*. A Spanish translation of his story collection, *Presentarse En Forma Grata*, was published in 2018 by Editorial Dos Bigotes. He is Books Editor at *The Brooklyn Rail* and a frequent contributor to *The New York Times Sunday Book Review*. His fiction has appeared in, among other places, *The Collagist, Dossier, Epiphany, New York Tyrant, Open City, Post Road, Salt Hill, Sleeping Fish*, and *Willow Springs*. His criticism has appeared in the *Los Angeles Times, Rain Taxi*, the *Routledge International Encyclopedia of Queer Culture, Angels of the Americlypse: An Anthology of New Latin@ Writing*, the *Believer Logger*, and elsewhere. He is an associate professor of writing at The New School in New York City, where he received the University Distinguished Teaching Award, and was the founding editor of the literary journal *LIT*. He lives in Queens.

LIESL SCHILLINGER

Liesl Schillinger is a writer, literary translator, podcaster, and professor of journalism at The New School in New York City. Her writing has appeared in *The New York Times, The Washington Post, Foreign Policy, The Atlantic, The New Yorker, The New York Review of Books, Lit Hub*, and elsewhere. She is the author of the book of neologisms, *Wordbirds*. In 2017, she was named a Chevalier de l'Ordre des Arts et des Lettres of France.

ANDREA SCRIMA

Statorec editor in chief Andrea Scrima studied fine arts at the School of Visual Arts in New York and the Hochschule der Künste, Berlin, Germany, where she lives and works. A German translation of her first book, *A Lesser Day* (Spuyten Duyvil), was published by Literaturverlag Droschl, Graz, in 2018 under the title *Wie viele Tage*. Scrima writes literary criticism for *The*

Brooklyn Rail, Music & Literature, Schreibheft, Manuskripte, and other publications. She publishes a monthly column for *3Quarks Daily* and is currently working on her third book. Her second book, a novel titled *Like Lips, Like Skins,* is due to come out in a German edition in the fall of 2021.

ALICE STEPHENS

Alice Stephens's debut novel, *Famous Adopted People,* was published in 2018 by Unnamed Press. Her work has appeared in *LitHub, The Los Angeles Review of Books, The Margins,* and other publications. She is the editor of *Bloom* and writes book reviews and a column, *Alice in Wordland,* for the *Washington Independent Review of Books.*

CHERYL PEARL SUCHER

Cheryl Pearl Sucher is an award-winning novelist, journalist, and broadcast interviewer. A recipient of a National Endowment of the Arts Fellowship in fiction, her first novel, *The Rescue of Memory,* was published by Scribner; she hopes that her second, *Alive Among the Ruins,* will be in print before her cousin Julia turns 90. She lives between New Jersey and New Zealand and has been a frequent contributor to such publications as *The New Zealand Listener, The New Zealand Sunday Star-Times,* and *The Forward.* She is the curator for McNally Jackson's "Between Two Worlds" author conversation series, where she has interviewed Min Jin Lee, Sigrid Nuñez, Susan Choi, and Sally Rooney, among others.

CLIFFORD THOMPSON

Clifford Thompson is the author, most recently, of *What It Is: Race, Family, and One Thinking Black Man's Blues* (2019), published by Other Press.

SASKIA VOGEL

Saskia Vogel is a writer and Swedish translator from Los Angeles. Her debut novel *Permission* was published in four languages in 2019 and is forthcoming in German. Her translation of Johannes Anyuru's *They Will Drown in Their Mothers' Tears* won the 2020 Firecracker Award for Fiction. She lives in Berlin.

MATTHEW VOLLMER

Matthew Vollmer is the author of *Future Missionaries of America, inscriptions for headstones, Gateway to Paradise,* and *Permanent Exhibit.* As an Associate Professor of English, he teaches creative writing and literature at Virginia Tech.

DAVID DARIO WINNER

David Winner is the author of *Tyler's Last* and *The Cannibal of Guadalajara.* His work has appeared in *The Village Voice, The Kenyon Review, The Iowa Review, The Millions,* and other publications in the US and the UK. He is the fiction editor of the Rome-based magazine, *The American,* senior editor for *Statorec,* and a regular contributor to the *The Brooklyn Rail.*

TIFFANY WINTERS

Tiffany Winters has spent most of her adult life writing ad copy and news stories by day and publishing micro-fiction, photo essays, satire, and badly drawn comics anonymously at night. She's trying to use pseudonyms a little less; submit a little more; and live like the world is on fire.

ACKNOWLEDGMENTS

The editors would like to thank the 31 authors of this collection for their outstanding contributions, many of which were written under considerable pressure. We'd also like to thank StatORec's publisher, John Reed, for his steadfast support of the magazine, as well as Jon Roemer for having had the foresight to leave a slot free in his fall program for precisely this kind of publication: born of the moment, fueled by adrenaline, and literally down to the wire.

Our gratitude goes to Founding Artistic Director Kristin Marting and the talented designers at HERE Arts Center in downtown Manhattan for hosting the #stillHERE with StatORec playlist of video clips of our authors reading from their works. We'd also very much like to extend our heartfelt thanks to managing editor Rebecca Chace for interviewing us for *The Brooklyn Rail*, during the course of which we were able to make sense of the cacophony of experiences and impressions of the past five months as we acquired, edited, published, and promoted an average of two texts each week. Thanks, too, to our editorial assistants Zeynep Camuşcu, Rachel Marble, and Charlotte Slivka for their expertise at various times during the making of the issue and anthology. A humble thank you also goes to our neglected partners and kids—Angela, Christian, and Paul—for putting up with us as we worked through lockdown, social distancing, and the inevitable normalization of risk to put together an issue and an anthology that felt, to us, to be necessary and crucial.

Finally, we owe a great debt to the essential workers who have kept the world running over the past eight months at great personal risk to themselves and their families. It's to you that we dedicate this anthology, and to you that we most wish a better, fairer, safer future.